PHIL JASNER
"ON THE CASE"

PHIL JASNER
"ON THE CASE"

· · · · · ·

*His Best Writing on
the Sixers, the Dream Team,
and Beyond*

· · · · · ·

Edited by **ANDY JASNER**

TEMPLE UNIVERSITY PRESS
Philadelphia • Rome • Tokyo

TEMPLE UNIVERSITY PRESS
Philadelphia, Pennsylvania 19122
www.temple.edu/tempress

Library of Congress Cataloging-in-Publication Data

Names: Jasner, Andy, 1969-
Title: Phil Jasner "on the case" : his best writing on the Sixers, the dream
    team, and beyond / edited by Andy Jasner.
Description: Philadelphia, Pennsylvania : Temple University Press, 2017. |
    Includes index.
Identifiers: LCCN 2017033585 | ISBN 9781439914946 (hardback (alk. paper))
Subjects: LCSH: Jasner, Phil, 1942-2010. | Sportswriters—United States. |
    Sports journalism—United States. |
    Sports—Pennsylvania—Philadelphia—History. | Professional
    sports—Pennsylvania—Philadelphia—History. | BISAC: SPORTS & RECREATION
    / Essays. | HISTORY / United States / State & Local / Middle Atlantic (DC,
    DE, MD, NJ, NY, PA). | LANGUAGE ARTS & DISCIPLINES / Journalism.
Classification: LCC GV742.42.J37 A3 2017 | DDC 796.09748—dc23 LC record
    available at https://lccn.loc.gov/2017033585

♾ The paper used in this publication meets the requirements of the American
National Standard for Information Sciences—Permanence of Paper for Printed
Library Materials, ANSI Z39.48-1992

Printed in the United States of America

9 8 7 6 5 4 3 2 1

CONTENTS

CHAPTER 6 • THE '83 CHAMPIONSHIP SEASON
Introduction by Billy Cunningham

CHAPTER 7 • THE SIXERS BETWEEN FINALS RUNS: OCTOBER 1983–2000
Introduction by Earl Cureton

CHAPTER 8 • THE DREAM TEAM
Introduction by Charles Barkley

CHAPTER 9 • IVERSON AND THE 2001 FINALS RUN

Introduction by Allen Iverson

CODA • PROFILING GIANTS

A photo gallery follows page 126.

FOREWORD

By Andy Jasner

I T NEVER ENDS.

I was sitting on the beach a few years ago in Ocean City, N.J., and a man walked by me and said, "Hi Phil."

There was the time I woke up early on a vacation day at a resort in the Poconos. I walked across the grounds into the main building, and as I reached the front door, a man said, "Nice job in the paper today, Phil."

Oh, and how about the day I went to fetch some early morning coffee at a café on Long Beach Island. I was awakened quite early by one of our daughters and was in desperate need of a pick-me-up. As I opened the door, two men had parked their bicycles. One said, "Are the Sixers making a trade soon, Phil?"

Now, I've been told through the years that I resemble my dad, Phil Jasner. When someone is remembered so often in the years after passing away, that's the ultimate compliment. Dad was taken far soon on December 3, 2010, after a near two-year courageous battle with cancer at the young age of 68.

But his memory will live on forever. He made such an indelible stamp on people through his work as a sportswriter, most famous for covering the Philadelphia 76ers from 1981 until his final days in 2010.

I get approached several times per month asking if I'm related to Phil. My daughters—Jordana (11), Shira (7), and Leah (4) get asked about their last name. It's not a common name, but nothing about Phil Jasner was common.

Dad never punched a time clock. He couldn't. He never treated his job like a chore. Because he wouldn't. His job was a true labor of love. My dad never felt like he had done enough. He was always searching for more, the next interview, the next call, the next breaking story. Before Doug Collins was hired as the Sixers' coach before the 2010–2011 season, my dad texted Collins every single day imploring him to give him the scoop before anyone else. Dad was passionate. Relentless. Persistent. Aggressive. All of those traits made him a respected journalist. Dad wanted the story first. But he also wanted every fact to be correct.

My dad was a rarity in this day and age. Even at the end, he was more passionate about his career than he was when he first started. You don't see that too much anymore. If at all. Being a sportswriter is all he ever wanted to be. His dream job was to work as a sportswriter in the city of Philadelphia. He lived out his dream virtually every day.

Dad was never a conventional person. Whether the workweek demanded 40 hours or 90 hours, he was there plugging away at his computer—or his typewriter back in the day.

For all these years of hard work and dedication, Dad was inducted into six—count 'em six—Halls of Fame. In addition to his induction in the Naismith Memorial Basketball Hall of Fame, Dad was also added to the Philadelphia Sports Hall of Fame, the Philadelphia Jewish Sports Hall of Fame, the Big 5 Hall of Fame, and the halls at both Overbrook High School and Temple University.

A Temple University graduate, my dad spent the early part of his career at the Pottstown (Pa.) *Mercury*, Montgomery Newspapers (Fort Washington, Pa.), as well as the Norristown *Times Herald* and *The Trentonian*.

Then he found his true niche in the workforce when he joined the *Philadelphia Daily News* in 1972. He never left. He never thought about leaving. This was it, the perfect situation, the perfect place with a staff he came to call his colleagues and lifelong friends.

Dad began covering the 76ers on a full-time basis in 1981. From Caldwell Jones to Bobby Jones to Julius Erving to Charles Barkley to Allen Iverson to Evan Turner, Phil Jasner was "on the case."

That was his catchphrase.

When his editor called our house, Dad would say, "I'm on the case."

And I knew that he always was.

Long before cell phones were invented, Dad would rack up a gargantuan phone bill with calls to Hong Kong, Japan, Australia—wherever, to track down a pressing story. He wouldn't quit until he got every fact for that story. Even if it meant working in the wee hours of the morning while I was sleeping in the adjacent bedroom.

"Andy, do you think they will be upset with my phone bill?" Dad asked me all the time.

He was always worried about minutia like this, but he was never worried about getting it right. He got it right for 38-plus years at the *Daily News.*

In an era where so many newspaper reporters burn out, dad kept on churning with an energy level unmatched by those even in their 20s and 30s. To this day, reporters from other cities ask me where his energy came from.

Dad and I were the first father-son combination to cover an NBA All-Star Game in 1992 in Orlando when Magic Johnson won over the fans with an MVP performance. I remember sitting courtside with my father, who had this wide-eyed look on his face. While other reporters were complaining about deadlines or the business in general, Dad was in utopia.

When he returned to Philadelphia, he bought as many copies of the *Daily News* as he could find and mailed them to family members and friends scattered throughout the country. He was that proud of his work.

I was also fortunate to have covered three NBA Finals and numerous other All-Star Games with my dad. The NBA, namely Brian McIntyre, was always incredibly gracious in seating the two of us next to each other even when I was just starting my career in my early 20s.

My career took me in one direction and dad's career continued to blossom as the years passed. As he got older, he worked even harder, which is tough to believe. In 1996, the Sixers drafted this young whirling dervish named Allen Iverson with the No. 1 overall pick in the draft.

From there, a unique relationship developed between A. I. and Dad.

In the early days, Iverson and Dad didn't always get along. When you're a beat writer covering a team every single day, there are bound to be disagreements. The biggest argument came on May 10, 2002, during Iverson's famous practice rant.

Here's an excerpt . . .

Iverson: "I don't know Phil. I don't know you as a basketball player. I know you as a columnist, but I have never heard of you as a player, though."

Dad: "Why is that an issue?"

Iverson: "Why is that an issue? Because we're talking about basketball."

Dad: "Let me ask my question."

Iverson: "Go ahead, Phillip."

Dad: "Suppose you shot 44 percent . . ."

Iverson: "I don't know about that. That is in God's hands. I do not know if that will help me or not. That's God. God does that. It ain't up to you to say if Allen Iverson does this then he'll do that. That's up to God. It ain't up to anyone in here. That is up to God. He handles that."

Dad took umbrage that Iverson challenged him about the line of questioning. As the years progressed, they continued to build a mutual relationship. They respected each other.

When Dad passed away on December 3, 2010, Iverson was one of the first people to send a tweet out to the world. Iverson sent his condolences to me and my entire family. It was a sign of a human being who had matured in so many ways.

Iverson has shouted out Phil's name at every single press conference in recent years. He chose to talk about Dad and how much he missed him. It is always so touching. It's also very rare in today's world. Reporters and players don't always get along. Sometimes they do. It's rare when a player has this much love for a journalist.

Iverson has always been an emotional person. So was my dad. At times, they were just like family members—they battled with each other, bickered with each other. But each one respected the other's profession.

Dad always said that Iverson was an electrifying player, and pound-for-pound, an incredible basketball player.

Iverson has talked about Dad being a giant in the world of sports journalism. He's right.

As an only child, being a sportswriter was the only thing I ever wanted to do. For years, I was able to work side-by-side with my dad at numerous NBA All-Star Games and three NBA Finals. I was there with my wife, Taryn, in 2004, when Dad was inducted into the Basketball Hall of Fame in Springfield, Mass.

Back then, Iverson was in the prime of his career. My dad was still covering the Sixers. Not even a Hall-of-Fame induction would slow Dad down.

It's surreal to think that nearly seven years have gone by since Dad passed away. I think about him every time I walk into the arena. That will never go away. I sit in his seat courtside and in the press room. I look up at heaven every time the starting lineups are announced and point to dad. I know he's watching.

Every time the Sixers make a major announcement, or win a big game, or trade away a player, I think of dad.

It never ends. The memories will never fade. Your imprint will live on through me and your three amazing granddaughters and wonderful daughter-in-law.

Love,

Andy, Taryn, Jordana, Shira, and Leah

PHIL JASNER
"ON THE CASE"

CHAPTER 1

THE EARLY YEARS

Introduction by Merrill Reese

Phil Jasner was born to be a sportswriter. That's all he ever wanted to be from day one. We weren't in the same class, but we did go to Beeber Junior High School and Overbrook High during the same years. Phil was sports editor of both the Beeber *Oracle* and the Overbrook *Beacon*. At some point, we met in schoolyard basketball games. That led to football where I was always the quarterback and at 6-foot-3, Phil was a great target at receiver. Even then, Phil thought about a career as a sportswriter. I wasn't nearly as mature. At 5-foot-8, I still believed I would grow another four or five inches and end up on the cover of *Sports Illustrated* with my right wrist cocked as I looked downfield. Oh well.

By the time I entered college, I had determined that the closest I would ever get to the line of scrimmage was the broadcast booth. There I could enjoy my passion and share my love of sports with millions of fans. Phil stayed faithful to his original course. At Temple, I majored in communications (radio-TV) while Phil focused on journalism.

At the end of my freshman year, I was appointed sports director of WRTI (the student-run FM radio station). As a sophomore, I got to broadcast Temple football, almost all losses, and Temple basketball, a lot of wins. That year, the Owls got off to a great start. There was great anticipation as they prepared for a trip to Kentucky to meet the number one team in the country. WRTI only covered home games because there was no budget for broadcast lines and travel expenses. I got up my courage and went begging to the alumni association to finance the broadcast. I almost dropped over when they said yes. Now all I needed was a color analyst. No problem. Phil was covering for the *Temple News*.

I was excited for another reason. I had never been on an airplane. The day of the flight it snowed . . . and it snowed . . . and it snowed some more. The flight was canceled and we were put on a train at 30th Street station. Phil and I shared a Pullman car. Along the route, a man jumped onto the tracks and the train hit him. We were halted for over two hours. By the time we arrived in Lexington, it was almost 27 hours later. When you're confined to close quarters for that long, you either end up despising each other or become very close friends. Phil and I shared our dreams and career paths. Phil's biggest hero was the brilliant sportswriter at the *Daily News*—Stan Hochman. Mine was Eagles play-by-play voice Bill Campbell. Stan played a major role in Phil's biggest career move. Bill and I became very close friends years later as I had established myself as the Eagles voice.

Throughout the years, Phil and I remained close. Our lives took us in different directions. The day-to-day pressure of real life coupled with the demanding careers made it difficult to stay in constant touch, but we knew we were always there for one another. All it took was a phone call and we were up-to-date on everything.

I don't think there was ever one story that Phil wrote in the *Daily News* that I didn't read. And I appreciated his tenacity as a reporter, his clear grab-you-by-the-veins writing style and his sense of fairness and journalistic ethics. If Phil wrote it, I knew it was true. He never threw rumors and innuendoes against a wall and hoped that they stick. Phil told me that Stan Hochman's edict—"Get it first, get it right"—was etched in stone.

In this business, it's easy to make enemies. Coaches and players are often very sensitive to criticism and Phil never minced words. His personal feelings about someone never affected his evaluation of their performance. Phil wasn't a ripper. He didn't enjoy tearing people apart, but he felt responsible to his readers and he told them what he saw. I'm sure there were ruffled feelings from time to time, but I don't remember Phil ever making an enemy. Allen Iverson's famous "Practice" press conference where he said "We're talking about practice!" led to a famous exchange with Phil. We will remember that as long as we live.

Nobody has ever made a more indelible impression on my life than Phil. When something happens, I still, for a brief second, think about calling him. And then it hits me hard again—that Phil is no longer with us. But then again, his memories that were left will always be there and his special presence will forever impact our lives.

MERRILL REESE *has spent 40 seasons as the play-by-play voice of the Philadelphia Eagles and was recently inducted into the franchise's Hall of Fame.*

· · · · · ·

ACCENT ON YOUTH

The Philadelphia Jewish Times
August 31, 1962

WALK DOWN A STREET in Philadelphia. Any street, any day, any time. Something's different. It's still summer, but something's not the same.

They're kids all over.

In the playgrounds, the swimming pools, parks, back drives, on the street corners, outside the bowling alleys. All over the place. They're home from the seashore, from Europe, from camp. From all over.

And their parents, for about an hour and forty-five minutes, are beset with ecstasy and glee at the return of their little loved ones. But soon, almost unbelievably soon, the initial shock plunges to its nadir and you hear in a quiet, almost whispered tone, the plainful, mournful wail of bored youth: "Hey Mom! I don't have anything to do!"

"Oh happy days," mother mumbles as she shoos her young ones out the door. "Go find your friends and play till dinnertime."

So when you walk down a street in Wynnefield, Overbrook Park, Oxford Circle, Logan, South Philly, or anywhere, you see kids. They're all out playing till dinnertime.

That kid throwing the ball against the wall, you think. Maybe he'll be President someday, or maybe he'll play second base for the Yankees . . . whichever pays more. And how about that little girl? Maybe a model? . . . or the First Lady?

You're thinking about all this, and suddenly you stop. Because just ahead in a driveway between two row homes are 18 kids, and instead of messing up the sidewalk, they're staging an outdoor musical to raise money for charity. With 14-year-old Harry Freedman directing, the kids display their talents via songs, dances, choruses and skits. In 1961, you learn, they earned $85 for the Retarded Children Association, and this year they sold $87 worth of advance admissions.

Susan Freedman, Andrea and Tina Silverman, Meryl and Joel Podolsky, Harriet Weisman, Stephen Kafin and Jeffrey Borland were some of the performing youngsters. They range in age from 11 to 16, and now you feel a little more secure when you think those kids are the adults of tomorrow.

"Kool Kats Productions" was the name of the teenage version of the Great White Way, and as you think about it, you wonder if this day will be noted in the annals of American History as "The day 18 potential cool cats became Kool Kats?"

Smorgasbord . . . Karen Sherman, a junior at Temple, has received the Presser Scholarship to the university's School of Music. It's the second music scholarship for the Roxboroughite. She won a Board of Education music scholarship when she graduated from Girls' High. . . . Merrie and Bruce Kristol, of Merion, recently returned from a trip to Florida with their parents, Mr. and Mrs. Benjamin Kristol. Merrie returns to Harcum Jr. College in the fall, and Bruce embarks on a collegiate career at Pennsylvania Military Academy. . . . Miss Beatrice Buten, also of Merion, has returned from a European summer. Miss Buten graduated from Brandeis University in June, and leaves in September to study for her master's degree at Berkley. While in Italy this summer, she had a brief reunion with some of her Brandeis classmates. . . . Robert Weinberg, son of department store owner Sol Weinberg, will resume studies for his master's degree in business administration at Harvard. He spent the summer doing research for a New York firm. . . . Levittown's Jane Frankel will be in the cast of the final Children's Show of the season at St. John Terrell's Lambertville Music Circus. The musical revue will have songs, dances and novelty acts for the kiddies, and the performers will all be under 18. Abe Neff joined forces with the Al Small orchestra, of the country villa in Bushkill, Pa., to put on an entertainment program for the kids at the Golden Slipper Square Club Camp. . . . The Rhawnhurst Jewish Young Adults are holding a social Sunday, Sept. 9, at 2312 Loney St. Dress is casual, but no slacks. Anyone interested should contact Norman Master, at 2501 S. 10th St., or Joe Shour, at 356 Rockland St.

Sports note . . . Spike those rumors about Dan Swartz leading the American Basketball League Tapers if they play in Philadelphia next season (if they play at all). Dan just inked his name on a contract with the Boston Celtics.

PERGINE GAINS SOUTH BEND GRID PRAISE

Montgomery Newspapers (part of the fall 1966 football preview)
September 15, 1966

WHEN JOHN PERGINE WAS a junior at Plymouth-Whitemarsh, Notre Dame Athletic Director Hugh Devore mailed him tickets to a South Bend spectacular. When he was a senior, Ara Parseghian offered him a scholarship.

It was like telling Roy Rogers he could have Trigger.

Pergine was an outstanding quarterback for the Colonials, an All-State basketball player and a promising baseball performer. He's 6'1", 215 these days, and strictly an inside linebacker.

"Don't be too quick to pass judgement on John because he's no longer a quarterback," Parseghian cautioned. "People have been passing judgement on John Huarte as a pro, but they forget it took him four years to develop into a Heisman Trophy winner."

Responds to Challenge: Colonial coach Ron Landes, who has had several players climb into college prominence recently, echoed Parseghian's comment.

"Everybody seems to be more concerned with John becoming a linebacker than John is," Landes pointed out. "His fans are pretty disappointed that he's no longer a quarterback, but John is happy with his new position. He likes the challenge."

He has also responded to it, although he sheepishly minimizes his accomplishments. What he did was win a Player of the Week honor during Spring Practice.

"It's not really an award, or anything fancy," Pergine explained. "They pick an outstanding player each week, and hang his picture on the bulletin board. I guess I did okay one week."

You can't afford to guess when you glance at the kamikaze flight plan that doubles as the Notre Dame schedule. Parseghian says you have to win a bowl game to be allowed to play the Irish. Duke, Army, Navy, Purdue, Northwestern, Michigan State and Southern Cal are some of the qualifiers.

Pride Major Ingredient: "There's never any problem getting up for the games," Pergine noted. "Football season provides the best weekends of the year. There are students, fans and tourists all over the place. The coaches help us a lot, too. They're sincere, and don't play any favorites. They see what you can do, and they work with you steadily. It's a terrific football atmosphere, and pride is a big thing."

Pergine seriously started thinking about college when he was a junior in high school.

"I had a good season, and began believing I could make it in college ball," he remembered. "I have pro ball in the back of my mind now, but first I want to do well in college. Every year, I learn more. If I keep learning, well . . ."

Parseghian, Pergine noted, stresses guts and courage—ingredients that many overly sophisticated fans secretly regard with a smirk.

"I don't know about that," Pergine said quietly. "All I know is it works with us."

ROGER GRIMES: EVERY GAME IS WORLD SERIES

Norristown Times Herald
October 31, 1968

ROGER GRIMES IS A Philadelphia Eagle taxi squader, and everybody knows National Football League teams don't keep extra ballplayers around because they photograph well or look nifty standing on the sidelines.

Roger Grimes is also a star runner and receiver for the Pottstown Firebirds, and Dave DeFilippo knows Atlantic Coast League teams don't use NFL or AFL taxi men because their names look cute on the roster.

Pottstown thumped the Lowell Giants 25–14 last Saturday night, and Roger Grimes netted 62 yards in 11 carries and caught four passes for 156 yards and two touchdowns. In the halfback's private World Series, it was a bigger victory.

For the former Penn State wunderkind, the road has been long and treacherous. But he is almost back. He knows it, and DeFilippo thinks the Eagles know it.

"Look, they don't sign guys because they're nice fellas," the Firebirds' coach and general manager said pointedly. "Roger is a good running back—a thumper who rarely takes any punishment on his knees because he's always driving forward.

"And he can catch the ball. I'm not Roger Grimes' publicity man, but the boy's got great hands for the normal passes to swing men coming out of the backfield. He can take the screens and flares, but he can also run the deep patterns.

"I guess it'd be fairly easy for the taxi guys to come up here two nights a week and just go through the motions. But this kid plays every game like it was the World Series."

Things started for Roger Grimes at tiny Cornwall High, about 13 miles east of Hershey. There were 85 people in his graduating class. Not 85 ballplayers, 85 people. But he played his way onto the Big 33 roster and into Penn State.

They were saying all the usual superlative things about the gritty sophomore, but he never made it through his second college "World Series."

"I twisted my knee in the second game of my sophomore season against UCLA," he remembered. "It took some time, but I recuperated and tried to finish the year without getting an operation.

"Next thing I knew, I had mononucleosis. And then the knee went again.

"I still wasn't sure whether I was going to get that operation. I was working out in the gym before Spring Practice and hurt it again. They operated in May.

"I really didn't think too much about it, though. I knew plenty of other players who had had the operation and had no problems later. I was more relieved than anything else. I was finally getting it over with."

The story does not get all bright and shiny and Walt Disneyish from there. Not for a while.

Roger Grimes felt he was healthy and ready, but he was a grim spot performer for the next two Nittany Lion seasons. He graduated in June and was signed as a free agent by Dallas.

Six weeks and several roster cuts later, he was finally placed on waivers. An hour after he cleared the offering-around procedure, the Eagles were on the phone.

"They took a quick look and asked me to join their taxi squad," he said. "It wasn't the same as getting the chance to play someplace, but I was happy.

"I know I didn't play much for two years and I got here too late to play in any of the Eagles' exhibitions. That's why I was glad for the opportunity to join the Firebirds. When you don't play, you begin to lose confidence. You start to wonder whether you can do the things you thought you could do.

"Now I'm playing and learning, and that's what I need more than anything. It's a little tough, working out four days with the Eagles and twice with the Firebirds, but it won't hurt me. You need a break to play in the major leagues, and maybe this will be mine."

Once there was a tumult and shouting around University Park for Roger Grimes. Now it is for Ted Kwalik and Charlie Pittman and Bobby Campbell.

When the knee goes, the tumult subsides and the shouting becomes a whisper.

Instead of All-East or All-American honors and perhaps a bonus contract and a spot in a big league backfield, he is scrambling for success and recognition at a lower level. And looking for a way to the top.

It is Roger Grimes' private World Series. Keep tuned.

OLAF VON SCHILLING—VILLANOVA FROSH SWIMMER WHO'S GOING PLACES

Norristown Times Herald
May 1, 1968

YOU ASK OLAF VON SCHILLING to name the places he's been and he just smiles sheepishly and says it's easier to name the places he hasn't been. There are only a couple.

Olaf Von Schilling—Ollie—is a freshman at Villanova. He is a swimmer, and a good one. A very good one.

He is 24 years old and will probably compete for the West German Olympic team this summer. When his country needs him for a meet, all it has to do is ask.

His country asked about six weeks ago.

"I got a cablegram at the dormitory on Thursday telling me that West Germany was competing in a triangular meet with East Germany and Russia at Tiffelis, on the Black Sea," Ollie explained. "They wanted me to swim for them. I was planning to go home the following week for the West German Nationals, so it just meant leaving a little sooner."

Really, it meant more. A lot more.

What it meant was about two dozen hours on airplanes, several more hours waiting restlessly in airports, having breakfast in Germany—he had to stop home for some equipment—and dinner in Moscow.

It went something like this—

"I left Philadelphia late Saturday afternoon, and arrived in Frankfurt early Sunday morning," Ollie began. "I had to pick up some additional plane tickets and some equipment, and fly from there to Copenhagen. I was only in Frankfurt for about an hour.

"I had to wait two hours in Copenhagen to make the next connection—there was no faster direct way—and flew from there to Moscow. A man from the Russian Swimming Federation met me at the airport, took care of my visa—it usually takes about a week to get one—and took me out to dinner. I had some borscht, a small steak, peas and carrots and tea. They had a soft drink that was something like Coke, but it tasted terrible. I couldn't drink it.

"The flight from there to Tiffelis also took about seven hours, and the German coach met me at the airport. I got there about 1:30 in the morning on Monday.

"I thought the meet started on Tuesday, but they told me I had to swim Monday night. I was really tired, too. I couldn't sleep at all on the plane.

"I didn't get up until 1:30 in the afternoon. My body and stomach were pretty confused by the time and altitude changes, so I worked out for about an hour just to loosen up. The altitude on the Black Sea is about the same as Mexico."

In the storybooks, Olaf Von Schilling would have won three dramatic races and been greeted at the post-meet banquet with thunderous applause and glistening medals.

Ollie had to settle for a 4:18 victory in the 400 meter race and second place finishes in the 100 and 200 meter competition.

He didn't have time to attend the banquet.

"The West German Nationals were Saturday and Sunday, so I left for home right after the meet," he explained.

He won all three there, slicing six seconds off his 400 meter time.

Tuesday morning he was back at Villanova.

"They interviewed me on West German television before I left," Ollie remembered. "They think a college athlete in the United States lives like a professional but I set it straight. I guess it's probably like that, but it's not that way at Villanova.

"I have 21 hours of classes a week, I swim 21 hours and I study for two or three hours every night. I get pretty fair grades—Bs and Cs—and I think I could get better ones if I studied more.

"But two or three hours a night is enough, unless you have a special exam or a final. I feel you should work hard, but still be able to enjoy life, and I enjoy my life at Villanova."

He is a swimmer partly by default, and he wound up at Villanova through a wave of clinics, friendships and an automobile accident that nearly ended his athletic career.

"I met the U.S. Olympic coach, George Haines, at a clinic in Germany," Ollie said. "He liked me, and wanted me to come to California, where he was the coach at the Santa Clara Swim Club.

"I came, and when it was time for me to go home, he wanted me to stay and go to college here."

Ed Geisz, the Wildcat coach, took it from there.

"We were interested in Bob Burke, a backstroker from Brooklyn Prep who had taken up residence in California to train under Haines," Geisz explained. "Burke and Ollie became friends and roommates and decided they wanted to go to college together, Burke was interested in Villanova, and Ollie said he would come, too."

But Ollie returned to Germany for a visit. He was sitting in a parked Volkswagen when the other car hit him. He was in traction and a cast, and didn't swim again for four months.

And while he was in the hospital, Burke enrolled at Michigan State.

"Swimming was the only thing left for me," Ollie said. "The doctors told me I shouldn't do too much running around or play any contact sports. I had liked soccer as a youngster, but I hurt my foot and had to give that up.

"The accident ruled out water polo—and I was pretty good at that, too—tennis or track. So I concentrated on swimming.

"I had said I was coming to Villanova, and I kept my commitment."

The 'Cats were 4–6 in freshman dual meets, but Ollie swept 29 of his 30 events. His only second came by a tenth of a second in the 100 yard freestyle against Princeton.

"I really like it here," Ollie said. "In German universities, they want you to always be the best, no matter what you're studying. There's not really much time for sports.

"Here, you study, you compete and have time for some fun. I like that."

He has been to Russia 10 times as a swimmer, and competed in places like Turkey, France, Israel, Angola, Japan, Hong Kong and Liberia.

You ask him where he has not competed, and he stops to think.

"South America," he said. "I have never competed in South America. Or in Ireland."

But if the next cablegram says West Germany is swimming against the Irish Nationals, he'll be there.

Just leave the tickets and bathing suit at the airport. For Ollie, the rest is routine.

UMPS HELP TAR PHILS

Trentonian
July 29, 1970

PHILADELPHIA—JIM BUNNING DID NOT win his 100th National League game last night.

He lost his 77th.

He did it with nothing on the ball.

It took the Los Angeles Dodgers to pin the 6–2 defeat on Bunning and the Phillies. It took John Kibler, Chris Pelekoudas, Augie Donatelli and Don Davidson to make sure.

The four umpires surrounded Bunning at the start of the fourth inning, examining the 39-year-old pitcher's hands for evidence of pine tar, the sticky substance that helps hitters and pitchers grip a baseball.

Examine him? Make that minor surgery.

Clean hands: "They said he was using pine tar," Phils' manager Frank Lucchesi grumbled afterward. "I said, 'Look at his hands. They're clean.'

"Pelekoudas (the third base umpire) said 'Whatever he's using, tell him to wipe it off.' Hell, they all said it. It was silly. I said 'Prove he has something.' They said they didn't have to prove anything."

Lucchesi was upset, but relatively calm. Bunning was in a quiet rage.

Jim: "I had nothing on my hands. Nothing. They (the umpires) got caught with their pants down. They made me wipe my hands to protect themselves. There was nothing there. Absolutely nothing.

"The Dodgers didn't bring it up, the umpires did. Pelekoudas over-umpired again, that's all. Kibler (the home plate man) was satisfied. He looked at my hands and said let's go. Pelekoudas said no."

The umpires finally asked for a towel from the Phillies' dugout. Pitching coach Ray Rippelmeyer quickly scurried out, then just as quickly scurried back, towel still in hand.

Rip: "They made me take it back and pour alcohol on it. Was the towel sticky when I brought it back? I don't know. I didn't pay much attention after that. All I know is pine tar isn't going to make a bit of difference as far as action on the ball. You need something slippery to do that."

Dodgers upset?: Amazingly, the Dodgers were at least as publicly upset as Bunning.

Manager Walt Alston: "I can't believe anything like that could affect Jim's pitching. He's far too good a competitor to let a thing like that bother him."

Shortstop Maury Wills: "I have a lot of respect for umpires, but I hate to see a man of Bunning's caliber shaken down like that. I didn't have to happen."

Winner Joe Moeller: "I had enough problems of my own to notice what Jim was doing. But whatever he uses, I sure could have used it myself. Anyway, if the problem is simply gripping the ball, you can get almost the same effect by using a lot of rosin. At least I can."

Moeller got his fifth win last night, Jim Brewer got his 15th save and Bunning had a final comment.

"Am I disappointed about the 100th win? I didn't build this up. Everybody else did. I hate to lose, sure, but I'll start again Saturday."

The first inning was a minus downstairs when the Dodgers scored two runs on a single by Wills, a bunt single by Manny Mota, and RBI double to right-center by Wes Parker and an infield out by Jim Lefebvre.

Key bunt: Mota's bunt was the key to the rally. Manny dropped one down the third base line, but Don Money made a fluid charge-and-throw, bringing an "out" call from first base ump Davidson. A split second later, Davidson reversed himself, apparently claiming first baseman Deron Johnson had left the bag too soon.

All told, that cost the Phils an out and a first base coach. Billy DeMars was ejected an inning later for questioning Davidson's judgement.

Bunning was tough for the next three frames, then staggered in the fifth when Ron Stone played Willie Crawford's liner to right into a double. Moeller sacrificed and Wills singled past a drawn-in Denny Doyle.

Singles by Mota and Davis and a sacrifice fly by Parker gave the Dodgers their fourth run. Tom Haller tripled and scored on an error by Doyle in the sixth.

Billy Grabarkewitz welcomed reliever Barry Lersch with a two-out homer to centerfield in the eighth, his 11th of the season.

Waste chance: The Phils solved Moeller for single runs in the second and third, but could not produce the big early rally despite sending seven men to the plate in the third. A single by Stone and a double by Larry Hisle accounted for the first tally, and singles by Tony Taylor and Doyle, a stolen base by Taylor and an infield out by Johnson brought in the second.

Stone and Hisle followed Johnson's ground ball with walks to load the bases, but Terry Harmon struck out to keep Moeller in command.

The Phils loaded the bases again in the seventh on Johnny Briggs' pinch walk, Doyle's single and Johnson's two-out walk.

Moeller said good night, Brewer said good evening and Lucchesi said Jim Hutto (right-handed, .206) would bat for Stone (lefty, .296).

Are you listening, Gil Hodges?

Jim Hutto, who has twice won the game with pinch homers, struck out looking. It was revenge for Brewer, who yielded a grand slam to Hutto in Los Angeles last week.

Jim Brewer, obviously, had more on the ball than Jim Bunning.

THE EXPLORERS GO WESTHEAD

Trentonian
March 10, 1970

DREXEL HILL, PA.—PAUL WESTHEAD is no choir boy, but nobody ever asked a choir boy to coach La Salle College's basketball team.

Paul Westhead signed a four-year contract yesterday as the Explorers' sixth coach in eight years. He made it through the late morning press conference and the seemingly endless media interviews, phone calls and appointments.

Late Homecoming: He was an hour-and-a-half late getting home, and his wife told a persistent caller that he very possibly might've stopped to talk to a high school player.

Paul Westhead laughed.

"She asked me if I was nervous when I left for the press conference, and I told her this would be the easiest day I'll ever have. It's tough to keep forcing smiles for photographers, to keep answering the same questions for radio and television and newspaper people, but what lies ahead is infinitely tougher."

Refers to Ban: He meant the NCAA probation, the shadowy dealings that had supplied Explorer athletes with innocuous jobs, the snickers when knowledgeable fans wondered how this player or that player ever got into college in the first place.

"I thought about all of it," the 31-year-old former West Catholic High, Malvern Prep and St. Joseph's athlete explained. "I decided you can't judge people by just what you read.

"You have to find out for yourself. I found out that they've done some things which I could not have done, but they asked me to be their coach—my way.

"I'm not naive, but my way is the legal, aboveboard, moral way. I wanted the new start as a head coach, they wanted the new start as a head coach, they wanted the new start in terms of approach and reputation. I can't guarantee tournament teams, but I will guarantee—absolutely—that my players will carry the integrity and respect of a student-athlete. Whatever La Salle's image has been . . . well, images can be changed."

La Salle finished Tom Gola's second season with a 14–12 record. Paul Westhead will inherit Ken Durrett, Bobby Fields, Ron Kennedy, Greg Cannon, a collection of sparsely used reserves and perhaps two or three freshmen. Hopefully, he will also have academic casualties Bill Pleas and Jeff Piccone.

"To rebuild the program here . . . to get it back to the right level . . . realistically will take no less than three years, probably four and maybe longer," the new coach said. "But if you're an aspiring coach, and you believe in yourself, the Big 5 is where you want to be. My opportunity is now. All I ask is a fair chance."

Coach Hawk Frosh: Westhead coached the 1969–70 St. Joseph's freshmen (Mike Bantom, Mike Moody, Pat McFarland, Bobby Haas, Bobby Sabol, Jack Krustick) to a 21–2 record, tying Penn for the Big 5 title. He had been assistant athletic director and assistant basketball coach at his alma mater since 1968, after spending a year as an assistant at Dayton and five successful years at Cheltenham High. In 1968–69, he guided Cheltenham to the PIAA Class A eastern championship.

"People ask me if I can really be La Salle's coach with my close ties at St. Joseph's," he said. "My real interest is in coaching, and that involves total allegiance to wherever my career takes me.

"The coaching, the recruiting, the work . . . they're basically the same everywhere. My interest is in coaching and dealing with young men. Only the cover of the book has changed."

JACK HAS SOMETHING IN RESERVE (CUNNINGHAM)

Trentonian
April 28, 1970

PHILADELPHIA—BILLY CUNNINGHAM WILL PLAY for the Philadelphia 76ers during the 1970–71 season. Positively. Definitely. Absolutely.

Billy Cunningham expects to play for the Carolina Cougars during the 1971–72 season. Maybe. Possibly. Less than absolutely.

A lot less than absolutely.

Cunningham and the 76ers have agreed to terms for the next National Basketball Association season. That is not the same as signing a contract, because then you get into the gray, shadowy, yet-to-be-tested area of the NBA reserve clause.

Philadelphia owner Irv Kosloff refused to announce Cunningham's salary, but it is safe to assume that he is now the team's highest-paid player. He earned approximately $55,000 last season and has signed a three-year pact with the ABA Cougars that is reportedly one of the richest and best in professional sports.

Jack Ramsay, the 76ers' acting general manager, did not act like a coach who had just been saved from the bottom of the Eastern Division.

"I can't say that I'm surprised, because I always expected Billy to play here," Ramsay here. "I know he had never said definitely that he would play for the 76ers next season, but he had told me several times that he was 'planning on it.' That was good enough for me.

"I expect he'll be with Philadelphia a lot longer than one season, too. The reserve clause in the NBA contract binds him to us, and when he signed his last contract with us, it included a statement agreeing to the reserve clause.

"The press and media have written and said a lot about the legality of the reserve clause, but it's never been proved anything but legal. When a player signs, he agrees to it—every player in the league.

"For Billy to go Carolina after next season would be breaking a contract, and then we'd have to go to court to settle it."

The way the standard NBA contract is written, the club's obligation is to mail a player a contract by September 1 of each year. The player does not have to sign to make it legal, but a club can pay an unsigned player 75 percent of the sum in the last signed agreement.

Isn't that the same as slavery, Jack?

"Slavery? At these prices?," Ramsay questioned. "NBA players are the highest paid athletes anywhere. What kind of slavery is that?"

Cunningham agreed to terms early yesterday afternoon, then met the press with Kosloff, Ramsay, Cunningham, counsel Shelley Bendit and 76ers' counsel Nat Budin.

"I thought about all the possibilities," Billy admitted. "I thought about staying here, about playing for the Cougars next year, about sitting out the season.

"I came up with an answer that it would hurt me as a ballplayer to sit out a year. I thought about Rick Barry (who sat out a season before playing for Oakland in the ABA), how it took him a while to come back, how he got hurt when he finally did get started.

"Jim Gardner (the Cougars' owner) told me he'd have preferred to have me play there next year, but that this was fine. He felt it'd be better for me to play in Philly and keep my name before the public than to sit out. In the long run, he feels it'll help the Cougars."

Ramsay says a merger of the NBA and ABA would have no effect on Cunningham's status. Cunningham says he simply has an agreement with the Cougars, and that he fully intends to honor both. Positively. Definitely. Absolutely.

Stay tuned. All these positivelys, definitelys and absolutelys have a history of fluctuation.

PLAYERS ANTI-MERGER

Trentonian
June 19, 1970

PHILADELPHIA—THE NBA AND THE ABA have asked Congress to ap-
prove a merger of the two professional basketball leagues.

Does that mean anything to Luke Jackson?

Keep in mind that Jackson has two years remaining on a Philadelphia
76er contract that reportedly pays him $100,000 per season.

Also, keep in mind that the 6-9 former Olympian "agreed to terms"
with the Carolina Cougars just before he signed with the 76ers.

"I don't expect the merger to affect me . . . I don't see how it can," Luke
said last night. "There's no litigation against me (from Carolina), and I
want to stay right where I am. It could come to a court decision, though,
and I suppose if the courts ruled that I had to play for them I would.

"I'm not surprised that the merger is finally going through. The other
league (ABA) has shown it can survive, and it has some good talent. It's
not up to the NBA level yet, but let's face it, the NBA has been around
forever. You can't expect a new league to be that good right away."

Has Luke been anti-merger?

"I think most of the players are," he answered. "They feel they're being
deprived the right of negotiating with other clubs. After all, playing pro
basketball is nothing more than a job, and a guy with a job should at least
be able to determine who he wants to work for."

The Cougars have probably never filed litigation against Jackson
because the forward-center has since suffered two crippling leg injuries
and has never regained the form and potential he showed during the
1967–68 championship season.

"I feel well," Luke said. "I haven't had any trouble with my leg at all,
but I'm not going to play ball this summer either."

By summer ball, he meant the Charles Baker pro league.

Is that because he wants to rest his leg?

"No, it's because I just don't want to play in the Baker League."

If no litigation is forthcoming against Jackson, you can bet the merger
money that the Cougars and 76ers will wind up in court concerning Billy
Cunningham.

Cunningham has agreed to play one more season with the 76ers, then
plans to honor a three-year pact with Carolina. Billy spent last night in
business discussions with attorney Sheldon Bendit.

Philadelphia coach Jack Ramsay has contended from the start that
Cunningham is bound to the 76ers by the NBA reserve clause.

And how familiar does that sound?

CHAPTER 2

· · · · · ·

THE EAGLES YEARS

Introduction by Vince Papale

Phil was so cool. He was so calm in his work environment. He couldn't be rattled. I was the young nervous guy trying to find my way. Phil came up to me and treated me like I was an All-Pro player. I'll never forget that. I loved that. Here's this crazy young player like me and Phil was so calm, sat down next to me, and started talking. I was going a mile a minute, just trying to earn my spot on the Eagles. I didn't know anything. I was young and raw. Phil came in and had this calming influence for me to trust him. That's not easy being interviewed. Instantly, I felt like this reporter was my friend. He had this great wit with little tactical things he would use when he was interviewing you. I could tell he enjoyed his role as a reporter as much as I did trying to earn my way onto the Eagles. This was all new to me. I could tell right away it wasn't new to Phil. He knew what he was doing and came prepared. His trust gave me trust on my end to tell him anecdotes. I was this long shot kid and thank God Phil wrote these stories because I felt like it gave me more of an opportunity to make my way and work my way on the Eagles as that long shot. He told my story.

I can't say that I trusted everyone back then. Some guys wrote articles that weren't always fair in my eyes. That wasn't Phil. He told every story the right way. You knew that you could trust him. It wouldn't go to press until Phil had all the facts straight. There wasn't one thing that Phil left out or you felt like should have been included in the story. Phil didn't do anything for show. He wasn't like that. His stories told the stories of the players and coaches that the readers could understand. He was amazing in that way. When you read his stories, you felt like you were on the inside. The trust was never broken, either. That was rare.

I was this intense 30- to 31-year-old guy who wanted to make his mark and didn't want to offend anyone. I felt like I could tell Phil anything. He would take everything in and wouldn't write anything that would hurt me in any way. If he had a question, he would ask. I always enjoyed reading Phil's articles. You knew the finished product would be terrific. Every time. He treated me the same as a Hall of Fame player. He was the epitome of class. He saw a side of me that was a great story to tell and he recognized the interest it would generate. I trusted him from the first time I saw him and that trust developed into a beautiful friendship for many years. He asked me what I thought about situations. I was this unknown guy, not an All-Pro by any means. He gave me such respect that you gave that same respect back to him. I knew that I couldn't go wrong.

I took pride in what I did. Phil took such great pride in what he did. That mentality never changed in either of us. Phil looked at the good in people. He wanted to tell the good stories in all of us. He would write critical stories when necessary, but they were always fair. He hung out so much that he was part of us. The guys in that locker room trusted him because of his work ethic and diligence. He was part of the culture. We knew we could trust him. When he wrote his stories, we were excited because we knew the product would match the prep work.

I got to know Phil very well. As the years passed, if we would cross paths, it was as if time never passed. The friendship increased. He was everything you could ask for—trustworthy, honest, friendly, diligent. Just a great man. I miss him every day.

VINCE PAPALE *earned a roster spot on the Philadelphia Eagles as an undrafted rookie in 1976 and went on to play for three seasons. Papale's story was so inspiring that a movie titled* Invincible *was released in 2006, describing Papale's remarkable journey from a part-time bartender and substitute teacher to becoming an Eagle.*

• • • • • •

THE HAWK IS VERY MUCH ALIVE . . . AND TRAINING WITH EAGLES

Philadelphia Daily News
June 26, 1976

ONE OF THE INGLORIOUS AXIOMS of a professional football training camp is that rookies must sing during meals. Their songs may be raucous, their voices weary and gravelly, their tunes almost unrecognizable.

Every once in a while, the feeling is there, and one of the sport's rites of summer glares back at the veterans who demand the performances. Like when Vince Papale, the 30-year-old rookie receiver, insisted on singing a tribute to a boyhood hero.

Papale brightly climbed on a chair and rumbled through the St. Joseph's College spiritual that carried the Hawks to many of their greatest basketball victories at the Palestra. The words were mildly adjusted to paint a picture of 32-year-old Ben Hawkins, a man on the way back.

Glory, glory, hallelujah, the Hawk will never die.

And he might not.

"I think I'm doing all right so far," Ben Hawkins said during a break in the regimen of the Eagles' training camp at Widener College. "My leg's been holding up (it was broken during the 1973 season), and if I was gettin' kinda tired the first week I'm coming back okay now."

Ben Hawkins. A third-round draft choice from Arizona State in 1966. A spectacular receiver, flourishing against man-to-man defenses that he could outrun, outmaneuver or outjump. He became the Hawk, with his chinstrap dangling, and his x's and o's bedeviling a defender.

He was traded to Cleveland in 1974, stayed four weeks, then returned to the periphery of his profession, visiting frequently with old teammates and friends. He surfaced last year with the Bell in the World Football League, an athlete with enough experience and identity to survive in a struggling new league.

"As far as the receivers go, we're just doing a lot of running, staying on our feet a lot," he said. "There's a lot more hitting than ever, except maybe the year Eddie (Khayat) had all that hitting and (Lee) Bouggess and some others got hurt. Then he stopped.

"But I know most of the guys out here, because one way or another I've stayed in touch. It's been a lot of years, but not really that much of a change. I think to myself, I'm one of the old guys around, and when I came up in '66 I saw all the old guys there then.

"What the future holds is all up in the air. Your age doesn't matter, it's that you have to be able to play. The ones who can are the ones who will be here. . . . I think maybe I have 2–3 years left, and I just wanted to come back and play some more. Anyway, about this time, you get the fever.

"But I also know when the end of this stream is here, that's gonna be it. When your water runs low, it's over. If an athlete doesn't know when it's over, it's because he doesn't want to face up to it. If I can't play anymore, then I can't. No sense worrying about it."

The trade to Cleveland could have been the beginning of the end, except that he would not allow it to happen.

"I was in Cleveland four weeks, and I don't think I really got a shot," he said. "I won't say anything else. That's as far as I want to go."

"The WFL? It was an experience. You saw things in a different light, but on the field it was still the same. A lot of the stuff, as far as the organizations went, hurt, but the caliber was good.

"What I want to do now, though, is just come in and play, perform, do my job. I've seen all the fanfare, and it doesn't mean that much, because I'd rather be taken as a person, for what I am now. The rest of it is secondary."

If he is older than many of the players in camp, he doesn't always feel it.

"Kids'll say I remember you when I was in grade school," he said. "They'll say they used to see me on television. But you've got to realize, when they say it, it's true. It was the same with me, when I was coming up. I'd come into camp, pick out people, say I'd like to be like somebody else. I always listened to the older people, tried to learn. All the stuff I heard before is coming back around now, only sometimes it's me telling a younger guy instead of the other way around."

He is open to change, willing to adjust, believing enough of the Hawk remains with Ben Hawkins to resume a career of excellence.

Ironically, he was just entering the dining hall when Papale finished his musical tribute.

"I would've liked to have heard it," he conceded. "It's not too many people they write songs about."

Vince Papale's carefully chosen words had been for him, but for Ben Hawkins the music spills out onto the playing field, filtering into the patterns and the moves that once made him one of the best at his trade.

He is 32 and believing there is more to be done. Which is why he is here. Trying to get the feeling is another of professional football's inglorious rites of summer.

ROMAN CAN'T TELL HOW CLOSE HE IS TO COMEBACK

Philadelphia Daily News
July 26, 1976

ROMAN GABRIEL IS IN Rancho Mirage, Calif., contemplating his—and the Eagles'—future, wondering if his surgically repaired right knee will ever again be as strong as his will to someday return to the playing field.

Joe Gardi is in Hempstead, Long Island, occasionally reviewing the flurry of frantic circumstances that finally earned him space as an assistant coach in the National Football League, then determinedly going about the business of teaching the New York Jets' special teamers and tight ends.

Gabriel will soon be 36, knowing he cannot resume his career as a quarterback for a minimum of several weeks, possibly not until next season, and perhaps not at all. If his options are less than spectacular, his approach is, at the very least, admirable.

"I'll go on doing what I'm doing," Gabriel said, meaning he will stoically continue the tortuous four-hour daily workouts, starting generally at 6:30 a.m., a concession to the grim desert heat.

"I know I'm not ready to play football right now, but I haven't totally ruled out the season. A few weeks ago, I felt I was close, and I still have that feeling. But 'close' to me can still be far away, and close isn't good enough. You'd have to know me very well to understand all of what I mean.

"But I'm not downtrodden, and I haven't retired, because I haven't ruled anything out. What it is, is an empty feeling, the first time in my career I've been unable to come to training camp. I'm just glad I'm smart enough to separate feelings and emotions from reality.

"But whether I play football or not, I'll continue this program. If I can't ever again play football, I still need my right leg to do other things. Retired? Not yet. Just say I've graduated to a new area."

Eagles' Coach Dick Vermeil talked with Gabriel late last week, before taking his team to Hofstra for a Saturday afternoon scrimmage with the Jets.

"Dick caught me a bit unaware," Gabriel admitted. "I was going to wait a couple more days, then call him, but if anything our discussion left me with a refreshing and another reason to continue.

"There are supposed to be all sorts of obstacles in my way. I'm about 36, I have knee trouble. I have more rehabilitation to go through, I may have to wait a whole year to play. I like the challenge of all that, and I might overcome it. I just might."

The incumbent quarterback now is Mike Boryla, a former Stanford star, a first-round draft choice, and for two years a teammate of Gabriel.

"I've given him some advice over that time," Gabriel said. "I've told him he has great talent, a great touch, but that he has to get stronger. A lot of young quarterbacks get knocked out of games early, then need too much time to come back. A quarterback is going to be hit by big, strong people in the NFL, so he has to be strong and resilient.

"Another feeling comes from my talks with Dick Vermeil. He's told me things are coming together well, but that he'll need cooperation to make the progress he wants. I know enough about the coach to know he builds winners, and that if people around him work as hard as he does, it will happen with the Eagles."

If there is a trace of despondency in being unable to perform, Joe Gardi knows the euphoria of being in the league at all.

Gardi was the special teams coach with the Bell, during the adventurous, unfortunate short life of the World Football League. He became the team's interim coach when Ron Waller was relieved, then became a popular, successful coach of the struggling Portland Thunder.

Out of work through no fault of his own, he pursued various college jobs, was twice interviewed by the front office of the expansionist Seattle Seahawks, and even contacted Vermeil about room on the Eagles' staff.

"Dick was very, very nice, but he said he had a list of 65 friends who all wanted jobs," Gardi recalled. "He was open and honest with me, and I was a guy he just didn't know that much about.

"I had known Lou Holtz (the Jets' new coach) from my time at Maryland, when he was at North Carolina State, so I decided to call, hope he'd remember. I woke him up at 7 in the morning, and wouldn't let him off the phone until he promised to talk to me.

"He agreed to see me, but I think he was just being courteous at that point. I finally asked him to let me make a presentation, and five hours later I had a job."

"Ahhh, so what if some unusual things happened in the WFL? It was the greatest experience of my life. With the Bell, Willie Wood got a job that I wanted, then I got a job in Portland, then the league couldn't go on. I think back, and I wouldn't trade a minute of it. If not for that, I wouldn't be here."

Joe Gardi says he could not be in a better, more positive situation, that he has found rejuvenation, a new life.

In Rancho Mirage, Calif., where the Eagles have left a playbook and special weight and exercise machines in Roman Gabriel's garage, the search continues.

Roman Gabriel would settle for what Joe Gardi has found.

JOACHIM AND GROSSMAN: THEY'RE CROSSING PATHS AGAIN

Philadelphia Daily News
August 9, 1976

THE SUMMER SAND of Stone Harbor, N.J. Warm. Reassuring. Deceptive. Hot at the top, cold and dark beneath.

Randy Grossman, the Pittsburgh Steelers' backup tight end and special teamer, would run through his patterns. On the beach. And Steve Joachim, the quarterback from Temple, still seeking an opportunity somewhere, would throw. And throw. And throw.

"Had to be a tough summer for Steve," Randy Grossman was saying between Steelers' workouts to prepare for tonight's exhibition with the Eagles at Veterans Stadium.

"I mean, I've played two years, but Steve had been through some tough luck with Baltimore and Toronto. He was up there in the early part of the summer, got out and came home worried, with things on his mind."

Grossman and Joachim. Joachim and Grossman. They had intertwined their careers, first at Haverford High, then at Temple, the success coming first, the ironies developing later.

Grossman went to the Steelers, quickly signing a two-year contract the day after the draft. Joachim, having led the nation in offense, and having won the Maxwell Award a year later, lingered until the seventh round, then had only the briefest opportunity with the Colts.

Grossman comes into tonight's game with six preseason catches, leading the Steelers. Joachim will arrive in the second half, replacing Mike Boryla as the Eagles' quarterback.

"Long overdue for him," Grossman said. "But in the summer, he was throwing stronger and better than ever. He has a much better idea now of where to throw, when to throw.

"Sometimes the explanations for why a player does or doesn't succeed are so well hidden, you wonder if anybody can explain them. There are hundreds of variables, but no formula of fact. No right, no wrong, just situations. And they're never the same."

Grossman is the more secure of the summer duo. He has caught 24 passes in his two regular seasons, played in two Super Bowls, caught a touchdown pass from Terry Bradshaw in one.

Secure? He has a new two-year contract, but he has veteran Larry Brown ahead of him, and rookie Bennie Cunningham scrambling behind him. Secure? He wonders if he'll be a Steeler at all.

"I guess I'm doing all right," he conceded, "but it's gonna be tough to make this team, pretty much the same situation I've always been in. A little disappointing, but all part of the business, too.

"It's not the situation you picture as a kid, but after a while you realize it's the way things are done. It's not a bad situation, just different.

"I have no feeling of security at all. . . . I won't even look for an apartment until the regular season starts. The new contract is nice, but it has no value until I survive all the cuts. It's why I cope with pro football on a day-to-day basis. I can't afford to plan ahead real far."

He wondered if he might be selected in the expansion draft by Seattle or Tampa Bay. He asked himself if the Steelers would possibly make a personnel decision, trade a tight end, waive one, whatever.

"I'm just as happy to be here, though," he said. "I'd as soon be a Steeler on the second team as be a starter for someone else. At least that's the way I feel right now.

"It's funny, but I have my own evaluations of how good I am, how much I can accomplish, but the coaches evidently look for different things, and I haven't measured up to what they want in a starting tight end.

"They say I'd have to block much better, something I never took that seriously. Blocking was something I could do well enough to get by, but not something at which I excelled. I catch the ball as well as anyone, but that's not enough."

It is a dismal, and, at the same time, illuminating feeling.

"Don't get the idea that I'm happy or that I don't think I can make it," said Grossman, "because I've already accomplished a major portion of what I set out to do. I'm here. I've played. I've shown my capabilities. Still, I'm a second-team tight end. Second-team players are expendable, and if you take it personally, it could be difficult to live with."

The Steelers crushed the College All-Stars, 24–0, in a rain-shortened opener.

"Rain?" Randy Grossman said. "That was the most rain I've ever been in at one time. It was like trying to play football in a swimming pool."

They rumbled past New Orleans, 24–14 (the Saints dressed 81 players, had 19 others injured and unavailable), and have outgained the two opponents, 645 yards to 296.

"I don't know that the two games can tell you that much," Grossman suggested. "The College All-Star game, nobody's wild about playing The All-Stars would rather be in the camps of the teams that drafted them, the pro team would prefer to be in camp or at least playing another pro team. The Saints? Well, we're supposed to do well against teams like that."

His early lead among receivers, he insists, tells us less.

"I didn't even know," he said, "and with all the receivers and backs we've been using, is probably more a freak of the numbers than anything else. I'm happy, sure, but I'd be happier if I was still there several weeks from now."

If it is a time to stay, it must also be a time to quickly develop. The summer workouts with Steve Joachim on the Stone Harbor beaches were worthwhile, but only a very small beginning.

Randy Grossman's instincts tell him a second-team tight end on even a Super Bowl team can afford no sand castles.

EAGLES' ROOKIE TORAN HAS FILL OF BAD TRIPS

Philadelphia Daily News
July 7, 1977

NATE TORAN WAS RUTGERS' All-American. A symbol on an undefeated team. A leader of a defense that led the nation in three categories. He led his team in quarterback sacks, he finished second in tackles.

And did he get snapped up in the NFL draft?

Well, did he?

"I spent three days in Washington, before and during the draft," Toran recalled during a break in his preparation for the Eagles' training camp that opens Monday at Widener College for rookies, free agents, quarterbacks and selected veterans.

"Three days . . . I mean, they sent me a plane ticket and I jumped at it. I had to believe if they were that interested, then it was likely they were going to draft me. The way it turned out, though, was not what you could call a refreshing experience.

"There were five of us . . . players from various schools, all in similar situations. They had hotel space for us, took care of our meals, showed us around town, but it was like being all alone when you suddenly realized you should've really been with your coach, your friends, your lawyer. Somebody."

He was a 6-1, 227-pound defensive end at Rutgers, and Washington did not draft him.

Neither did anyone else. The 12 rounds of picking and choosing and ferreting through computer analyses deteriorated into a private agony for an athlete who had contributed 17 sacks for 115 yards in net losses, 53 primary hits and 26 assists in an 11–0 senior season.

"As each round passed and no one took me the first day," Toran said, "I looked ahead to the later rounds, when the Redskins had some picks.

"When the last round was over, and I hadn't been picked I sort of stood there, startled, with my mouth open, wondering what in the world was going on.

"A little later, they sent some people down to talk to us, explain each guy's situation. They told me they had considered taking me, but a couple of times the player they had wanted sooner was taken by some other team and they had had to change their plans.

"I'll admit it all sounded logical, and when they were done, they wanted me to sign as a free agent. I thought about that, and remembered that George Allen seems to hold veterans in especially high regard, so I felt that might not be the right place for a rookie or a free agent."

At the other end of the telephone line came a voice from the Eagles.

"And all things being equal, I figured that might be a good place to try," said Toran. "For one thing, when a team isn't winning there's usually a large turnover in personnel, another way of saying they have to try something new, someone different. If I perform I could be a part of that."

Not that there won't be some swift adjustments. The Eagles signed Toran as a projected linebacker, an area where they are strong among the regulars (Bill Bergey, Frank LeMaster, John Bunting), where they have four other veteran returnees (Terry Tautolo, Tom Ehlers, Drew Mahalic and Dean Halverson), where they have signed nine additional rookies and free agents.

"Why didn't he get drafted?" asked Herman Ball, the Eagles' director of player personnel. "You look for reasons, and the first is probably size. Not many teams are gonna get hopped up about a defensive end who's 6-1, 227, and some teams don't like to draft athletes that they have to project to a new position.

"When we have a guy in that category, we give him some drills, some instruction, accept the fact that he has no experience and see how he assimilates the information, how he adjusts, how easily he understands. If the signs are good, he has a chance. If he has a chance, why not take him?"

Toran wonders about the clickety-clack of the computer readouts.

"How can you argue with a machine?" he said. "They can measure your size, your weight, but they can't know what's inside you, how much you want to play, how hard you're willing to work. I won't judge a computer, because I'm mortal. I'm fallible. I only wish people understood that computers can be fallible, too.

"Like, people have asked if Rutgers going to a postseason bowl might have enhanced my situation in the draft. The answer is, I was a two-year All-American, a three-year All-East, I played on an unbeaten club as a senior, I played well in our games on TV. I don't know that any more publicity could have helped me, made any difference at all.

"The way people looked at Rutgers football, all I can say is if you're gonna go 11–0, leading the league in yards allowed per game, rushing yards per game, and fewest points yielded . . . in order to be all of that, you've gotta be good. I don't care if you're doing it on a sandlot, you've got to be able to play."

So he will try with the Eagles, helmet in hand, so to speak.

"I don't want to come in and be a star," Nate Toran said. "I just want a job, a year for a pro team to nurture me along, help me develop.

"One of the things I learned from my three days in Washington is a big reason I'm trying it with this team. I remember the ride home from there after expecting big things and not getting drafted at all. . . . It was very long and very lonely, and if I ever have to make a trip like that again I'd prefer it to be a short ride."

Finally, Nate Toran paused in his thoughts.

"On the other hand," he said hopefully, "I'd just as soon they let me stay. That's what I really want."

NO DOGS, BUT THE EAGLES HAVE BOW-WOW

Philadelphia Daily News
July 7, 1976

HIS NAME IS WOJTKIEWICZ. S. WOJTKIEWICZ. Pronounces it Wo-jehho-witch Woit-kev-ich.

"Polish," he said after lunch yesterday in the Eagles' training camp at Widener College. "Means ruling a kingdom. A Polish prince. My father once told me, 'You've got a name, don't ever change it, but make something out of it.'"

It is an impossible name. Unpronounceable. You see it written out, you ask if it's an animal, vegetable or mineral. But there is a quick, painless way to handle it.

"Call me," he says unabashedly, "Bow-Wow."

Bow-Wow? He is a close friend of Dick Vermeil. Says he is a close friend to the UCLA athletic family. Says he is independently wealthy, that he can afford to take a month or two and live in the Eagles' camp, watching Vermeil, assessing the situation. Mike McCormack used to worry that there were too many dogs on his roster, and Vermeil shows up with a watchdog.

Bow-Wow will not say how old he is, but he recalls he had an older brother who played briefly at Notre Dame.

"Knute Rockne nicknamed him Big Bow-Wow, because he played center and seemed to snap the ball and get through the line so fast maybe it seemed like a dog was at the other team's heels. Screamed as he went through. I was Little Bow-Wow, because I was always hanging around.

"Best thing you can say about me is, I'm not ordinary. I got started years ago, when Howard Hughes sold RKO, started Trancas Producing Co. Now we shoot movies, commercials, training films for big companies and put 'em on cassettes.

"We're gonna go into peoples' homes pretty soon. Put a box on the television, a place to drop in a cassette and you have full-length films on home TV. It'll cost maybe 50–75 cents a movie . . . use 'em once, then mail 'em back for us to rewind. Costs $18 to install the box. It belongs to us, but once it's in, there's no rental fee.

"We'll have cartoons, other stuff for 10 cents . . . As a come-on, because it'll cost 26 cents just to mail them. But you hope the customer likes it, then orders other more expensive stuff. Liz Taylor did two movies for us. Richard Burton's doing one, with the salaries deferred for a percentage of the cassette use.

"It's a funny situation, because it's Howard Hughes' corporation. I'm the president and the owner is dead. I've got a pretty good idea where the will is though . . . at least the portion that pertains to us. There's an old judge down in Texas has the answers."

Bow-Wow says he is also a writer.

"I'm writing a book called 'The Tramp Athlete,'" he said. "It's about me, because I went to 12 colleges, using fake transcripts. I got thrown out of 13 military schools. Ahh, at the time I was wild and ornery, I wanted to outsmart everybody. I didn't try to get kicked out, I just did things I thought were funny. Schools are stricter now.

"I had a friend at a junior college, got me all the transcripts I wanted. I played under eight or nine different names, but I caused problems for myself because I'd sometimes forget who I was at which school. I'm the reason you see photos on transcripts now."

He says he has been involved at UCLA for 31 years, in no specific area or capacity.

"Help recruit, drives coaches around, help out whenever, wherever," he said. "Now, I'm usually in my studio in California at 5 a.m., go over to the college maybe 2:30. Gets me away from the movie people.

"I watched Dick Vermeil when he first came to UCLA and knew he was a winner. I mean, UCLA was in the same basic situation as the Eagles are in now . . . They couldn't beat Southern Cal, couldn't get to the Rose Bowl. He did it all in two years. The players almost revolted, and he told them they'd shed tears together, then beat Ohio State. He did it there, he'll do it here.

"The guy works so hard, if he were at General Motors or 20th Century Fox, he'd be a president. He's a driver. He'll outwork anybody. I'd say 80 percent of the people I've known work at maybe 30 percent of their capacity. He works at 110 percent. I used to drive him home from UCLA at 1–2 in the morning, because if he went himself he might fall asleep at the wheel. Then he'd wake up at 5, figure as long as he was up he may as well get some work done."

Bow-Wow says he eventually earned a degree at UCLA.

"Then Jack Warner helped me get started, and I began to write," he said. "My wife was Sheila Graham, who did a newspaper column for years. I wrote the thing for her for five of those years, and I wrote, 'Beloved Infidel' for her. It came down to UCLA or her, and I finally took UCLA.

"People ask me if I knew Howard Hughes, and I answer by saying he was the greatest American ever with the least credit. He was involved in so many things to help this country. Charity work, cancer research, everything.

"There was a point years ago when he had to go before a Congressional Committee, and the way it was handled disgusted him, so he dropped out of sight. But he got $50 million worth of publicity by not being around. He read everything printed about him. I saw him maybe 4–5 months ago in Acapulco. He looked healthy."

And what else does he say about Dick Vermeil?

"I know he's gonna win here," Bow-Wow says. "This city has a reputation for fans who boo. Well, if his players don't perform, that's one thing, but if those same people applaud when his players gave a spirited, 100 percent effort, then the fans will be contributing, too.

"I know it's gonna be tough, because every club in the division has improved itself and all the Eagles have added are a bunch of coaches. Well, it's a start. I know Dick Vermeil. His family is my family. I see his first team here winning seven games. I think it'll happen."

Will the Eagles' bite finally be worse than their bark? Will Bow-Wow ever leave?

Bow-Wow would only answer the last question.

"Can only stay about four weeks," he said. "Then I've got to get back. Too much to do, too far behind in the movies, the cassettes, my book. But I'll be around. If Dick Vermeil needs me, I'm always around."

ECHO FOR BIRDS: MAYBE NEXT YEAR

Philadelphia Daily News
December 14, 1976

DICK VERMEIL WILL HAVE somewhere between 15 and 20 new athletes on his 43-man roster for 1977, a logical step toward rebuilding the Eagles at least two games closer to .500 in the fiercely competitive NFC East.

Not that anyone should make any judgments based on Sunday's 27–10 victory over 2–12 Seattle.

"Well, Sunday demonstrated more clearly the kind of football we'd like to be able to play . . . the style, the good, sound running game, the high-percentage passing game, getting after people," Vermeil said yesterday.

"Fortunately, we played a team that allowed us to do what we wanted to do, what we actually tried to do every time we lined up all season. We haven't gone as far as I'd like to have been able to, but if I could program a game for 14 games, that's what I'd like to do.

"Maybe you have to have better personnel. I don't know you have to be better disciplined, because in that style no one guy wins for you. (But) I know we've played a better schedule than 25-26-27 other teams . . . you'll see a team going to the playoffs next week that's played three teams like that (the ones we played), lost two and tied one."

Lurking in the midst of Vermeil's postseason commentary is the basic truth that he has now given his players the season he promised them. He kept some when he could have taken slightly better ones off waiver lists or in minor deals, but he steadfastly protected his people, rewarding them for loyalty in a brutal summer that began July 3 at Widener.

"I did what I wanted," Vermeil said. "I gave every player a chance to prove what he could and couldn't do. Now, I'll do my best to upgrade everything. I've been fair . . . as fair as anyone I know in coaching."

And the answer is . . . what?

"I would say almost all these guys can play in this league," the coach replied. "But you don't want them all on the same team at the same time. Then it's touch when you start playing the Cowboys . . . the winning teams.

"Some guys, no matter how much you coach 'em, are not gonna be good enough to beat Dallas if you've got 10 other guys lining up with them playing average football. But I've also seen average guys go somewhere else in a trade or something, and suddenly go like hell because the guys around them are so much better, they fit right in, not as much is expected just from them."

To improve, the Eagles have a fifth-round draft choice and three sixth-round picks (if there is a draft at all). Then they will sign a high number of free agents, perhaps more than last year, possibly pursue a player or two who has fulfilled contractual obligations elsewhere, possibly even attempt to dangle some combination of current players (Charlie Smith? James McAlister? Tom Sullivan?) that could bring either an experienced player or something as high as a second-round pick.

Guards Tom Luken and John Niland, kick returner Larry Marshall, running back Art Malone and puzzling defensive lineman Cliff Frazier will come off the injured reserve list. Next I think Vermeil will search for an experienced quarterback, and if he cannot get Dan Pastorini from Houston, would he consider Jesse Freitas from San Diego? Or Ron Jaworski from Los Angeles?

Vermeil believes his team could have—should have—won six games, but no one is surprised that it did not.

"We played the Monday Night game (against Washington) and should have found a way to win," he said. "The (second) St. Louis game, we should have found a way to win. If we had done a super job coaching, we should've found a way to win at least six."

Maybe next year. Maybe if all the new people are good enough. Whoever they are.

CHAPTER 3

THE BIG 5 YEARS

Introduction by Paul Westhead

knew and respected Phil for a lot of years; from his days in Trenton, and even before, that is when I first met him. I actually first met Phil when I was coaching at Cheltenham High School. He later covered colleges, but it was then at Cheltenham when I first got to know Phil. We were the bottom of the barrel in the league, and the league has changed so much over the years. Phil was covering a lot of high school sports in Norristown and wrote a lot of articles, including a number for our home games. We were at the bottom, but here comes this guy with big curly locks of hair asking me a lot of questions to get the story he was looking for. He was fair and pointed and showed us respect. I felt right away that I could trust him. I interacted a lot with Phil and he showed up prepared, having done his homework. He asked good questions, sometimes hard questions. I just felt like from the beginning, I could trust him, that he wouldn't write something that hurt me. He would be fair and always was fair. I saw that from the very beginning at Cheltenham. So we became fast friends and maintained that friendship for the rest of his time.

I was a young buck at the time. He was a young buck at the time. We were both doing our things. Right from the beginning, Phil was very personable and hit me with question after question after question. By the time the interview was over, he got what he needed. He wouldn't finish until he had every single fact straightened out. If it meant asking another question, he would do it. Since it was Phil, you just never minded because you knew it came from a place of hard work and diligence. Phil wanted to get it right, no matter how long it took.

He would look at you and give you that glare as I called it with a come-on-give-me-an-answer type of look. You couldn't avoid that honesty in Phil. He would never dig up dirt on you or anyone. But if there was a tough story to write, he would do it in a responsible way that you had to respect. You knew Phil had checked every fact, dotted every "i," and crossed every "t." If the story was published, you knew it was accurate. There was no question. Usually, writers and coaches didn't always get along. There were issues and problems. Not with Phil. He never, ever did anything shady. If he was going to write something tough, he would present it to me and tell me. I respected that. It was a major reason we became fast friends and remained such good friends the years beyond.

In later years, as he advanced and I advanced to college and then the NBA, we talked a lot both professionally and personally. Phil never changed. He covered games and wrote stories the same way—with respect, integrity, and fairness. Phil was so unique and rare. There weren't many like him. I'm proud to say that Phil and I were such good friends. Even if there was a critical article, it would never change how I felt about Phil and how Phil felt about me. It all started at Cheltenham, and Phil was the same reporter and friend decades later. I was shocked when I heard he was sick, and I miss him. He was truly one of the all-time greats.

PAUL WESTHEAD *had a long and storied coaching career that saw him guide the La Salle Explorers from 1970–1979. He later coached at Loyola Marymount and George Mason on the collegiate level.*

· · · · · ·

WESTHEAD: BIG 5 PULLS FOR MCKINNEY

Philadelphia Daily News
November 8, 1979

THE PLANT WAS HAND-DELIVERED to Little Company of Mary Hospital in Torrance, Calif., to be presented at an appropriate point of recuperation to Jack McKinney, the Los Angeles Lakers' coach.

"I saw it," said Paul Westhead, who will coach the team tonight in San Diego, "and I noticed it was impressive in size, that it had five big leaves. Only five.

"Then I saw the attached note, and it was from the Big 5."

McKinney is the former St. Joseph's College player and coach who was injured in a bicycling accident last week. Jack paid his dues as an NBA assistant in Milwaukee and Portland, then succeeded Jerry West this season with the Lakers.

McKinney remains hospitalized while doctors continue testing and treatment, and while that goes on, Westhead has stepped in with admirable effectiveness.

"There have been some signs of improvement in Jack," said Paul, who left La Salle after nine years to become McKinney's assistant, "and those developments have had an uplifting effect on everyone. We all seem to feel better, knowing Jack is getting better.

"Things were kind of touch-and-go for three–four days, but now he's regaining consciousness for two–three minutes at a time, showing some signs of recognition, knowing who's in the room, knowing his own name.

"He hasn't reached any sort of conversational level, but each day seems to being something more. The doctors are running tests and seem relatively certain he'll recuperate."

McKinney had been en route to Westhead's home, where the two had a tennis date. But McKinney fell from his bicycle and suffered a head injury and a fracture in his elbow.

"I still don't have all the details," said Westhead, "but a fella saw Jack coming down the hill, apparently at a moderate speed . . . I say that, knowing it's a steep hill, that if a car just rolled from the top it might be going 70 MPH by the time it reached the bottom.

"In any case, there must've been a malfunction in the bike, the report said he went flying, slid a good 20 feet. The fella who saw it rushed to the nearest house, had whoever answered the doorbell call the police.

"The prognosis is still really indeterminate, because the doctors were sort of riding out the first several days. I know they'll make more evaluations now, but I don't know much more than that."

In the meantime, Westhead, who played at West Catholic, Malvern Prep and St. Joseph's, is 2–0 as the interim coach.

"Jack had done a terrific job programming the players, in terms of responding to winning or losing," Paul said. "There are situations where teams tend to get disjointed or all bent out of shape when they lose a couple, but Jack was very aware of that, and they've picked it up well.

"I obviously don't like the circumstance of seeing Jack hurt and hospitalized, but the work he did early has made it much easier for me to fill in now. I refer to the role of the gambler, who, when the chips are there, he plays them."

That's one major reason the team's owner, Jerry Buss, and GM Bill Sharman decided against bringing in an additional assistant to share the workload with Westhead.

"We didn't want to do anything to change the atmosphere of the team," Paul said, "although Jerry West has done a lot to help.

"Jerry sits in the stands, then talks to me at halftime. The day of a game, he'll talk to me about certain tendencies of an opposing team or a particular player, and, when we go on the road, he's going to do some scouting. He's been excellent about it, volunteering to do whatever might be needed.

"That's about the way the whole experience has been. When I took this job, I heard all the truisms and clichés about the overpaid, unresponsive pros, the guys who take the position that they know it all, but that hasn't been the way it's been here. Jack and I found excited, eager players, willing to do whatever it might take to win.

"That's been the approach from Kareem (Abdul-Jabbar) on down. If anything, these guys have been more cooperative than the college kids. When we bring in a scouting report, they want to know everything they can, they've been all ears. Sometimes the college guys think they're already there.

"If this is my pro experience, I'm excited about it, because these guys play outside themselves. They don't seem to care who does it, as long as the team does it. And the more they act that way, the better they play."

Which brings us to Laker rookie Earvin (Magic) Johnson, the NBA's player of the week.

Magic earned the honor with a four-game stretch that included 89 points, 35 rebounds, 34 assists and 68 percent shooting from the floor. In last Sunday's 140–126 victory over Cleveland, he scorched the Cavaliers with 24 points, 16 rebounds and 12 assists.

"If there ever was an appropriate nickname in sports," Westhead said, "he has it. He's a delight to coach, and he has the town in the palm of his hand. He helps us have a new excitement about playing ball.

WESTHEAD: BIG 5 PULLS FOR McKINNEY • 43

"I had been told here the fans didn't get excited, that they were hard to please, but they're revved up because of him. He has the nickname, but what I really like is, he backs up everything with production.

"I'm around these guys in all kinds of circumstances, and they're nothing like what people may have been led to believe. I see athletes taking care of their bodies, meticulous about their diets, doing whatever they have to do to improve. I'm not sure that that's the image the fans . . . the average basketball guy . . . perceives about this league."

Somebody wondered if the eyewitness to McKinney's accident had been offered season tickets.

"What I would like to offer him, more than that," said Paul Westhead, "would be tickets for the night that Jack McKinney returns."

DON'T THE OWLS DESERVE TOP 20 CONSIDERATION?

Philadelphia Daily News
January 2, 1979

HERE WAS REDD FOXX, kibitzing in the lobby of the Landmark Hotel with the Temple basketball team. And there was Don Casey, the Owls' coach, off visiting historic Hoover Dam.

And at courtside, in the Las Vegas Convention Center, Joe DiMaggio was watching the action, obviously prepared to take in the breathtaking adventures of the Runnin' Rebels.

Las Vegas, you may recall, is capable of running off 25 or 30 points before old Joe could brew a pot of coffee. These guys pop shots the way you and I pop corn.

So what would Casey have bet that his enterprising young team could have hustled home with the Las Vegas Tournament championship, a 9–0 record, Rick Reed's MVP trophy and the likelihood of space in somebody's Top 20 poll?

"It's funny, but I didn't bet a dime the entire time we were there," Casey was saying after an 89–79 upset of the Runnin' Rebels and a harrowing New Year's trip home by way of snowbound Chicago, Cleveland, New York and the Jersey Turnpike.

"The kids were kidding me, asking how I could keep walking past the tables, past the slot machines. Well, after we won, we were waiting in the airport and I succumbed.

"I dropped three quarters in a slot, I came up with an apple, a bar and a kangaroo. I thought it was ridiculous. And then John Everts, our publicist, walked up next to me, dropped in a silver dollar and won $100."

That's OK, Case. Sweeping this tournament is like breaking the bank at Monte Carlo. Baylor was there with heralded Vinnie Johnson as a likely finalist, and Marymount was in the field as the sacrificial lamb.

But as the evening of the finals wore on, the standing joke became: How was Vegas gonna scrape Temple's name off the second-place trophy in time?

Worse, the Rebels suddenly were having a problem scraping together that stick-of-dynamite offense. Reed, who also scored 18 points, was cracking the Vegas pressure with regularity, and Neal Robinson (18), Bruce Harrold (17), Walter Montford (15) and Alton McCullough (11) were filling up the basket at the opposite end.

"Going into our game," Casey said, "Vegas was 92–4 over the last five years in that building, and I could see why."

So much for the backdrop. The Rebels were 9–2 going into the title game, and had earlier scored 117 points against freestyle San Francisco. Twenty minutes later, they had 31 against Temple.

"Jerry Tarkanian (the Vegas coach) said he had never seen a point guard break down his defense the way Reed did," Casey said.

"You've gotta understand how they play to appreciate what we did. The full-court press at one end, and just run and shoot with reckless abandon at the other. Rip off 3–4 baskets in a row, throwing them up from 30–35 feet.

"But our kids would answer a run of four baskets with two or three of their own, bit their lips and stay close. Then we got into our zone slides, went from 2–3 to 3–2 to match-up, extending the angles, packing it in. Between Reed's control and Harrold's constant adjustment, we began to confuse them.

"We were diving on the floor, leaping into the stands, doing whatever had to be done. I looked up in the second half, and we were winning by 17. I know we haven't come to the end of our journey, but I knew then that we had taken a major step on this particular portion of it."

Now, nobody can blame the Owls for asking for room in the Top 20. The game was televised in the Los Angeles and San Diego areas, ironically allowing Penn Coach Bob Weinhauer to see the final five minutes.

"And what I saw was a Temple team in the total control of the situation," Weinhauer said. "It was very gratifying for Philadelphia, for the Big 5 and for the East, because there wasn't any question about who was winning that one."

No one had beaten Vegas in the tournament since 1971, and this year's team was averaging 98 points. Golden State Warriors' Coach Al Attles had checked in to watch Vinnie Johnson and came away making notations on Reed. Broadcaster Chick Hearn was gushing about Reed being among the better guards he had seen in his career.

"Personally," Reed said, "I thought the place was like a big Atlantic City, not a lot of stuff I hadn't seen before.

"They talk about that gym as a Tank for the Shark, cause Tarkanian's called Tark The Shark, and I could understand that. As soon as we got there I felt like the enemy.

"Those are hard people, they come at you before you ever come out to play. But I hope what we've done gets us some recognition, because we've earned it."

You think people in Vegas weren't badgering Casey about that?

"No one there understood how we could be 7–0 coming in and getting no attention," he said. "I explained about the lack of clout, that we don't operate like some of the big conferences, that the East is a fragmented situation at best. Mass producing stuff to get us up in the polls, that's not our style."

Nor is it their style to forget that the Owls won nine games when Reed and Montford were freshmen.

"They were going to try and get home in time for a New Year's celebration," said Dwynne Casey, Don's wife.

"And then Don called to say the Chicago airport was closed, that they were changing their plans, that he didn't know when he'd be in. I told him we already had about 20 people in the house, that we had a victory party ready to go. He might be the guy bringing home the trophy, but we were gonna start the party without him."

When the party finally did get under way, Casey and the Owls were somewhere over Cleveland.

"I knew he'd be here eventually," said Dwynne. "The way that team is going, I thought they might be able to fly home without even using a plane."

PENN WILL TEST TEMPLE'S RANKING

Philadelphia Daily News
January 10, 1979

"WHO ARE WE PLAYING NEXT? Which team?" Penn Coach Bob Weinhauer said, straining to keep a straight face.

"Oh yeah, Temple I had to look it up."

Smile when you say that, Bob. The Quakers, coming off a weekend blitz of Ivy have nots Harvard and Dartmouth, draw nationally ranked and unbeaten Temple tonight at 9 in the Palestra.

That's nationally ranked, as in finally. The Owls turned up 18th in the AP poll and 15th in the UPI after squeezing past St. John's Saturday night for their 11th straight win.

"Let's be honest," Weinhauer said, "Temple is by far the class of the city right now, on the strength of their record. They've certainly proven equal to every task so far."

Strangely, until an abortive 0–2 trip through the Cabrillo Classic with Iowa and San Diego State, some people thought the Quakers were the Big 5's most dynamic entry.

Now Weinhauer's team is 7–2 and Weinhauer is hoping that Saturday night's struggle against Dartmouth's zone was solid preparation.

"I would say that playing Dartmouth offers fantastic preparation to face Temple's zone," he said. "Temple has by far more quality players for the style, but Dartmouth's offense is equally a challenge. They don't make all those passes necessarily to score, it's more them saying that as long as they have the ball, WE can't score."

But Penn survived, 52–44, committing only eight personals. The next test, of course, is tantamount to a mid-term exam.

"Marty Stahurski, who was with us the last four years, visited our hotel during the weekend in New York," said Don Casey, the Temple coach, "and he said he always felt that the zone was something of a weapon. It was like the kids could look down the road at whoever they might be playing and know the zone could keep them in the game."

And these Owls are playing it beautifully, getting leadership from Rick Reed and Bruce Harrold, tough inside play from Walter Montford, help from Keith Parham and scrambling nose-for-the-ball contributions at both ends from Neal Robinson and Alton McCullough.

The elusive rankings?

"I'm just happy that we finally got it," said Casey, "for ourselves selfishly, but also for the Big 5, for the ECC, for the East."

"Now, a team doing well that make us succumb, beating us would be a shot in the arm for them. I think that all leads up to a terrific Temple-Penn game."

Even the first game might not be bad, regrouping La Salle meeting 7–3 Western Kentucky.

The Explorers blew away Lafayette last Saturday as Michael Brooks totaled 36 points and 18 rebounds, but the Hilltoppers once known primarily for their high-powered offense, are averaging the 60s.

But what to expect?

"Joe O'Connor went down to Nashville to scout them," said La Salle Coach Paul Westhead, "got caught in an ice storm, sat in the airport and brought home a Western Kentucky brochure and handed it to me. That, and a bill for the trip."

ST. JOE'S WIN A HALL OF FAMER

Philadelphia Daily News
January 29, 1981

FRAGMENTS OF THE GAME rumbled through John Smith's frazzled mind, pieces of a dream, portions of a tapestry.

His mind raced. His heart raced. And, after a grueling 63–61 St. Joseph's victory over Penn in the Palestra, he did not know which to face first.

He sat on the floor of the locker room, legs stretched out, back propped against a cold, bare wall. His team was now 14–2, had won seven in a row, and he was one of the captains.

"My heart," Smith said softly, "tends to go too fast sometimes. It feels like it's happening now. But it's happened before, too.

"I was supposed to get an EKG and a chest X-ray the other day. I guess I'll do it Friday. There just wasn't time . . . so much schoolwork, such an important game."

If there is a category in the Big 5 Hall of Fame for entire games, this one's a serious candidate. The Hawks had nearly suffocated in a firestorm of Penn emotion, falling behind 10–2 and getting blown off the boards in the opening five minutes.

But reality is what you have left when the initial burst of feeling dissipates. And that is when St. Joseph's went to work.

If the work ethic was the answer, luck was the savior. The Hawks won when David Lardner, a sweet-shooting Penn sophomore, missed the front end of a one-and-one with three seconds left. The shot caught the front of the rim and caromed long, rolling out of bounds as the buzzer sounded.

"I'm gonna say pride won for us," Smith said. "Pride, and our coach (Jim Lynam) screaming down our throats, reminding us of all the little things we didn't do early, that we had to do at the end.

"We beat 'em last year in three overtimes, on foul shots (by Boo Williams), on a tough call (against the Quakers' George Noon). Coach said, 'If you're gonna put the uniform on tonight, you gotta go after it, because they certainly will.

"The way it started, though, they got up so quick. Then Tony (6-10 freshman Tony Costner) picked us up, got some clutch points and rebounds, and it became contagious. We'd run up the court, Bryan (guard Bryan Warrick) kept reminding us that we're the Big 5's defending champions, so we had to play like it."

Rocky Balboa doesn't have much on John Smith. He's a strong, broad, durable kid from South Philly, and he knows what it means to take a jolt. But Smith finished the evening looking like he had taken one too many.

"I'm talkin' to Larry Lembo, the ref, during the game," John said. "I told him I love contact, that that's the way I like to play, but I was on the floor six times out of seven plays, and the whistle isn't blowing. And I'm not exactly a weakling.

"I'm out there, I'm supposed to be contributing, and for a whole half I didn't feel like I was. So I started tellin' guys, 'We gotta play 40 St. Joe minutes. Not 25. Not 30. If we're not playin' the way we can, then the rest has to come from within.' Hey, I think that's where it came from."

Wherever, it flourished in a raucous, sometimes brutal arena. A St. Joe's student, identified as Kevin McCaughan, was hit in the head by a cow bell hurled out of the stands. McCaughan was reportedly taken to the Hospital of the University of Pennsylvania for treatment.

Another cow bell came whizzing out of the stands at center court with 2:44 remaining, narrowly missing Lynam.

"There was another one thrown," Penn Coach Bob Weinhauer said later, "that landed between Jimmy and me. It hit the floor maybe five feet from me."

Costner, who had a terrific first half and ended with 14 points, said he had been pelted by smaller objects, possibly gumdrops.

"We've gotta play like champions," said Warrick, who had a game-high 23 points and shot 8-for-20. "I had this in high school, too [In Burlington Township, N.J.]. If you're the champion, you've gotta defend it."

So he turned aggressive at the offensive end, clicking off a flurry of pressurized jumpers, challenging bigger people in the lane.

"He's more a scorer than a shooter," suggested Hawks assistant Brad Greenberg. "He'll get points with hands in his face, when he's getting hit, when there's a crowd. It's just something he's capable of doing."

Bryan needed only someone to strike the first spark.

"The guys on the Penn bench were saying I wasn't a shooter," he said. "So I shot. And now we're 14–2, and I'm happy.

"Somebody asked the other day, after we beat North Carolina-Charlotte, whether we should be in the Top 20. Well, maybe we don't need that. We've just gotta win, and if we do that often enough, we'll get to the NCAA tournament, we'll get our share of credit. I look in the papers for South Alabama scores. They keep winning, too, but seem to have the same identity crisis we have. Hey, if you're good, you're good, it doesn't matter if you're ranked."

How fierce was it? With 4:45 left, Smith, Costner, and Penn's Noon, Vincent Ross and Paul Little all had four fouls, and St. Joe's had a four-point lead.

That stretched to seven (60–53) at 1:14.

But Kenny Hall and Lardner each hit two free throws, and when Costner fouled out at 0:40, the advantage had been sliced to 61–57. Warrick made one free throw, and Hall retaliated with two tough field goals, the second off a steal.

It was 62–61, at 0:14, when Hall fouled out and Warrick converted only the first part of a one-on-one.

But Angelo Reynolds missed a corner jumper and Lardner scrambled into the lane. Referee Charlie Diehl confidently waved off an apparent field goal and three-point play opportunity, calling a foul on the Hawks' Jeffery Clark.

That left Lardner facing a one-and-one.

"There's always contact under the boards, bodies banging," Lardner said afterward. "They've got to call what they see . . . I can't complain.

"I don't think I lost the game. I just didn't win it. What upsets me most is that I had the shots and didn't come through. I feel bad for myself, the team and 5,000 students in the stands."

Meanwhile, Williams, the Hawks' other co-captain, accepted the win and immediately examined it for flaws.

"We're lucky," Boo sighed. "How many times will a shooter like Lardner miss one like that? Usually, if you miss at that point, the ball hits the back of the rim, goes up, maybe there's a rebound. This one hit short, just flew away."

The winners talked about pride, poise, togetherness, and spirit.

"Pressure," Tony Costner said finally, "is mental. If you tell yourself you're not scared, then you're not.

"What did I think of the game? Well, not because it's the first City Series game I ever played in, but I would say this one certainly deserves to be on the back page of the Daily News."

BIG 5 TEAMS, TURNSTILES LOOK GOOD

Philadelphia Daily News
January 22, 1979

"I CAME IN HERE yesterday," the weary coach said, "looked around and said this was one of the fine old relics of college basketball.

"Then we played today, and I said, back when I played we used to have games like this in here all the time."

Which coach said that? John Thompson? Rollie Massimino? Surely not Paul Westhead?

John Thompson said it, and he was glad, because Georgetown beat Penn, 78–76, because the Hoyas' Craig Shelton may have put a death grip on the trophy that goes to the outstanding visitor to the building.

"They don't call Shelton 'Big Sky' for nothing," marveled St. Joseph's Coach Jim Lynam after scanning the Sunday papers. "That's about as apt a nickname as I've ever heard for a player."

Shelton was impeccable, shooting 9-for-12, scoring 21 points and taking eight rebounds in a game that has to be penciled in next to Penn-Temple as the finest moments in the city all season.

"When we go on the road," Shelton said after the 10th-ranked Hoyas climbed to 14–2, "we expect the unexpected, then tell ourselves we can't play the other team's way, we've gotta play Georgetown's way."

That meant exploiting the individual strengths of the starters, even to the sublime point of getting 11 points, 8 rebounds and 9 blocked shots from 6-11 Tom Scales, who was averaging less than two points a game.

"People ask me all the time why he's playing," John Thompson shrugged, "and I said he was like a volcano waiting to erupt."

How good was this game? Well, how many times have you heard a coach say his team deserves Top 20 recognition after a loss?

"If we can beat the team that is now ranked 12th (Temple) and play the No. 10 team to a tough two-point game decided in the last 10 seconds," Bob Weinhauer said, "then I have to say we deserve to be noticed.

"I won't say it if it's not true, but it is. We're as good as any team we've played, we're as good as many of the teams already in the Top 20, but I didn't say anything earlier because we were playing seven games in 15 days."

"Now we've got 12 days off, we've shown what we can do, and if we don't get noticed now, then I don't care if we ever get noticed."

And that could be the next problem.

"Now we've gotta look ahead at 10 Ivy League games, one City Series game (against Villanova)," said Tim Smith, "and if we do what we're supposed to do, we could be in the NCAAs again, maybe see Georgetown again someplace.

"I think we're a Top 20 team, but I don't know if we'll be ranked. And I don't think the voters look at the Ivy as a strong league, so if we go on and, say, beat Brown, it's not going to get us a lot of votes. I agree with the coach, that we should've been in the Top 20 a lot earlier, but if we don't get in after this, then maybe we never will."

In the sport's court of last resorts, the Quakers are gambling that the prestige of the Big 5 and the tournament berth that accompanies the Ivy title may yet work in their favor.

"So our main objective," said guard Booney Salters, "has to be win 'em both, get the value of each.

"I think the Top 20 is just personal opinions, and some of the voters may like to see the big-name schools up there. To break that line, you've got to beat one of the big names, and in the minds of the voters, Penn must not be a big name, I don't think they'd look to see that Penn-Georgetown, if we played again and again, could go either way each time."

The ticket-buying public has noticed, because the Palestra has filled nearly 36,000 seats in its last four dates, and Villanova lured another 3,000-plus to the Field House Saturday night.

Rollie Massimino affectionately refers to the building on Lancaster Ave. as The Cat House, but are they cats or chameleons?

Whichever, they surprised George Washington, 89–77, and the team that is 0–5 in the Palestra climbed to 3–0 on campus and a remarkable 5–0 in the Eastern Eight, where the first four finishers draw a playoff date advantage.

"Some people talk about the struggle we're facing," Massimino said, "but I say 9–7 for this group is damn good. Picked fifth in the league, fourth in the Big 5, and, outside of Merrimack, every night is beyond belief."

So Massimino eased the self-inflicted torture with the latest in a series of midweek meetings.

"Coaches had a meeting, then we had a team meeting, then we had some individual meetings," he said, "but that's no big deal, because we'd do that anyway."

Still, he wouldn't deny the immediate benefits.

"Tom Sienkiewicz had 26 points," he said, "but, more important, he had maybe the highest efficiency grade we've given in six years."

And Alex Bradley scored 21 without trying to carry the weight of the world on his shoulders, and senior Larry Sock jumped in with eight points and four rebounds.

"And our fans came out in droves," said Massimino. "The bad weather didn't matter, I knew they were coming."

Unfortunately, the massive attendance figures were only a rumor to the La Salle players, because roughly half the Palestra emptied out after the opener.

"We were ready and willing to play before a nice big crowd," said the Explorers' Michael Brooks after a grueling 90–89 loss to Duquesne, "but we came out for warm-ups, and it was like everybody had just disappeared."

And then the Explorers' winning streak disappeared, too, when Miguel Davila banked home a six-foot follow-up with two seconds left.

"I know all those guys, I played for Paul Westhead's team in Puerto Rico (Caguas)," Davila said. "Funny that the ball came to me at the end, because I hadn't taken a shot all game. I didn't want to be the one, but I was."

"We got down by 20," said Mo Connolly, "and the coach told us Duquesne plays hard, like street fighters, that they've had that reputation for 10 years, so we could either roll over or try to come back.

"Maybe instead of looking at this as a loss, we'll look at it as a game that shows we can come back on anyone. Maybe 2–3 games from now, we'll really be the team we can be."

At least the teams and the turnstiles are finally singing the same song. Whatever lingering deficiencies the Big 5 may still have, it's nice to see them reaching for notes we all once thought were out of their league.

. . . . . .

CHAPTER 4

THE SOCCER YEARS

Introduction by Al Miller

I remember first getting to know Phil, and we got to know each other very well. From the first time I talked with Phil, he had a personality that was infectious, and you got the immediate feeling that you could trust him. He wanted to tell the inside story of the Atoms, and he worked tirelessly to come up with information. Even while he went after that inside scoop, you knew Phil would never write an article that burned you. Phil would never do that. I remember a story on Casey Bahr . . . Phil did so much research and asked every question he could. He wanted to tell the story, the personality side of the story, and he did it brilliantly. By the time you read the profile stories that Phil wrote, you just felt like you knew the person so well. We weren't as high profile as the other sports in town, but Phil treated us like royalty. When he came on the beat, he treated us as if we were the most important thing going on in a huge sports market. That meant the world to me and to the players. It led to an instant friendship being struck with all of us, and it was the beginning of a beautiful relationship between our organization and Phil with his role at the *Daily News*. We didn't have the same type of fan base as the other sports. Phil treated every single story he wrote as the most important one. He spent so much time with us, and the players got used to seeing Phil around. He would show up day after day after day. You knew once Phil had the soccer beat, he was going to be there. He captured the human interest side of our team so amazingly.

To be honest, I don't think there was one story, one angle that Phil didn't capture. There were three writers, I believe, who covered our team. Phil worked harder than any of them. He would just not be outworked. He did his research and his homework and came to practice with the questions he had prepared for gathering his stories. He would call me and come up with extra information until he felt like he had what he needed to get the proper stories in the paper. He never interfered with what we were doing. You had the respect and trust for Phil because of that work ethic. I mean, he worked so hard and wanted to tell these personal stories of our players. It was wonderful for me to see because I hadn't always had the greatest relationships with every writer I had ever come across. Phil was different. There was a look in his eye and a trust you felt. When you read the stories in the paper, it just made you smile. He practiced what he preached. He did it right. And he did it right all the time.

Being around Phil as much as I was, I don't think this was work for Phil. He worked so hard. He was with us all the time. He called me late at night checking on facts. He was working on multiple stories at once. The combination made Phil the best. The proof was in the paper. We were instant friends and that friendship developed further as the years went on. My relationship with Phil was a one-of-a-kind special bond that will never be broken even with Phil's passing. Phil got me. He got the players. He got everything. He missed nothing.

When we won the championship, I felt like Phil won it, too. He couldn't wait to write the stories from the championship. He worked like that from the beginning. Every day was the same. His work ethic was unmatched. I really never lost track of him when he moved on from the soccer beat. Every banquet we had through the years to honor our championship team, I had to include Phil. I never trusted the media all that much. To include Phil shows how much he was loved and respected. I felt like he played an integral role in that season from start to finish. I wasn't aware he was sick at the end, and I received an e-mail from him one day telling me he had cancer, was very sick, and might never see me again. It floored me and knocked my socks off. I know that I responded but I don't really remember what I wrote. Without Phil's presence and influence, that championship season wouldn't have meant as much. He was the most passionate journalist I have ever met to this day. I loved Phil and always will.

AL MILLER *was a terrific longtime soccer coach who led the Philadelphia Atoms of the North American Soccer League to the championship in 1973.*

• • • • • •

BUILDING SOLID FOUNDATION PUT KICK IN ATOMS

Philadelphia Daily News
August 18, 1973

"WHEN TOM MCCLOSKEY DECIDED to hire me," Al Miller was saying, "he told me, 'When I build buildings, they've got to stand for years. I depend heavily on proper foundations.'

"What he was saying was, he had already analyzed the situation. He is a builder, so he had put it in relative terms. He was telling me he was a successful man, and that if he was going this deep into a venture he could not afford to have it fail.

"He was saying, in essence, go out and do the right kind of job. I couldn't add a thing to that. It was all I ever really wanted."

Tom McCloskey is, above all else, a builder. That, perhaps, is the singular reason he chose Al Miller as the head coach of the Philadelphia Atoms. McCloskey paid $25,000 for the North American Soccer League franchise, roughly $16 million less than his abortive bid for the Eagles in 1969.

"The first couple games," he admits, "I sat in the press box and didn't have any idea what it was about. Now I don't think you can surpass it.

"First, you don't have to be 6-10 or 6-11. You don't have to be 6-4, 270. You don't have run the 40 yard dash in 4.4, and you don't have to wear a lot of protective padding.

"These kids are like middleweights, and I've always felt that's the best division, pound for pound. I'm not telling you I came into this knowing anything about soccer, but I began to notice things. I'd drive up the (Roosevelt) Boulevard and I used to see a lot of touch football games. Now I see soccer.

"I told myself there must be something to this game. I'm learning."

"I suppose every soccer person would prefer an owner who knows the game," Al Miller was saying. "I was worried at the beginning . . . that he wouldn't understand our game or our players.

"He watched our (talent) trials and he had a bit of a dazed look. I knew it was impossible to tell him everything there was to know about the game in a short time, but I eventually learned I didn't have to.

"He began to find out for himself. He educated himself, and he did it because he wanted to.

"When I first met him, I thought he was a typical businessman, hard and fast. I've learned he is a very humane individual, strong when he has to be, but always sincerely caring about us, far beyond whether we simply win or lose. How many teams can say that about an owner?"

The premise of a second major league soccer franchise in Philadelphia—the Spartans has failed clumsily seven years earlier—had begun with a call from Lamar Hunt. There had been a meeting at the Fairmount Hotel in San Francisco, another meeting with a Hunt representative at the Marriott, and several phone conversations.

"At the beginning of the year," McCloskey said, "I hired Bob Ehlinger as a full-time public relations consultant for McCloskey & Co. I sent him to New York to look into the soccer thing. He's a very careful, tenacious man and I knew he could sort it out.

"He came back and said we ought to take a hard look at the possibilities. Our investigation showed, among other things, there were 44 colleges in the Delaware Valley playing soccer, that interest in the game was growing remarkably on the high school and age group level. Finally, I said let's go."

After some early scrambling, he settled on Ehlinger as his general manager and Miller as the league's only American coach. The Atoms—an expansion franchise—scorched the Eastern Division with a 9–2–8 record, stepping boldly into tonight's semifinal playoff with Toronto at Veterans Stadium.

"When you think about it," McCloskey says, "the only thing I can honestly take credit for is picking the two guys who are running the club. Oh, we meet and we talk all the time, but they're the guys doing the executing."

The Atoms lead the league in attendance and, probably, in total promotional expenditures.

"There's no way this is a money making operation yet," McCloskey said. "We spent more than we originally anticipated, and even though we brought in more than we had hoped, it's not enough to turn things around that quickly. That could happen next year, though.

"People tell me Philadelphia is a hard city, but I don't believe that. I believe we have a product to sell, and that it's gonna go. You know, in 1960, you could buy an AFL franchise for $25,000, and Lamar Hunt tells me he thinks this has a better chance now than that did then."

He paused for a moment, projecting no deeper than two games into the future.

"Suppose we were to beat Toronto, then go on and win the title?" he said. "What could we do to match it, win every game? In February, we had nothing. In August, we have a chance to win it all. Whatever happens, it's going to be a hard act to follow."

BOB RIGBY TO FURY IN NICK OF TIME

Philadelphia Daily News
July 9, 1979

NOW TOM FLECK KNOWS what it is like to think the heavenly thoughts of a concert maestro, only to discover you're waving a baton at a dead issue.

And he knows what it would have been like had Fury secretary Nancy Rose Bohl not punched up the key question on the NASL telex machine early Saturday morning.

It's no fun facing desperation, which is all the new general manager thought he had as he, publicist Thom Meredith and Rose Bohl scanned the bits of information arriving as the league's 3 a.m. trade deadline approached.

"Nancy hit the button to get us the correct time," Meredith recalled sleepily from San Jose yesterday, arriving after a dismal 4–2 loss in Houston the evening before.

"We figured we had maybe 10 minutes left, and we knew we didn't have Bob Rigby yet, and we were at a point of total frustration. But Nancy hit the time button and it came up 1:48. In effect, we were saved because the telex was programmed for standard time rather than daylight saving. That extra hour helped us finally make a deal with Los Angeles."

Unhappily, Fleck's blockbuster package that involved LA and Tulsa had dissolved earlier, wiped away by a decision in England (by Bolton Manager Ian Greaves) that kept forward Frank Worthington frozen on the Fury roster.

That deal would have sent goalkeeper Rigby from LA to Tulsa to the Fury; Worthington and Richie Reice to Tulsa; and Iraj Danaifard, Bill Sautter and Steve Earle from Tulsa to the Fury.

As it was, Fleck didn't get league approval on the moves he did make until noon Saturday, tracking down that much with a call to the NASL administrator Ted Howard in a Detroit restaurant.

Here's what the Fury got:

Midfielder Curtis Leeper and a third-round draft choice in 1981 from Fort Lauderdale for defender Kevin Murphy.

Rigby from LA for cash.

Free agent midfielder Karoly Kremer, from a midweek tryout at the Vet.

Fleck passed on opportunities to retain former Temple forward Sautter from Tulsa (the price was too high) and Minnesota forward Greg

Ella (sold to Tulsa), and was blown away in a bid to add Jan Soerensen, a Spanish international winger.

"Soerensen signed again to play in Denmark," Fleck shrugged. "I wanted him, but he wanted a ton of money just to finish the season. I didn't mind paying the guy, but I wasn't gonna give him a ton."

He's gambling that Leeper (the Pan Am captain) will give the Fury the active, aggressive midfielder they've lacked since Tony Glavin was hurt, and that Kremer will emerge as a Cinderella story.

"He's 30, from Hungary, and looked hungry, and I don't mean that as a pun," Fleck said. "The guy doesn't speak an ounce of English, but I'm hoping he'll tell a hell of a story.

"I've seen lots of ink on him, our coaches liked him in a brief workout last Thursday. The guy had just gotten off a plane, thinking he was going to Washington because he has a friend (Joe Horvath) who plays there.

"But the agent called ahead, discovered Washington didn't need midfielders, and brought him to us. We didn't initiate this, but we'll take him and hope like hell."

If Kremer can get an updated ID from Immigration in time, he conceivably could play in San Jose Wednesday night.

Oh, and you thought we might forget that this star-crossed team was still on the road? Or that it tied a dubious league record Saturday night by losing its 10th-straight away from home?

"I can't help what has already happened, or even what hasn't happened," Fleck said. "I can only work ahead, I can only deal with what is.

"I'm hoping what we came away with gives us four ingredients: The three new players, plus a professional attitude from Worthington. He wanted to leave, we tried to accommodate him, we failed through no fault of our own.

"Now he's with us for the remainder of the season, and he says he'll give us all he has. His manager in England wouldn't OK a trade to Tulsa because he feared Tulsa would go deeper into the playoffs than we might. If we don't make it, he's home sooner. Ahh, I just hope we get in, keep Frank with us a little longer."

Send the guy a telex, Tom. But taunt him with it. Don't tell him what time it is.

Free kicks: Don't ask about Marko Valok's logic starting travel-weary Bob Rigby ahead of Keith Van Eron in Houston. And where that fits in the coach's philosophy of having players win jobs in practice. And isn't that one reason forward Pat Fidelia isn't on this trip?

Houston, a tough 10–0 at home, buried Rigby with two early goals in the first half, then got a beauty from former Textile star Dale Russell in the final moments of the half. Van Eron started the second half and may start again in San Jose.

Fran O'Brien moved from defense to midfield and scored both goals. Jim McKeown played the final 32:53 as a replacement for Richie Reice and climbed a couple notches on the depth chart. And rookie forward Tom Wieboldt played for the first time, replacing Miro Djordjevic for the last 16:41.

LONG DISTANCE TRIP TO ATOMS NO MINOR PROBLEM

Philadelphia Daily News
August 23, 1973

THE INTERSTATES AND TOLL HIGHWAYS connecting Baltimore and Philadelphia do not necessarily qualify as sleek, scenic routes. There are long, dreary sections of construction and redevelopment entanglement. There are your basic peak hour traffic obscenities, tinged darkly with incredible added starters.

There is, for example, the tight little stretch of Chester Pike coming past the Widener College complex and winding back toward International Airport. If you are a late afternoon driver moving in the direction of Veterans Stadium, you do not roll, you slither. To make the trip on a daily basis can become an achievement of unusual proportions.

For three emotion-wrenching months, the highways have become Karl Minor's crucible. For the intelligent, aggressive Atoms' forward, life behind the wheel was deteriorating into a debilitating, defiant lifestyle. It became, in a very real sense, an endless summer.

"To understand how I felt, you have to understand how I joined this team in the first place," Minor suggested before an early evening training session. "When I first tried out, I explained to Al (head coach Al Miller) that, at the same time, I was checking out the situation for a couple of other players in Baltimore.

"I expected to find the Atoms practicing in some schoolyard, with a coach handing out T-shirts. I got here and I saw what they had, and I was impressed. Then somebody said the coach was an American and I thought, 'Here we go.' After a while, my response to Al changed. It was more like, 'Where did you learn the game?' It was obvious the man knew.

"But the ride . . . well, it takes about an hour and 45 minutes, but five minutes difference reaching a key point can mean a 15 or 20 minutes delay.

"Crossing the Penrose Ave. Bridge, for example, can seem like a month. I'd be late for practice and Al would get on me. He knew where I was coming from, but he simply hated tardiness."

Seemingly insignificant irritations on the highways had a way of magnifying. Karl Minor found himself handcuffed to an imperfect machine. He began, admittedly, talking to himself.

"I'd find myself getting angry, then angrier as I got closer to the stadium," he said. "I'd get wild. I'd get worked up by what I thought Al might say. Curiously, it affected my training. I've never worked harder. By the time I'd get out on the field, I'd be so upset I'd be ready to take on the world."

Instead, he took on the North American Soccer League, contributing four goals and five assists in a scramble that has already brought Philadelphia a divisional title. The key, though, came on May 19, when he drilled home the decisive goal in a 2–1 triumph over Dallas, the team the Atoms must beat again Saturday night (9 o'clock, Channel 17) to sweep the playoff championship.

"We were having our pregame meal, and a guy came to Al saying he was from Argentina and that he had some players to offer," Minor remembered. "Again, I thought, 'Here we go,' but Al said our roster was full and thanks anyway. The fellow insisted these were good players, but Al said he had all the players he needed. It took a great deal of courage for him to do that, and I know what it meant to my confidence."

Meanwhile, Miller was handling Minor with an aggressive, if low-key, approach.

"Bob (general manager Bob Ehlinger) and I had both predicted it would be a tough road for Karl to haul," Miller said, the clever analogy perhaps unintentional. "He insisted it would not be, but he learned it could be a big burden. What happened was, he began to feel sorry for himself.

"Part of it was certainly understandable. Other players would be going to dinner or to the theater and he'd be in his car driving to Baltimore. He said he felt like he wasn't a part of the team.

"We talked a long time, ironing out most of the problems. We found we could easily eliminate some of the little annoyances. Like, if we were flying back from a road game, we'd arrange for Karl to fly directly home. He made some concessions and I made some.

"I told him if he wanted to pack it in, he could, but that we'd prefer him to stay. I'll tell you this, he does things on the field now I didn't think he was capable of doing. He's basically a goal scorer. All that was missing was some conditioning and the proper mental attitude. I think, now, he has both."

Karl Minor will go into Saturday night's game as the Atoms' best available scorer, the drudgery of three-and-a-half hours in a car each day buried somewhere in the outer reaches of his consciousness. Life on the interstates, he is learning, can have its moments.

CAN ATOMS NOW BECOME MORE ROWDY

Philadelphia Daily News
June 14, 1975

THE ATOMS HAVE GROUP RATES for their excursions to Veterans Stadium. Group rates? Last night the group wore a T-shirt, Bermudas, tennis shoes and no socks.

No sock, that's what the Atoms' problem is. They lost, 2–1, to the Tampa Bay Rowdies, giving up a goal to Clyde Best in the first minute of the second half, then giving away a goal to Stew Scullion with 5:29 left.

The Atoms are 4–4 and a distant third in the NASL East, and the rowdiest part of the evening might've been the turmoil raging inside Al Miller.

In eight games, his team has seven goals, two on penalty shots and none by a forward. If Tom Gola had been a soccer player, no one ever would have heard of "Gola Goal."

If Miller brought in every guy claiming to be the answer, he'd have more refugees than Indiantown Gap. If the Atoms went on What's My Line, they'd stump the panel. Two years after their championship, they're an Atom Bomb.

"We can't exist this way," Miller said. "We have to make changes. I wanted to make them a long time ago. We're gonna do it now. We have to do it."

The New York Cosmos imported Pele, the Atoms brought in Peter Smith, a mailman and English semi-pro, and John Cummings, a club player from Jersey. Smith was overmatched. Cummings has played decently, but decency was never the question.

"There are four guys I'm working on," Miller said, "but you can't believe the complications. The English season ends, the players take vacations, the managers take vacations, you can't find the people you want. And let's face it, what I want is a scorer. It's too early for panic or depression or desperation, but it's a problem that has to be resolved. If I have a forward who can give me four goals in our first eight games, we might be undefeated."

"Isn't this a bleeping cheerful place?" defender Bobby Smith said. "This is bleeping ridiculous. That's why winning is where it's at. This is a bleeping waste of time. The finish is missing. It's not morale, it's not internal problems, it's goals. Bleeping goals."

The formula for a struggling franchise is basic. No scoring, no victories. No victories, no people in the stands. No people, maybe no franchise. Last night's group was announced as 5,819. There may have been more people at the nearest McDonald's. There may have been more enthusiasm in the street hockey game outside your house.

"If we lose, if we don't have crowds, it has to be at least partly my fault," Miller said. "But people won't appreciate us if they don't see us. I'm just afraid people left here tonight thinking we were terrible. And 5,000 people in a 55,000-seat stadium is terrible enough. It's empty, and the players have to notice. Nothing gets going. I heard the public address system all night, and I never hear that."

The Atoms have had more chances than the Pennsylvania Lottery. Al Miller left the stadium last night determined to prove their number wasn't up.

WILL THE ATOMS AND WINGS BE CROWDED OUT?
FANS COOL TO SOCCER ...

Philadelphia Daily News
June 20, 1975

LAST TUESDAY'S 3–2 OVERTIME VICTORY over the Washington Diplomats at Veterans Stadium might have been the most crucial win in the two-and-a-half-year history of the Atoms.

"It crossed my mind during the game," coach Al Miller confessed before leaving for tonight's game in Chicago. "We were down, 1–0, the crowd wasn't very big and the Flyers weren't able to take part in the halftime promotion. I knew if we didn't win, give the people some excitement, we were in big trouble."

How big? Big enough for speculation to spread through the city that the North American Soccer League franchise might be for sale or even about to dissolve.

It's happened before. The Freedoms lasted a season. Something called the Patriots was here for about 15 minutes, a tiny misdirected softball caravan hurrying through South Philadelphia, its creditors not far behind.

Across the street from Veterans Stadium, the Wings have struggled for identity and acceptance, not to mention crowds. The Bell's first year was Great Adventure in helmets and pads.

"We'd like to be 9–0 and instead we're 5–4," said Atoms owner Tom McCloskey. "It's frustrating, sure, but we meet, we talk. It's Al Miller's team, and I've put no restrictions on him. Same thing with Hal (GM Hal Freeman). I don't like to lose, but I don't want to sell, either. I haven't talked to anyone about that. I haven't even had an offer."

Still, the Atoms announced 28,978 for their first three home games with Miami, the Israeli World Cup team and Toronto. The paid figure, the People Paper has learned, is 19,593, more than 9,000 less than the announced.

The club has announced 20,124, 5,819 and 7,510 for its last three dates.

"We've been stricter than ever with comps," said business manager Jim Michener. "Last year, when people asked for big blocks, we said yes. This year, we're not doing nearly as much of that. Hal doesn't want people holding back waiting for free tickets. We feel that attendance is about what we expected. We're still pretty close to our budget."

McCloskey felt personally hurt when Pele did not play for New York here June 10. Pele did make an appearance, helping draw an announced 20,124, but McCloskey feels the crowd could have been much greater.

"We didn't know until the last 24 hours that he definitely wouldn't play," McCloskey said. "I called (league commissioner) Phil Woosnam, and asked him to intercede. I felt the league owed us a favor, because we released Miller from other duties to coach the U.S. World Cup team on a special tour. Phil said he tried, and couldn't work it out."

With the Atoms and Cosmos playing in different divisions, it's conceivable that a 1976 schedule wouldn't include a New York appearance here, but McCloskey seems to think it will. The projected crowd and public interest excites him, even though the Cosmos would get 50 percent of the gate receipts over the pre-Pele attendance average.

"The people who come to our games love it," McCloskey said. "Give them the right thing, and a lot more will love it. You can't ask people to constantly watch 1–0 games. But this team is a bounce away. Give them a couple of guys who can score, and the fans would have somebody to relate to. We understand that problem."

Two years after winning the championship, Miller doesn't want his team caricatured as a shot in the dark, but the elements are there. The Atoms don't get many goals, but they try hard. They don't get the extra players they need, but they search frantically. They appeal to their public, but they can't find them.

Al Miller is not Peter Sellers. The identification problems infuriate him, the vacant reaches of the stadium trouble him. He is one of the country's definitive soccer people, and his third summer in Philadelphia has become his crucible.

He is, for the moment, coaching a team whose best credentials are its past. Resting on its laurels was never a consideration. Not even laurels can grow in AstroTurf.

Write it in graffiti. The Phantom is an Atoms fan.

AL MILLER FINALLY WINS A BIG AWARD

Philadelphia Daily News
August 17, 1973

AL MILLER GLIDED INTO Philadelphia as an integral, if almost totally anonymous, portion of the Atoms' basic blueprint. He arrived largely unknown, other than in the most knowledgeable soccer circles. More curiously, he arrived unencumbered by the gaggle of plaques, trophies, silverplates and other award paraphernalia you might ordinarily associate with a terribly successful and supremely dedicated coach.

"The only thing I ever really got was a game ball from my players at Hartwick last year after my 100th victory," the Atoms' head coach said after the North American Soccer League's players and coaches voted him Coach of the Year.

"Honestly, it got to the point where my wife would kid me about it. We'd stop over to see some friends, and if they were bowlers or golfers they'd have a bundle of awards in their dens or on their mantelpieces. Me, I didn't have a thing."

He came to Philadelphia and things immediately got better. Before the regular season ended before the Atoms clinched a playoff berth, Miller was fondling his first piece of hardware.

"I played in a golf tournament at Squires with (Atoms' owner) Tom McCloskey, an architect named Jim Nolen and Joe Walters," he said. "We finished second and came home with a loving cup. I was really happy."

The Atoms finished 9–2–8 and won the Eastern Division title and he was happier. They meet Northern champion Toronto tomorrow night at Veterans Stadium and Miller has his award in magnificent perspective.

"My honest response is that a lot of people earned this and I'm the guy picking up the award," he said. "McCloskey is the first guy. He had the guts to pick an American coach, and then he allowed me to go after the players I wanted. That's the key right there. If the players don't do the job, well, these awards just don't come about, do they?"

Miller officially accepted the award at a news conference this morning. The premise sent some early impressions and some vivid memories churning giddily through the meticulous mind of general manager Bob Ehlinger.

"Before the votes were computed," Ehlinger said, "I told Al that if the winner was anyone but him it'd be a miscarriage of justice. What he's accomplished here, in an impossibly short length of time, has to be one of the all-time coaching jobs.

"My initial impression of the man concerned his obvious commitment. When we interviewed him, he reminded me of guys like Joe Paterno . . . extremely intelligent, well organized, inspirational and, perhaps above all, committed to excellence."

Barry Barto, a scuffling, efficient defender, knows Miller on the field and off. Barto is an assistant coach at Philadelphia Textile and is developing the Atoms' youth programs. He has played in 11 international matches and understands the styles and idiosyncracies of the profession.

"I don't think there's a perfect ANYTHING," Barto decided, "but the man has certainly done an admirable job. He works. He must. Look where we are."

CHAPTER 5

. . . . . .

THE SIXERS BEFORE 1983

Introduction by Doug Collins

First of all, getting to know Phil is one of the great thrills of my life. We were in the same boat: we both loved basketball. He represented everything honest about his profession and the journalist-player-coach relationship was a special one with Phil. Reporters have a job to do, and no one did it better than Phil. You're never going to love everything a writer is going to write. Phil was so honest, and if he had to write something critical, you knew it would be fair. As a coach, that's all you can hope for. I got to know Phil so well, and also his wife, Susie, because I was her favorite player. So I'd always send her Sixers gear, and I know it was greatly appreciated. When Susie was really sick, Phil and Andy had to be such rocks to handle it. Phil and I were a great team when we had that player-reporter relationship and later as a coach-reporter relationship. He had a passionate professionalism for his work, yet he was a guy who was always fair. There wasn't one time I can ever remember where I didn't think he was fair. Some writers cold be mean-spirited and there wasn't a balance in the stories that were written. Phil always had that perfect balance where he checked a fact, double-checked it, triple-checked it. He was never mean-spirited. He never, ever made it personal. He always got the story right.

Here was this guy with this big, curly hair and a notepad and there was this way that you just had to trust him. He took such pride in his work day after day after day. He would keep me in the loop if there was a tough story to write. He was dignified with how he handled himself, and there was a professional way he carried himself every day.

I'll never forget at the end when he was very sick. I couldn't go see him because we had a game. I talked to him on the phone right before the game started. Phil told me as part of his job, he was never allowed to cheer, but said, "I'm going to break my rule tonight." There was a mutual friendship that was built over many years. Phil said, "Don't you have a game to coach?" I said, "Nothing is more important than talking to you right now." That was the type of friendship that we had and the respect we had for one another.

As a coach in the NBA, the criticism you get comes every night. You feel like some people have agendas, and even when you win a game, you get questions that are critical and pointed. Phil was never like that. He was so professional and never wavered from that. If he needed something and felt like he had to call me at midnight, he'd do it. I never minded because I knew where this was coming from. He wanted every fact to be right.

I trusted Phil. I don't toss that word around lightly. I saw that in him from the very beginning. Never once did I think I couldn't trust him. I knew if he wanted to tell a story, he was going to get every single fact right. We became friends from the beginning when I was a player, and it carried through all the years later to when I coached the Sixers. I told the media that I wanted to make the Sixers relevant again. Phil and I talked all the time about the team and then off the record about our lives. I knew his wife was very sick and how that affected Andy and Phil and how difficult it could be. She was the toughest person I ever met. Phil had so much on his plate personally as did Andy.

Through it all was a wonderful friendship with Phil. I had the utmost respect for him in every way. I miss Susie and Phil terribly. Phil was the most honest journalist I think I ever met. Our friendship blossomed through the years. When he was sick, I would talk to him and we did talk a lot about basketball and family. That last phone call was so hard for me because I could tell how sick he was. I wanted Phil to know how much he meant and that he was part of the family. He was. I'm proud to say that Phil and I were such great friends and I miss him dearly.

DOUG COLLINS *was the No. 1 overall pick by the Philadelphia 76ers in the 1973 draft from Illinois State. He played eight seasons with the Sixers and was an All-Star three times. Collins later became head coach of the Sixers in 2010, where he would remain for three seasons.*

. . . . . .

OWNER FITZ DIXON GETS CAUGHT UP IN SIXERS' FEVER AND THE EXCITEMENT OF JULIUS ERVING

Philadelphia Daily News
June 3, 1977

IN THE 76ERS' PLUSH OFFICES on City Line Ave., club vice president Hunter McMullin has a payload of blueprints and artists' drawings of the projected new, spacious, modernistic quarters that will be built on the ground level of Veterans Stadium.

"One of the things I'm looking into," club owner Fitz Eugene Dixon Jr. said, "is an entrance-way of some kind into the stadium itself, where we could erect a screen, a projector, lighting and slow-motion and stop-action camera equipment. Keep the thing constantly working . . . as our way of letting our fans, and the ones that didn't see him, an opportunity to relive some of Julius Erving's greatest moments.

"I think that would be a way of maintaining interest and winning over new fans, to show them Doctor J, as we've seen him through the season . . . the unbelievable moments, the times we thought that when he began his leap toward the basket that perhaps he couldn't reach it, and then that he could. Watching him is the closest thing to ballet that I could possibly imagine."

Fitz Dixon appears to revel in the 76ers' season in the same fashion. Looking back, taking the moments in sequence, squeezing the joy from them and repackaging them for another evening's entertainment.

"One of the things I remember is opening night of the regular season," he said. "I will admit that, to that moment, I had never seen Julius Erving play basketball, possibly did not appreciate all it is that he can bring to a team.

"In any case, two young fans—sitting maybe two rows away from me—came by, asked if I was Fitz Dixon. I said I was, they said, 'Thank you for bringing us Doctor J.' I looked at them, asked why, and they said it meant that they didn't have to drive up to Uniondale to see him play anymore, that they could just come to the Spectrum.

"I was a bit incredulous. I said, 'You drive all the way to Long Island to see this man play?' When they said yes, that they did it often, I realized I had something special. I couldn't wait for the season to unfold, so that I could see just what it was about pro basketball, and about the Doctor."

When the 76ers purchased Erving from the beleaguered New York Nets, it was the sort of happening that splashed across your TV screens, jumped out at you from your newspaper, leaped into your consciousness from the radio. There was $3 million for Julius Erving, roughly the same amount for Nets' owner Roy Boe. Doctor J became The Six Million Dollar Man.

How?

"I think I was in the Spectrum offices one afternoon," Dixon recalled, and Pat (Vice President and General Manager Pat Williams) said, 'You won't believe this, but there's a possibility that Julius Erving might be available.'

"I'll confess that I didn't know exactly what that meant, but with explanations it appeared to me that he was the equivalent of a Mickey Mantle, a Babe Ruth, of another time and another sport, but obviously with tremendous impact.

"My first thought was, if this man is everything they say, or even close to it, why would they be letting him go? But I checked a little, and felt if he was there, if my people wanted him . . . if they felt we could add him without disrupting or injuring what we already had—which seemed to be a very strong team—then I would say go get him.

"I sometimes think if we hadn't done this, the media would have suggested that I was a cheapie. If some other team had taken him, they'd have said, 'Why didn't he do that? What sort of owner is he anyway?'

"We were down in the little locker area that the coaches used at training camp at Ursinus College. I asked, from a morale point, is this a good thing to do or a bad thing? I thought I saw a super attitude among the players we already had, and people were telling me how good a team it appeared to be.

"The consensus was, we should do it, but I alone made the final decision. After Pat and Gene (Coach Gene Shue) both said Doctor J could assimilate into a team situation, I said we should finalize the deal."

Dixon could look back confidently now, assessing his judgments. Williams and Shue had warned him that even an outlay of millions for Erving would not guarantee a playoff championship.

"They both carefully told me that it might not even assure of getting INTO the playoffs," Dixon said. "They told me about a San Francisco team with Wilt Chamberlain, Nate Thurmond and Wayne Hightower that had a terrible time, an awful record. Basically, they were telling me to keep my hopes under control."

The arrangement was consummated, and Julius Erving was en route to Philadelphia, to a press gathering at the Hilton Inn at 10th and Packer. Upstairs, an hour or so beforehand, on the seventh floor, the owner met his newest player for the first time.

"I saw him as a gentleman, well-spoken, delightful company," said Dixon.

"And then came opening night (against San Antonio), and a number of games after that, and I was told that the Doctor was not performing as he had in the ABA, but that I should just wait, that when the time was right, he would.

"I saw him come to the fore in the All-Star Game (in Milwaukee). Since then, he's been a rising star, if in fact you can say that about a man of his caliber. Ask me now if he was worth the money and I'd say yes. Absolutely."

And while he learned about the Doctor, Fitz Dixon continued his own education as an owner. He had owned parts of the Phillies, Flyers and Eagles at various times, had bankrolled the Wings in professional box lacrosse, but this was his own team, and there were details to be learned.

Most memorably, there was the night he stepped into the interview area, where Shue was meeting the press after a troubling loss.

"I'm waiting to hear your excuses," Dixon told Shue from the perimeter of the media.

Even now, the moment haunts the owner.

"A grievous error on my part, something I never should have done," he admitted. "I'm haunted by, 'What's your excuse?', a moment that has been blown out of proportion, but a moment that also should not have taken place.

"I'm more careful now, because of the embarrassment I caused. But at the same time, in the course of the season, I wondered about press coverage of our team. No matter how well we did, there always appeared to be a negative side.

"When Harvey Catchings was playing center regularly, and playing well, especially defensively, people constantly asked about Darryl Dawkins. Why wasn't HE playing? Somebody must have asked Darryl if he was satisfied with the way things were, Darryl said no, and the deadline became, 'Dawkins Dis-Satisfied.'

"And yet it's almost magic the way things have worked out. Harvey gave us what we had when we needed it, then Caldwell Jones, then Darryl. Darryl has come along superbly . . . Gene told me this is the way it would be, that he didn't plan to use him much for a while.

"The way Darryl has progressed is a justification for the way Gene handled it. Especially now. Especially when the chips are down, in the playoffs. The intensity I see in the games now, I know that with the same intensity many more games could have been won during the season, but I also understand now what people mean when they say the playoffs are different.

"But getting back to me asking Gene about his excuses . . . I had maybe 50 guests with me that night at a dinner party, and I over-reacted. I was anxious for the team to do well, disappointed when it didn't. But, be reasonable, am I going to ask Gene for excuses about basketball? Basketball is his area, not mine. I'm not seriously going to ask him a thing like that, not for all the tea in China. It was a mess, a mistake . . . a joke."

Later, another dimension of the new owner crept into the papers.

There was no one's contract in the organization that Fitz Dixon couldn't—or wouldn't—buy back.

If it sounded cold, harsh, demanding—given the time and circumstances—it was meant to be.

"I first made that statement at a staff meeting," Dixon said. "Probably a way of letting people know, but I was trying to meld two organizations . . . the 76ers, which I had just purchased, with the remainder of people from the Wings. And I wanted to keep as many people as possible, but I also had to let them know who the boss was, to avoid any confusion.

"Don't misunderstand, though . . . I was talking about the front office, the operation of the team. The players, that's Gene's job, Pat's job. I have the wherewithal to get them the men they need, but I would never tell them which men or how to utilize them."

And then Fitz Dixon permitted himself a rare moment.

"Ahh, if I was the coach, maybe I'd have used Darryl more early in the season," he said. "But I'm not the coach, and the one I have is a top-notch man in his field. I can think about things like this, but I must leave the decisions to him.

"Gene was in a difficult enough situation as it was. To mold together a team of superstars, that can't be easy. Every time they lost a game, people asked, 'How?' He couldn't win unless he won every game, and no one does that."

But the 76ers, the guys in the silk suits, have played their way into the championship round.

"I was one of the few people to watch the closed-doors practice where Gene installed the idea of Caldwell Jones bringing the ball upcourt," Dixon said.

"I'm still learning about the game, but (assistant coach) Jack McMahon explained the premise to me. I felt a sense of excitement, then felt even better when I saw how it worked against Portland.

"I was never a basketball lover, but I'm into the sport now. I was unable to go to Houston for all the games in that series, and—watching on TV—I became a pacer. My wife kept telling me to stop, that I was wearing a hole in the rug. I couldn't stay still.

"One thing I discovered that sets it apart from hockey is that every time up the court, something happens. A field goal, a foul, a steal. Something. The level of excitement, the intensity has reached me.

"I bought the controlling interest in the team from Irv Kosloff, and I see him at the games, amazed that he can watch and remain as calm as he appears to. I can't explain the total respect I have for that man . . . he's a gentleman, he's also a gentle man. I know he must be as happy, as pleased as I am."

Finally, there remain the continuing rumors about Fitz Dixon reaching out to purchase the Eagles from Leonard Tose.

"All I will say there is, the 76ers are a part of my holdings and will be as long as I live, as long as my son George lives," Dixon said.

"If, later on, the Eagles turn up on the market, we'd look at it, possibly be willing to head a syndicate of some sort. As of right now, NFL rules prohibit me taking majority control of one of their teams. A ridiculous rule, but a rule . . .

"At this point, I'm not buying the Eagles. They belong to Leonard."

So . . .

"One thing I do think about," Fitz Dixon said, "is how easy it would be for me to do nothing, to simply around, drink martinis for lunch. I can't do that . . . I won't do that. I have a mind, I feel I have to use it.

"I don't like to be called a rich man, I'd prefer to be referred to as a contributor. I don't want a life in an ivory tower . . . I want a life where I work without having to punch a time clock, a life where I can help others. With the 76ers, where I can bring a championship to the city. If we win the title, the success will belong to the players and coaches, but I would be happy to share it with them."

A FREE AND EASY WIN FOR THE SIXERS

Philadelphia Daily News
March 25, 1976

THE BROWNSVILLE BOMBER strutted out of the Spectrum in his basic Brownsville going-to-the-playground wardrobe; waist-length tan leather jacket, grey sweat pants, high-top white sneakers. Not the sort of threads you'd select with all those Jacob Reed gift certificates that filter through the sports establishment, but Lloyd Free will live in them as long and as merrily as he can.

"Hey, I'm from Brownsville, so what do I know about clothes?" the Brownsville Bomber giggled after his best night of the season in a 118–100 blowout of the lifeless, formless didn't-they-used-to-be-the New York Knicks. "Anyway, I was out in the park shooting around this afternoon. Didn't have time to get my good stuff."

The Brownsville Bomber was a starter last night, playing 34 minutes, scoring 22 points, taking 11 rebounds, handing out 5 assists. He challenges for stray rebounds on legs thicker than Gene Shue's playbook, hovering around the rim on an invisible ladder. He scores on a rainbow jumper and strong, dramatic moves inside, occasionally tangling himself in unnecessarily impossible situations.

But he's learning, and that's the good news.

"Seeing Lloyd produce tonight is really satisfying," said GM Pat Williams, "because we did a lot of chasing before we decided to draft him at all. The way he played tonight, if he's a senior, coming out of Guilford this year, he's ahead of Willie Smith, Quinn Buckner, Bobby Wilkerson, Chuckie Williams, Mo Howard, Armond Hill, Mike Dabnoy. Maybe everybody but Jonathan Lucas, and that's because Lucas is a true lead guard, a quarterback. But that's what Lloyd is becoming, too."

Free skipped his final year of college eligibility. He went from Canarsie High in New York to tiny Guilford, after nearly enrolling at Long Beach State. He forced his way higher in the draft hierarchy with three solid seasons, an NAIA MVP as a freshman, and an excellent effort in an AAU tournament last Spring in Baton Rouge.

Assistant Coach Jack McMahon was the investigating officer.

"Saw him early, was sure I liked him," McMahon recalled, "but then they didn't get to the NAIA, even with a good record. Lost a big game to Winston-Salem. But instead of ending the season, the whole team was invited to an AAU tournament in Louisiana. I was the only pro scout there. Outquicked everybody.

"I saw a penetrating guard, saw him shoot 26 free throws, saw him go wherever he wanted to go. I keep telling you guys, if Lloyd Free can't play, I don't know who can. He's 6-1, 6-2. Tonight he jumped like he was 6-8. As it turned out, getting knocked out of the NAIA was a great break for us. If he goes there and does his stuff, then everybody knows, maybe we never get him."

Free is a runner, a jumper, a mobile young athlete still learning the intricacies of pro defense and court awareness.

"I came that close to going to Long Beach," Free said, holding his thumb and index finger perhaps a millimeter apart. "My buddy, Greg Jackson, was at Guilford then, said he needed some help, couldn't win all those games by himself. You grow up in Brownsville, you learn to stick with your friends.

"What I remember about Baton Rouge is, playing in a gym that seated maybe 13,000, but there was never more than 100 people in the place. Scattered around, too. Looked like 10 people. But it was fun. If we couldn't go to the NAIA, may as well go someplace."

Which is what he's beginning to do.

"He's listening more," suggested veteran guard Wali Jones, "doing exactly what he should be doing, not going wild. He's a ball handler now. We need the ball, need it not thrown away. Turnovers come because the ball is standing in one guy's hand too long. The ball hums, the ball hops, you're gonna win more. That's the game I love to play."

McMahon knows how many times he has hurried to outrageous corners of the nation in search of talent and come up empty. Free is starting to flourish.

"I'm playing smarter," Free conceded. "I WAS playing stupid, comin' in, saying if I've only got a couple minutes, I'll do what I do and sit down. This is different. The thing now is to play better defense. In college I never played position defense. It was going behind a guy, gambling, slapping a ball free. I'll learn the pro way, too."

There is a whole lot ahead of him. Somebody pass the word up the Turnpike. The Brownsville Bomber has only just begun.

SIX SHOTS: Doug Collins, starting at forward, had 26 points, seven rebounds, negated Bill Bradley. Steve Mix had 16 points, 20 rebounds, as many as the entire Knicks' starting lineup. Fred Carter had a quick 24 points, Clyde Lee 12 on 6-for-6 shooting, Joe Bryant 12 points, eight rebounds. . . . Sixers' 41st victory moved a half-game ahead of Buffalo, in second place in the Atlantic Division, gave them a club record 29 wins at home.

THERE IS A TOMORROW FOR SIXERS

Philadelphia Daily News
April 17, 1976

BUFFALO—IT BEGAN AS [AN] EVENING of small, inescapable ironies. Nothing at stake . . . everything at stake. No pressure . . . fierce, unrelenting pressure. It developed quickly, unexpectedly, into a 48-minute celebration, the 76ers climbing excitedly toward the summit of their aggregate abilities.

The play-by-play sheets became etchings of value, the box score the team's window to the world. The Sixers evened their best-of-three playoff series with Buffalo, blowing past the Braves, 131–106, with the speed, power, consistency and concentration that Gene Shue has spent an entire season searching for.

"I've never come out of a game with this team believing every guy had performed to capacity, because it's never happened," said assistant coach Jack McMahon. "But tonight I would truly have to search if I was looking for something negative. From a coaching standpoint, this is everything you work for."

The study in excellence—just one day after the Sixers lost to the Braves in the Spectrum—forces a decisive third game in Philadelphia tomorrow at 1 p.m. The winner advances to the NBA's Eastern Conference semifinals, beginning Wednesday in Boston.

The Sixers got a spectacular 34 points from George McGinnis and eight points or more from seven other players. If the first game of this series—the first playoff experience ever for seven players—formed any scars, the Team of the Year showed remarkable, almost instantaneous, recuperative powers.

Fred Carter and Doug Collins, the starting guards, contributed 22 and 20 points, Steve Mix 14 and Harvey Catchings eight points, 10 rebounds and a game-high five offensive rebounds. Catchings was superb in the first half, making his most definitive contributions of the season.

"I can do better," Catchings said quietly. "In fact, I should do better. We were down a game, had to win . . . but when we came out for shooting practice in the afternoon, I liked the atmosphere. I could see guys ready . . . more ready than the day before . . . talking about what they would do tonight, what we would do tomorrow. Not looking ahead, just believing there would be another game after tonight."

In the first half, Catchings and Clyde Lee shadowed Bob McAdoo, who made two early field goals, then did not get another one for the final 20:43 of the half. He finished with 21 points, second only to Randy Smith's

27, but was largely ineffectual after the Sixers built a lead that reached 19 points after 2:08 of the third quarter.

"We played an absolutely super game, did all the right things, made 60 percent of our shots in the first half, then never let them closer than six points," said Shue. "And when it got down to six, we were able to take it right back up, something we were unable to do in the opener. We lost the game in Philly because we didn't make our shots, but tonight anytime they made a run at us we simply kept them at bay."

"Harvey's first half was his best of the season, George was absolutely super throughout, and we got production from everyone, including our people off the bench. The first game, perhaps because we were totally inexperienced in the playoffs, I thought we were jittery. Watching Doug jump around before the first game, I thought he was going to leave the earth. I mean leave and not come back. Afterward, I told the players, the playoffs WERE a bit different, but I thought we overdid it."

"I felt more intense tonight, or maybe just different," conceded Lloyd Free. "I knew I couldn't make a lot of little mistakes, that this was a night we ought to be out for blood. They had a chance to wrap it up. I was TOO fired up the first game, to the point where I couldn't do what I wanted. This game, as an all-around performance for everybody, was the best I've seen. I mean, even when we missed a shot, we crashed to get it back. Everybody."

In the fourth quarter, when the Braves climbed tenaciously within 95–89, Joe Bryant, Mix, McGinnis and Bryant again drilled field goals, expanding the lead swiftly to 14. Later, after the Braves' John Shumate had crashed to the floor and been unconscious for several seconds, Buffalo appeared ready to make another run at a two-game sweep. Instead, Collins made an important steal, turned it into a three-point play and forced any remaining life out of the opposition. With 3:17 to go, Buffalo coach Jack Ramsay cleared his bench, the NBA's version of concession.

"Outplayed them from the start, then continued to do it for 48 minutes," said Mix. "But it was honestly a night to relax, to just go out and play. Everybody's saying we're down one, going to Buffalo's court, that we're not a good road team, it seemed to take the pressure off.

"Now, it's different. Now, we're going home, where we're 34–8, where we need one victory to move on to the next series. We may have done some things wrong preparing for the first game, getting too keyed up, so today Doug and I just went for a long walk, played pinball for a while, anything to take our minds off the game."

"Ahh, the difference is still mistakes," insisted Carter. "We turned the ball over just 12 times, didn't get burned by our own errors. We're just an unpredictable team, to the point where there's no telling how we might play from night to night. On the other hand, we might come out and play two in a row like this."

That they even have the opportunity is mildly incredible.

"Buffalo had a chance to put us away," said Shue, "and they played super tonight. Don't downplay how well Buffalo played. But if they were super, we were super super. We got 131 points, shot 56 percent in a playoff game, that's more than you should hope for."

And if McGinnis didn't carry them, he certainly cleared the way.

"Thursday night, I took myself out of the offense in the second half," McGinnis said, "tonight I stayed in it. Early in the third quarter, I asked for a couple plays to be run for me, because I was determined not to let the same thing happen.

"When I stand around, guys tend to stand around and wait for me to do something. Tonight, McAdoo wasn't playing the way he can and maybe Buffalo began waiting for him. The playoffs, I have learned, are no place for me to stand around and wait."

DR. J MEETS OSCAR

Philadelphia Daily News
January 8, 1982

DETROIT—DR. J IS WHIRLING, skywalking, slam-dunking.

"I'm not tall enough," the kid says. "Can't do it."

"You can if we cooperate," the Doctor says soothingly. "I got the tall and you got the ball."

There is crashing and clattering reverberating out of Oscar's trash can.

Here is Oscar the Grouch, appearing at the top of the can to retrieve a basketball. A little later, Julius Erving appears.

Julius Erving?

"That's right," he says. "Now, may I have the ball. I have a game to get back to."

Over the years, the game has been his escape, and it is also his vehicle, his window to the world. If there are lessons to be learned from the inimitable Dr. J, maybe it makes sense that the little people, just forming work and recreational habits, can visit and learn—at their own level and speed—from a professional athlete who has become of their superheroes.

He is inundated with requests to appear, to discuss, to perform, and he chooses carefully, the way aficionados select wines and liqueurs. And now he has selected "Sesame Street," from the Children's Television Workshop. He'll tape his segments early next month.

Gordon, Maria, Susan, Donna, Big Bird, Oscar, Honker and Dr. J.

Dr. J?

"You don't do everything you're asked to do," the 76ers' captain was saying over the lunch the other day, "but when I was asked about this one, I couldn't see any downside. It's credible, there's no controversy, it offers a great deal of educational merit.

"I would think it's better for the kids to watch 'Sesame Street' than cartoons. The emphasis is on learning, on repetition, on associations with things they already know about. Colors, items they recognize, things they eat. To me, it's an opportunity to enhance my image as something other than as a basketball player. I've seen snatches of shows where they use Bill Cosby, Phyllis Diller, Gabe Kaplan, to get points across. The kids relate to it, so do the adults."

He is a star, in many ways a developing legend. But, at home, in Villanova, with his wife, Turquoise, 8-month-old Cory, 5-year-old Jazmin, 7-year-old Julius III and 9-year-old Cheo, he is Daddy. And he tries mightily to remember which comes first.

"During the season," Erving said, "I have no control of my time at home. Turq is mother and father to the kids, and it's the only life they've known. I used to travel maybe 70 percent of the time, now I've cut back to almost 50. In years to come, it may cut back to 25.

"Have I missed them? In the infancy stages, you miss your child if you don't see him every day. But that's something that had to be forfeited in my career. My absence, the necessity of it, will make me concentrate on the quality of our time later on.

"Even now, when I'm home, I really hear my kids. Some parents can be home seven days a week, but don't hear at all. It goes in one ear, out the other. When I'm home, I'm absolutely sure that won't happen to me."

So "Sesame Street," "The Electric Company," commercial TV and selected videotapes are available to the Erving kids. And when they want something, they ask.

"Turq and I have that in common, that when we were growing up, we did without," Julius said. "So we've pretty much told our kids that, if they really want something, ask and we'll do it. But make sure it's something you really want, or the meaning is lost. There's a risk involved, but if we've done our part, the risk is lessened considerably."

There is a TV room at home, and the tapes for the kids are in a drawer.

"Walt Disney, cartoons," Julius said. "And I let 'em look at some of the martial arts movies, the Bruce Lee types, although not necessarily with Bruce Lee in them.

"I'm not afraid of them watching violence. They see it in my profession, in terms of contact and collisions. If they decide to pursue it, it's OK. The first thing you learn from a martial arts instructor is patience, defense of self. Right now, the kids say they just like the movie, they don't want to really do it. But if they do later, at least they've been exposed to it."

He is a force in his household even when he is in Portland or Salt Lake City or Detroit.

"I made up my mind a long time ago," Erving said, "that I'm gonna be an influence in their lives, the dominant influence. Even now, when I'm home, I don't have to do so much as raise my voice. I can look at them, point a finger, arch an eyebrow, and they know to stop what they're doing, to look for further direction. I want that influence."

He says it is a blend of genuine love with responsibility, direction with knowledge of choices.

"It's a grand design," he said. "The kids grow, learn, develop, and then they leave, to pursue lives of their own. That's why, as you live as a couple, you also live as a family. You don't take care of one, and assume you'll pick up the other at some later point. Do that, the first thing you find is, it's too late.

"I like to think I'm living proof of my own philosophy . . . to try a lot of things, to taste options, discover new experiences. Whether our kids choose to be truck drivers, poets, politicians, whatever, as long as they have the prerequisites to make the decisions honestly and fairly, then we've done our job.

"Somewhere, I don't recall where, I read about Marques Johnson growing up. His parents, both educators, planned his schools, his college, his profession. For him, it worked, but how many people could have done that? I'd prefer to let our children see the spectrum, learn for themselves."

When the ball goes up, in special moments, he transforms into Dr. J. But he also remains human and vulnerable, subject to the same wounds as any of us. An argument with his wife, an angry word with one of his kids, a baffling rebellion at home.

"Lots of times, it's all I think about on my way to the arena," he said. "I'm distracted, the same way you would be. But when the game starts, it's different. Everything else blanks out."

It is the Doctor's yellow brick road, and he acknowledges its healing, calming effect.

"Through most of my life," he said, "I've used the game as an escape. I can recall one experience, at home, when I was maybe 16.

"It's Saturday morning, there's a high school game on TV at 11. I know some of the guys in the game, I really want to see it. I sleep late, get ready, but my stepfather comes in and tells me to go out and cut the grass.

"I said, 'OK, after the game.' He was a big, dominant guy, 6-2, 190. At 16, I was about 5-11, 150 at the most. I got the push mower out, got started on the grass. At 11, I wasn't done, but I came in anyway. I said I'd finish as soon as the game was over.

"My stepfather took his belt off, went to hit me. I wasn't going to let that happen, and caught the belt. He looked for a minute like he was gonna punch me, and I kinda pushed him. He stumbled, I left. I went out the door as my mother and sister came in. They had no idea what was happening, and I didn't stop to tell them.

"I went to the park, and just played ball. All day. I felt so good, so tired . . . At 6, I came home, forgetting about everything else. Dinner was over, my plate was on the stove. I ate, cleaned up, went upstairs. I forgot what had happened. That's what playing ball has always done for me.

"It still does. On the court, everything else goes out of my mind. Like I was born to play. I feel a freedom from reality, from the pressures of the moment. I just play. And I feel good."

It is not a lesson the kids will learn in a segment or two of "Sesame Street." But they will get a glimpse of the player, get a taste of the man, a look at Jazmin, Cory, Julius III and Cheo's daddy.

They will count shots, count round things, have fun, learn to be patient, to cooperate, to recognize the basic tendencies of a team. It is one more moment when Dr. J is bigger than life.

It is a chance to learn, and that, the Doctor says, is something no one should ever waste.

DOUG COLLINS IS A VOICE OF REASONS

Philadelphia Daily News
April 16, 1982

DOUG COLLINS CAME UP with a terrific piece of trivia the other day, listing three NBA players last season who had more than 100 points, rebounds, blocks, steals and assists.

Another time, he challenged anyone to recall an old Nets lineup against the 76ers that included five lefties.

He has lots of material about his time at Illinois State, in the Olympics, with the 76ers. His roots? He still subscribes to a Benton, Ill., newspaper.

Collins is filled with enthusiasm, details, X's and O's and anecdotes. He has spent the season developing his delivery and on-the-air personality as the WCAU-TV 48 analyst, and Sunday he'll cover Washington-Atlanta with Jim Kelly on CBS.

Ironically, Doug will be on TV here when the Sixers aren't, because their game with Milwaukee will be blacked out locally.

"I remember my first pregame show," Doug was saying the other day. "I did it cold. They just handed me a microphone and said, 'Go do it.'

"I interviewed Maurice Cheeks, and I guess I got through it, but the opening and closing was hard. I had been interviewed hundreds of times, but never had done the interviewing. So I started writing out a format for myself, and it's made a big difference.

"When CBS asked about my availability for three dates, I was as surprised as I was honored. Believe me, I understand that a lot of people go to school to learn this as a profession, and that it's awfully easy to get in front of a camera and embarrass yourself. So, if I'm gonna do it, I'm gonna do it the best I possibly can.

"I want to talk to the fans at a level they can accept, so they can watch the action more knowledgeably. I'm not big on statistics, I'd rather come up with reasons, tendencies. If a team's shooting 5-for-20, why? Is it defense? Is it poor shot selection? The wrong guys shooting? And as I'm doing that, I don't want to come off as a guy who thinks he knows everything.

"People have to understand that there's plenty the guys in the booth don't know, either."

Collins is working dutifully at a career transition. The former All-Star guard, who saw his career ended by a macabre string of foot and knee injuries, worked as a volunteer assistant at Penn, and is leaning toward becoming a college coach.

"Having so much to do has been a godsend," Doug admitted. "When you stop playing, you lose your little kid's exuberance. The playing, the camaraderie keep you young, but when it's over, the circle's closed to you. I still travel with the team now, but I'm part of the media. . . . It's a different game than college ball, and I'm not sure how I feel about that, either. Zam Frederick led the nation in scoring last year, and he's playing somewhere in Europe 'cause he couldn't adjust to the pro game. I went to scout a player one night, the opponent played a zone, and I never got to see the skills that the NBA would require. I'm learning that there's a great level of sophistication when it comes to evaluating talent."

What about Sunday? Collins knows the Bullets haven't beaten the Sixers in five attempts (they play again tonight in Landover, Md.), and that Atlanta was the first team to win twice in Philadelphia.

"When Atlanta's front line—John Drew, Dan Roundfield, Tree Rollins—is healthy, they're as strong as anyone," he said. "They're strong on the boards, and their No. 1 defense is the result of working together, helping out, rather than great individual skills. They use the clock to their advantage, and cleverly attack weaknesses in opponents.

"Washington's had a fine season, and I always felt that Gene Shue had great offensive plays, that if you execute them, you get great shots. They might not always go in, but if you use the screens and cuts, the right guys will get opportunities from comfortable areas.

"Jeff Ruland and Ricky Mahorn set strong picks, and Kevin Grevey and Greg Ballard get a lot of the shots. They've gotten great mileage from their talent. But if both teams are at their best, Atlanta's better. In fact, they're my dark horse in the East. They're confident, they believe they can play with anyone, they're good on the road. They could be frightening in a mini-series, which could be against the Sixers. I'm sure Billy Cunningham feels the same way."

If things go well, Collins could work two more games for the network, but there may not be any real future in it, because next season's coverage won't begin until after the NCAA's Final Four.

"All I'm doing," Doug said, "is exploring. Whatever happens later, happens.

"But I don't want anyone watching Sunday's game just because I'm on. It should be the game that draws the interest. Jim Kelly and Doug Collins shouldn't distract basketball fans from a great game, they should add to it."

MOTHER'S DAY MASSACRE

Philadelphia Daily News
May 10, 1982

BOSTON—WHERE WERE THE MASTERMINDS at Channel 10 when we really needed them? Anything would have been better for a national viewing audience. Even "Nurse." This was the Sixers' "Deathtrap," a 121–81 loss to dreaded Boston. In the opening game of the NBA's Eastern final, their arms were too short to box with the Celtics.

Could it possibly have been worse in Amityville? A team that won 10 regular-season games by 20 or more points, that never lost by more than 23, found itself buried in a 40-point embarrassment.

The Sixers never have scored fewer points against the Celtics in their playoff history and lost to them four times during the regular season by a total of 27.

"If there's any way to take consolation from something like this," Mike Bantom said afterward, "it's that this only counts as one victory for them. It's embarrassing, it's frustrating, but I know we're not this bad. I know we'll have this game on our minds, that we'll think about it and think about it.

"They hammered us. They got up by a lot (as many as 48 with 6:41 to go), and kept going for more. I don't know if you should be throwing lob passes and slam-dunking when you're up 40 . . . maybe you should, maybe it's what anyone would do. But it'll have us a little angrier, a lot more determined when we come back Wednesday night."

No Sixers game has ever become so absurd so fast. Center Darryl Dawkins left with 6:02 remaining in the second period, and didn't at all in the second half, insisting that his right leg was hurting. Dawkins suffered multiple fractures in his leg in January and periodically has complained of recurring pain since then. He went to Temple University Hospital last night for X-rays.

Next case, Caldwell Jones fouled out with 5:39 to go in the third period, the earliest he could ever remember being disqualified. Neither Caldwell nor Bobby Jones managed a field goal all day, Julius Erving had none in the second half, the Sixers scored just 11 points in the third period, and the starting lineup combined for four baskets in the final 24 minutes, all by Maurice Cheeks and Andrew Toney.

"What the Celtics did when they were up 40 (rookie Charles Bradley slammed home two points on an alley-oop lob from Chris Ford with 1:09 left), was their choice," said Bantom. "I know I'll remember it. To have it happen on national TV is something else to remember, but I've been on teams where guys have quit, and at least that didn't happen today. We just couldn't put an end to their scoring. They just did it and did it and did it."

(Let the record show that after Bradley's dunk, Cunningham called a time-out and deployed the Sixers into a four-corner stall. One possession later, though, he instructed sub guard Frank Edwards to resume a normal offense.)

The Sixers were coming off an emotional victory over Milwaukee in the sixth game of the quarterfinals, and hadn't practiced Saturday. The Celtics had been off since Wednesday night, after a double-overtime win that clinched their quarterfinal series against Washington.

Rub it in? Who, the Celtics?

"You don't rub it in in this league," said Bill Fitch, their coach, "because you're going to play six more times. If everything is going, if everything is falling, there isn't any way in pro basketball to stop it . . ."

The next quarter, Toney, who is not exactly a 98-pound weakling, tried Carr again and had to limp to the bench for his trouble. No foul, by the way.

"Hey, Hugh, is that a whistle you have?" barked Cunningham to Hugh Evans. "Is that a whistle you have?"

Evans, fingering his neck quizzically, said yeah. Then he caught on. "Oh, you don't think I'm using it enough?" he barked.

"No," Cunningham pronounced.

But it wasn't until 4:30 left in the half that we realized what Draculas the 76ers are dealing with. Mo Cheeks hit a 20-footer, then scored on a break. The sliced the Celtic margin to 52–35. Bill Fitch raged upward and called time-out. Time-out! No lead is too much, no bucket of blood too full, for these Boston stranglers.

"That might have (been) the key point of the game," Cedric Maxwell said. "What's the point of letting a 20-point lead get down to 10 before halftime? Only people that wanted this game to be close were CBS and maybe some 76er fans. Ask me whether I want to beat a team by four points or by 40, and I'll take 40. There's a certain humiliation factor involved."

At halftime it was 62–45. After three quarters it was 93–56. At game's end it was 121–81. Yes, there was a certain humiliation factor involved, kinda like Dunkirk. It could have been worse, too. If it had been up to M. L. Carr and Cedric Maxwell, it would have been.

In the third quarter, which was a neat 31–11, the Celtics let Philadelphia have its third field goal after six minutes and five seconds. With the score 81–51, Robert Parish blocked a shot out of bounds and Larry Bird did a broad jump into the courtside mob to keep it in. When the bodies were cleared, Bird helped one of the fans up. That was the Celtics' only human touch of the afternoon.

Some perceptive Celtics could see this coming Wednesday night. After they escaped the slow-motion Bullets in double-overtime, they learned the 76ers had allowed the Bucks to get within 3–2. That meant one extra flight, one extra game, one needless hardship leading into a series traditionally full of them.

"We were sitting here waiting," Maxwell said. "Sitting here waiting for them."

"Plus, it's easier for us to run up and down the court than it was against Washington," Carr said. "We were playing 89-point games against them." He leered with that boogie smile. "That ain't exactly our cup of tea."

"I would feel terrible if I'd been on a team that lost by 40," Maxwell said, now stepping down the party line. "Terrible. What happens then is that you dig down deep. If you lose by two or three, you maybe get some false comfort that you played well. I'd hate to be the opposition the next time the 76ers play."

Uh, Max, you are the opposition.

"Oh, yeah, I guess I am. Well, from our viewpoint, we want to go out there and do it again. Because if we don't do it again, we'll be down. I'm sure the media and the people around the Sixers will write and say things that will get them fired up. The next game won't be the same."

He said it with a touch of regret.

SIXER BID WILTS AWAY

Philadelphia Daily News
February 2, 1982

THE TELEGRAM TO HAROLD KATZ yesterday was brief, succinct, filled, Wilt Chamberlain says, with deeper regret than anyone may ever understand.

The Wilt Watch is over. He is not coming back to play for the 76ers.

"One of the biggest considerations . . . no, make that the biggest consideration, became controversy," Chamberlain said by phone yesterday from his suburban Los Angeles mansion.

"It's something I've had to live with all my life, something I've spoken about a zillion times. Because I am who I am, controversy has been associated with me, and it wasn't something I could control.

"I never believed all of it was warranted, and at this stage in my life, I'm not interested in it. I don't want to cause any unpleasantness for anyone, especially friends and family."

Still, at age 45, he had deliberated ending a nine-year retirement from the NBA to accept Katz' offer to finish this season with the Sixers.

He had enough feelings about the situation to meet with Katz over dinner last week in LA's posh Century Plaza Hotel. He later discussed it with the Sixers' owner by phone, and spoke three consecutive days with Dr. Stanley Lorber, who remains his own physician and close friend.

He listened intently to opinions from both sides, spending a half hour on the phone with Connie Hawkins, once a superstar in the sport.

"He said, 'Big fella, show 'em the way it was,'" Chamberlain said. "So many others called, saying basically the same thing.

"But my mother called, too, and she told me not to. Hey, she's no different than anyone else's mother. Love, care, emotion come into the picture. She said, 'Son, you've done what you had to do in that part of your life. It was enough. It's time to live the rest of your life and enjoy it. Don't make yourself miserable now, don't allow yourself to become vulnerable.' My sister called, said essentially the same things. Those are people who care about me as a person. Those are opinions I dearly value."

In other years, he had fielded NBA offers from Cleveland, Los Angeles, Chicago, Atlanta and San Antonio. As early as 1965, he had considered stepping into the ring against Muhammad Ali, and he had at least listened when a promoter suggested he could make a fortune as a barnstorming one-man decathlon show.

"All of those came up," Wilt said, "but I never gave any of them the thought I gave Mr. Katz' offer. I accepted it as totally complimentary to begin with, and it was easily the most unique, in a way made the most sense.

"First, it would only have locked me up for three months, not the full eight or nine months it takes to play an NBA season these days. It was in my home town, the place I started, with the only team I'd ever want to play for, with an opportunity to help them with a championship.

"Physically, there's not a doubt in my mind I could do it. But the regimentation of my time, the mental aspects. I could have endured it, but I would have done so reluctantly."

He had said he could come back and lead the league in rebounding and blocked shots, and didn't realize until later that his comments might have inferred things he had not intended.

"I've been away from the NBA nine long years," he said. "I had forgotten what levels of controversy Wilt Chamberlain seems to create. I don't want to deal with that anymore.

"When I said I could lead the league in those two areas, I didn't mean them as personal goals. If I had said I could lead the league in scoring, then they would have had a reason to worry.

"But defense? Rebounding? Blocking shots? Those are the attributes you need to build a champion, not tear it down. Bill Russell, it was said, did those things and he was called a great leader.

"I read a long story in the LA Times that indicated that Billy was against the idea of me playing because of the situation it might create. I read Julius Erving's comments, too. I realized that, no matter how I phrased it, it might be taken different ways by different people.

"Hey, if the guys on the street say, 'Ahhhh, Wilt can't do that anymore,' I'd have no problem. But people like Billy and Julius, with whom I'd be directly associated, I couldn't do that to them. I couldn't hurt them in any way. Billy's my friend. I don't know Julius that well, but I have great respect for him. I wouldn't do anything to change that.

"I thought about my mother's advice. Proving things? All I had intended to do was prove that 45 isn't too old to do anything, but I understand now that my days of proving things are over."

In other years, critics simply glossed over Wilt's theories, suggesting he was merely playing mind games, enjoying the mystery, intrigue and negotiating.

"This was never a mind game," Wilt insisted, "other than that any time you entertain an offer, it requires mental exercise. If I had chosen to play, it would've been for the fun of it. I didn't start playing basketball so many years ago to prove my greatness. I did it because it was fun.

"I don't play racquetball now to prove I can be a great racquetball player. I do it because it's fun. That's why when Mr. Katz wanted to talk about money, I said I didn't want to hear it. If I had gotten into that, then I would have been playing mind games. He'd have given me a figure, I'd probably have asked him to double it, just to see how much money he had, how interested he really was. You know, I never heard what he wanted to pay, and I don't want to now."

Katz had said several times he was willing to pay Wilt up to $500,000 for the remainder of the season, to pursue various endorsements for him, and to offer the opportunity to become "the most famous middle-aged man in the world."

"I wasn't afraid of falling on my face," Chamberlain said. "I was in my 30s when I decided to learn volleyball. I played against kids 12 and 13, and there I really did fall on my face for a while. I wanted to ski, I fell on my butt, the way anyone would until he learned the techniques. Trying . . . that's the name of the game.

"Didn't people say the same things when Gordie Howe was playing hockey in his 50s, on the same team with his sons? I'll probably come out a villain in all of this, but I have to say what I fel[t] . . . We're all individuals, and what's inside you is what you are. Play basketball? I know I can. But it mystifies me that people can only view situations through their own eyes, they have difficulty playing the devil's advocate, or seeing another person's point of view.

"That owners, promoters have come to me over the years . . . I have no control of their ideas, but when I decide not to do something, I get blamed. It's not right, but it's what happens. I'm involved right now with the Foundation for Athletic Research and Education, with its founder, De. Leroy Perry. We're studying preventive medicine, ways to build endurance, to help athletes lengthen and improve their careers, to show them it's possible to do more.

"I know more about myself than most people know about themselves. Most guys, at 45, can't even run around the block. I start each day with seven miles. I deeply resent people saying, if I came back, I'd be a shadow of what I once was. Those same people said I wasn't in shape when I played. Dick Young, the columnist in New York, said I couldn't play basketball. Where did he get that? Why would he arrive at an opinion like that? It bothers me that now, all those people seem to have opinions again, but they didn't even think I was so great when I was at the peak of my profession."

Wilt has a perfect understanding of what now has happened between himself and Harold Katz.

"He came to me, to a man set in his way of life, and asked me, even for a little while, to change," Chamberlain said. "It was never a matter of money. Hell, I could probably buy the Sixers. My consideration was to show the world that 45 is merely a number, not indicative of what a person can or can't do. But I realized that I like where I am and what I do. I won't kid you, my life's too nice the way it is.

"The pity of it all is, there's a percentage of people back in Philly, who would've loved to see me play. In a way, I feel like I'm letting them down. I just hope they don't take it personally."

So what should the Sixers now do? How much help do they need? And where might they find it?

"They might have all they need right there," Wilt said. "I know what's happening. They lost Darryl Dawkins with an injury, they lost a couple of games they feel they shouldn't have lost, and now it's time to regroup, reassess roles, maybe go get a player.

"Well, I have great faith in Caldwell Jones. He has the talent to play center, forward, guard, whatever they want. They have to give him the ball more, make him shoot, make him an offensive force. You think I don't know he's a reluctant shooter? Tell him I'll kick his butt if he doesn't. And he knows I can.

"If he'd shoot, he'd make Dr. J a greater threat, because teams couldn't double up as easily. Caldwell could easily do for the Sixers what Robert Parish does for Boston. Maybe he thinks he can't, but I know better. I'd like to see him go off and score 35–40 points. Not every night. Just once, just to let 'em know he can. It'd help maybe more than they realize.

"Caldwell wants to be an unselfish player, and I respect that, because not enough guys are. But you can be unselfish to a point of hurting your team. He's gotta go out there and establish himself. I've told CJ this a few times, and he always says, 'OK, big fella, I'll do it.' But now it's time. Hey, he could move 15–17 feet from the hoop and jump-shoot Kareem to death. I've seen lesser centers do it. I'm positive CJ could. And if he does, he might be giving the Sixers all they ever really needed."

CHAPTER 6

THE '83 CHAMPIONSHIP SEASON

Introduction by Billy Cunningham

Your dad was caring, loving, and a true professional. He always told both sides of every story and checked every fact for every story he ever wrote. I always felt that I had to be extra careful because not every story that was written came though like Phil's did. He was always professional with everything he did. He had a very difficult job to do. I had a very difficult job to do. We were very, very good and with that comes a lot of pressure. Phil treated me with respect and I knew when he was with our players, he had already done his research. He was prepared to do his job. If he had to double-check something, he would do it in a respectful way. He would call me late at night and I would say, "You're on the right track Phil," or "There's nothing to it, Phil." He would check and I appreciated it. Not everyone was like that. He would never test me with something that would be unfair in print.

He took such pride in that newspaper. He was so classy in his approach. He treated his job like I treated mine. We were cut from the same cloth in different professions. From that developed a mutual respect and trust.

Over time with your dad, as our relationship developed further, whatever I said, he used it properly. If something was off track, I'd tell him privately. If I'd fly off the handle, which I was prone to do, he'd reign me in and write the story in a respectful way. The pride he had for his newspaper was evident. Phil was in a different category in terms of how he handled himself and how he went about his business. I knew he had a tough job to do as a reporter, and he became someone I cared for so much as a person away from the court and as a friend.

We talked about your mom a lot as she was sick a good bit. My wife and your mom went to the same beauty parlor. Sometimes, your dad would go home from practice, pick up your mom and take her to the beauty parlor. They developed a nice friendship and ours developed as well. It was rather unique because a beat reporter has to write every day, and sometimes they are critical articles. We had this incredible trust built from the very beginning and it continued through the years. Your dad had such personal turmoil, but you would never know it by how he approached his job. He was so professional and honest. He was a special man.

When we won, you could feel the excitement in your dad's articles. He wanted to get every fact, every anecdote in the story. He wanted it to be correct. He wanted to be that connection with the fans. Philadelphia could be a tough sports town. Phil was a great connection between us and the fans. He was so fair. The energy he brought every day was unmatched. He took everything in stride and it came through in the newspaper. He was so different than the other writers. Like I said before, just a special, special man.

He would call me all the time. Did you hear this? Did you hear that? Is something brewing? I mean, he worked so darn hard. You had to steer him in the right direction and reward that hard work. There was not one fact that went unchecked. He was so persistent. He was honest. Phil Jasner didn't always write nice things. There were critical articles along the way even with us. But he always took an honest approach and was fair. He was respectful. He was factual and always wanted to confirm every fact. How could you not respect that in return?

Phil and I talked and e-mailed a lot through the years. From a personal standpoint, we were extraordinarily close. He would bounce things off me. I would bounce things off him. I miss him dearly. One of the all-time greats in every way. Just a special, special, special man.

BILLY CUNNINGHAM *spent 17 seasons with the Sixers—nine as a player and eight as a coach. Cunningham played for the Sixers from 1965–1972 and again from 1974–1976. He won an NBA championship in 1966–1967. Cunningham later coached the Sixers from 1977–1985 and won another championship in 1982–1983. His career coaching record with the Sixers was 454–196.*

• • • • • •

CLEAN SWEEP FOR 76ERS

Philadelphia Daily News
May 2, 1983

THEIR ENERGY WAS BEING siphoned off in pools of perspiration and gobs of emotion. They were, at one time, eager, anxious, frustrated and hungry.

The 76ers needed something more, raising their level of skill and will one more excruciating plateau because the New York Knicks were beaten and would not acknowledge it. The Knicks, even as they were being swept out of the NBA Eastern semifinals, would not go softly into the Manhattan night.

"This was a lot tougher than the last time we beat the Knicks, 4–0, in the playoffs (in 1977–78)," Julius Erving said after yesterday's 105–102 victory that sent the Sixers into the Eastern finals, most probably against the remarkably surging Milwaukee Bucks.

"The Knicks were prepared to play us, and we respected their ability. They came to win, we came to win. Neither team came merely to play, and that's where the conflict begins. We were a little better equipped, starting with the man in the middle (Moses Malone), the other starters, the guys off the end of the bench and, of course, Billy (coach Billy Cunningham), who pulled a lot of nice moves when it definitely could have gone the other way."

Madison Square Garden, through the course of the intense weekend, became a minefield, with both teams clawing up the floor like infantry troops, creating little explosions along the way, cleverly avoiding others. The Sixers won both games, and swept the series, because they were able to adjust their vaunted high-wire act. When they had to, they traveled on their stomachs.

When the Sixers left the building, it was as much to celebrate as it was to lick their wounds and contemplate their future. Andrew Toney sat out most of the second half when his left leg, weakened by a deep thigh bruise, stiffened. Maurice Cheeks was helped off the floor when he took a blow to the back of his knee that left his ankle momentarily numb. Clemon Johnson pulled up lame with a hamstring pull, Erving nursed himself through an assortment of bruises and pulls and Bobby Jones gamely played through the dregs of a bout with the flu.

"Every time I looked up," Cunningham said, "somebody was going down. I couldn't believe it. We looked like tenpins."

But a nightmare can transform itself into a dream, which is what Cunningham was experiencing. Malone thundered through 38 steamy minutes to generate 29 points and 14 rebounds; Erving scored 18 points; Toney contributed seven field goals in the first half; Cheeks handed out seven assists; and guards Clint Richardson and Frank Edwards played steadily off the bench. Even starting forward Marc Iavaroni, who has gone through the entire season searching for consistency, made all five of his shots and played an important 29 minutes.

"You must congratulate the winners," said Hubie Brown, the Knicks' coach. ". . . I told the team that we took them (the Sixers) to the maximum and it took a spectacular effort to beat us. They had to play to their outstanding athletic potential . . . No man likes to go out 0-and-4, but it was no knockout."

Maybe the result wasn't, but the Sixers' performance down the stretch was. They absorbed the Knicks' best shots and showed a resiliency, versatility and strength that previous Philadelphia teams were unable to display.

Long after the Sixers' locker room had emptied, Erving quietly iced down one knee and examined what has happened, and what remains to be done.

"I feel OK . . . kinda mellow," Dr. J said. "I feel very nice about what we just did, and I look forward to what's on the horizon.

"It's been a long, hard season, and all of these things—all the little injuries and problems—have gone on all year. To sweep this series just adds to the realization that, to be successful, a team has to adapt, adjust and sacrifice.

"But that's not a new trend. By finishing this series quickly, we've enabled ourselves to rest and get well. Even in winning, there's no room for cop-outs. We can't say, 'We've played so hard, come so far and now we're bandaged and battered.' We've got to perform.

"If we were to worry about such things, they would only serve as distractions. Injuries won't be our demise. We're going to think positive. We have our eye on a championship, and we won't be denied."

It was Erving's way of explaining that, regardless of the circumstances, the Sixers have the tools to win their first title since 1966–67. To get to the championship series now, they will have to defeat either the Bucks or the Boston Celtics, and the Bucks own an overwhelming 3–0 advantage in that series, with Game 4 scheduled tonight in Milwaukee.

"People," Erving said, "say Moses carried Houston to the championship have just one more (player) than that team, we're ahead of the game."

But they did not feel sufficiently ahead to bring champagne into the locker room for the second time this season. They filled their cups after clinching first place in the Atlantic Division, but kept the lid on yesterday.

"Winning the division and the conference, that was a mini-goal," Erving said. "Winning the first round of the playoffs was not a mini-goal. The championship remains now as a goal, the only one. In that regard, all the playoff games are being looked at in the same vein. We want 12 victories, because that is what is needed to win it all. We have four now. We need eight more."

The next series had been scheduled to begin Sunday—and the Sixers welcomed the rest—but some inquiries were made yesterday that could change that.

A CBS executive contacted the NBA yesterday to ask whether the Sixers would move up their Eastern Conference final opener to Friday night, if the remaining three semifinal series all were concluded.

Sixers GM Pat Williams said last night that no one had asked him yet. Nor did he know if the Spectrum was available Friday night. But he added, "If the league tells us to play, we will play."

If the other semifinal series end tonight and tomorrow, CBS would be left with no game for its Friday late-night telecast. Discussions are scheduled to continue today, but nothing can be decided until after tomorrow's Los Angeles-Portland game.

"Our biggest concern now," Cunningham said, "is that we have several people injured, and we want them to get well. We'll wait and hope they respond the way Moses did coming into this series."

Malone, who missed the last four games of the regular season with tendinitis in his right knee, then developed a problem in his left knee, scored 125 points in the four games against the Knicks, overpowering opposing centers Bill Cartwright and Marvin Webster.

"Today, when we needed him, Moses just took over the defensive board," Cunningham said. "You saw Moses ready for them. To have done what we did in this series is more than a surprise, it's a coach's dream. And what I saw from Moses, well, I'm not surprised by anything more. That's just the way he plays. Every game."

But the Knicks, getting 35 points from Bernard King, 15 rebounds from Truck Robinson and eight assists each from starting guards Rory Sparrow and Paul Westphal, tested virtually every phase of the Sixers' game, other than perhaps backcourt quickness. They refused to make it easy, even in the final, draining moments when the Madison Square Garden crowd was offering them a standing ovation.

"If we had stopped or let up, even for just a minute, we'd have lost," Richardson said. "We needed something from everybody, and what we got from Moses tells you why they pay him what they pay him. And why he's worth every penny. You have to give the Knicks credit for hanging in there against us. Hubie Brown got the most out of what they had.

"But we haven't peaked yet. We're just starting to run again. Andrew, Maurice, Clemon all were hurt, but it didn't stop us. We're gonna try to peak as we get to the championship series. When we do, we'll be unstoppable. We'll be the way we were when we came from 20 back to beat the Knicks the other night. We'll make the extra passes, play tenacious defense, everything we need. When you see it, you'll know."

Erving corroborated the feeling that swept through his teammates.

"In terms of past playoffs," Erving said, "this has been a slow start for me. But I want to start slow, finish fast. I'm kind of excited, because I know I can do more. The important thing is, through all of this, we're still winning. I'm feeling like a stick of dynamite, at any time ready to explode."

Yesterday, they blew up in the Knicks' faces. The swiftness of the sweep aside, not even Hubie Brown would argue that this is the way it was supposed to happen.

SOME THINGS NEVER CHANGE

Philadelphia Daily News
February 11, 1983

CHANGE, JULIUS ERVING SAYS, is to be expected, not feared.

Even if the change were to mean 12 NBA teams instead of 23. Or a radically revised salary structure.

The 76ers have changed. Julius Erving has changed. The game has changed. Can the league possibly be far behind?

Doctor J is going to his 12th consecutive pro All-Star Game, his seventh in the NBA. This one is Sunday in the Forum, where he will join Coach Billy Cunningham, assistants Jack McMahon and Matty Guokas, starters Maurice Cheeks and Moses Malone, and reserve Andrew Toney.

But wasn't it just yesterday when the Doctor took his first skywalk, when he unveiled his first 360-degree thunderdunk?

The purists tell us that, unless we saw Doc in his halcyon American Basketball Association days, we've really never seen him at all. Another faction insists we're now seeing an art form, a natural resource sublimating individual skills to allow team concepts to become dominant.

It has become a game that always offers the possibility of highlight-film explosiveness, but that more frequently remains even, careful, thoughtful. In a league that seems to spend the majority of its active moments searching for elusive logic and order, Doctor J remains a beacon of consistency.

Whatever difficulties his league is facing, he says the sport will endure.

"The game will go on," Erving was saying, "because it really is the true American sport. Somehow, some way, it will be preserved.

"Granted, there might be drastic changes. In years to come, it could go to 12 teams, there could be changes in the salary structure. But it's been here for 35 or 40 years, it'll be here another 35–40 years.

"Change, in itself, is not to be feared, but to be expected. I've already seen different brands of ball accepted, different rules, different team emphasis, different philosophies, almost like several eras. What invariably happens is the players make the adjustments necessary to make it work."

The Doctor's metamorphosis began back at Roosevelt High, on Long Island, where feelings and instincts began struggling for space on the surface.

"In high school and college," he recalled, "there were lots of things I felt like doing that the basketball purists didn't understand, wouldn't condone.

"In high school, we had a guard who, one day, threw me a lob pass. Accidentally, I think. But I scored on the play. The coach was furious. He said, 'Take that play back to the playground.' Now it's become an accepted way to beat a defense, by throwing the ball over it. Back then, we'd try to work around a defense, or, if we could, through it.

"Back then, committing yourself to the air was to take a shot or to make a specific pass, not to explore your options. It's funny, but when you're not encouraged to do something and you continue to do it, you start to feel you were destined to do it. It was something I couldn't explain."

Even a coach as analytical and demanding as Portland's Jack Ramsay doesn't search for explanations to define Erving's special skills.

"I remember that move along the baseline in the Championship Series with Los Angeles three years ago," Ramsay said. "He went up on one side of the rim and somehow floated underneath and laid it up on the other side. I've never seen anybody who could move laterally in the air like that. Nobody else ever has.

"I consider Bill Russell the greatest shot blocker of all time. A lot of shot blockers have tried to emulate him, but nobody's come close. It's the same thing with Julius. The things he does when he's airborne will never be done again. He takes off at the top of the circle, goes in the air and there's about six things that can happen. In Julius's case, they're generally all good things that can happen for him."

Erving accepts the inevitability of change, has gone with the flow, and has been known to force the flow in other, unexpected directions.

"One of the things we talked about in training camp was the possibility of having four guys from the ABA on this team if we hadn't had to give up Caldwell (Jones) for Moses (Malone). We'd have had them, myself and Bobby Jones. I sort of hoped we'd be able to make some sort of lasting statement, like a group of old warriors.

"I saw a report somewhere that said there were 25 players in the league now who were part of the last ABA season, when there were only six teams, and 28 players who were in the NBA at the same time. I suppose that's a statement, too."

But was there a time when he wondered if the vast majority of the country would ever be exposed to his talents?

"If there was a time like that," he said, "it was my first two years in Philly. That was because of the type of team we had. For me, it was a matter of learning to play another way.

"We all changed. Of course, they also cleaned house, but as it changed I found myself playing more often to my strengths rather than with reckless abandon. In a way, necessity parallels the shifting of styles.

"I still enjoy the physical part, and with the concept we have now, the nights we play the less fortunate teams tend to turn into easy nights. That's nicer than having to rely on heroics. Like last week in Portland, we had to try some heroics—mostly from Andrew Toney—to try and pull a game out at the end. But in recent years, a lot more games ended that way. Now we seem to play the same way every game, and that's more gratifying."

But owner Harold Katz has signed Malone for more than $13 million over six years, he is paying Erving roughly $1 million a season, and eventually will tender a rich new contract to Toney. There have been recent championship teams in Portland and Seattle that struggled with contractual hassles and were never the same. Can it happen to the Sixers?

"We haven't had a chance to be spoiled by success," Erving said. "If we had everybody back from last year, from the team that finished as the runner-up, added Moses and dropped the 12th man, then there might have been the potential to create problems. In that situation, I could have seen 11 guys knocking on Harold's door.

"But we didn't do it that way. This is a new team. Sure, there were some great big question marks about what we could do, and a lot of those questions have been answered, but we also haven't won anything yet. We haven't even won the division."

But the Sixers have had a spectacular first half, and Erving says that part of the destiny of this team correctly includes four All-Stars.

"I've always looked at All-Star Games as showcases of talent, but more than individual talent, the chance to show how easily top players can blend with one another. The spectator may think it's a one-on-one game, and at times it isolates that way, but it's really still a team sport.

"One of my most enjoyable All-Star experiences was the last ABA game in '76. The league was down to six teams, so the Denver Nuggets played everybody else. Marvin Barnes was on our All-Star squad, the only opportunity I ever had to play with him. I was the playmaker on four baskets for him, and afterward he thanked me for setting him up. I did it because the plays were there and he happened to be open, but he viewed it as me focusing in on him.

"My first NBA game was the next year, in Milwaukee. I was announced as the MVP, and the fans booed. We had lost the game, they obviously had their own favorites.

"But the ceremony was right there at center-court, so I addressed the crowd. I told them I hadn't come seeking the individual award, that I had come to represent my family and the league, that I thought I had played well enough to be the MVP, and that it was unfortunate that they didn't share that thought. They applauded.

"I just said what was in my heart at the time, didn't think about why, or the ramifications. But it did turn the crowd around. Later, I got a telegram from my college coach, telling me how much he enjoyed it."

It is the nature of Doctor J to add to the legend as he goes along. His personal challenge has become mastering his craft, and it is something he approaches eagerly.

"Today, I have a better balance between the physical and mental aspects," he said. "The possibility of overwhelming the opponent helps you win, but it's no longer something that must be done. Now, if I tried to do it every night we might win less. And, anyway, I can't play that way night in, night out any more. If I knew then what I know now, I might also have played differently then. Done less, won more. Brought out more in others around me.

"But you can't have it both ways, and it's not until you lose some of the physical that you develop the mental. And that's a stage you have to pass through before you can think about mastering your craft. When it's all physical, you just do it, you don't comprehend why or how. As I matured, I learned. In literary circles, they say if you use a word often enough, you own it. The same can be true of a move on the basketball court."

Finally, there is the matter of perspective.

"I hope," he said, "I have a universal perspective. It keeps me small, a speck of dust in the total universe. I never get the feeling of being more important than I should be.

"Each stage of my development has been broadening. At first, it was Long Island. Then regional, national, international, universal. But the bigger things get, the smaller I realize I am.

"On the nights when I don't play up to my own expectations, I tend to spend more time icing my knees, take longer showers, give myself time to sort it out. I can shoot 3-for-20 now, and when I leave the building, Julius Erving leaves and the 3-for-20 stays. The next night, I might just as easily be 17-for-20."

It is, simply, forever changing. To be expected, not feared.

BULLS CAN'T KEEP SIXERS DOWN

Philadelphia Daily News
February 26, 1983

WHEN HAROLD KATZ boldly brought Moses Malone to the 76ers, he was investing in a piece of the rock, leading Julius Erving to the fountain of youth, and prodding an entire franchise toward one more excruciating moment of truth.

This isn't just a basketball team any more, it's a seemingly impregnable fortress. Erving, the gemstone, left with 5:13 remaining in the second quarter, staggered by a scratched right cornea after an inadvertent poke from Chicago's Mark Olberding.

The Bulls, who had already been beaten four times this season by the Sixers and had lost five straight in the Spectrum, responded as if they had just been attacked by a swarm of locusts.

"Now we won't take anybody for granted the rest of the season," Clint Richardson suggested after Philadelphia erased a 13-point deficit, choking off virtually every conceivable Bulls' route to the basket in the stretch run. "I had a feeling we were going to have to rise to the occasion, because we had beaten this team so easily the other times. And the way they started off, they brought us back to reality pretty quickly."

Reality emerged as a 116–111 Sixers' victory, giving them a 48–7 record, the best start in their history and bringing them within one of matching the NBA's best-ever 49–7 start by Los Angeles in 1971–72. It was also their eighth straight win overall, their 18th in a row at home, and their 28th in their last 30.

And they did it without Doctor J, who was examined in the Spectrum by team physician Dr. Michael Clancy and ophthalmologist Dr. Jack Jeffers, then taken to Wills Eye Hospital for further evaluation. He was released from the hospital with a patch over the eye.

"What we did was for precautionary purposes," said Dr. Clancy. "He'll be re-evaluated each succeeding day, and conceivably could play Sunday (against Golden State) or Tuesday (in New York). Sending him to the hospital doesn't necessarily indicate that the injury was any more serious."

Perhaps it was only an optical illusion but Malone suddenly emerged in the center of the Sixers' patterns—larger, broader and, if possible, more imposing. He matched his season-high of 34 points (the 10th time this season he has had 30 or more) and swept 22 rebounds (the 10th time he has taken 20 or more). He also contributed five of the team's 13 blocks, giving the Sixers a total of 80 during the last seven games.

Everyone else revolved effectively around him. Maurice Cheeks shot 11-for-15 and matched his season-high of 24 points, Andrew Toney scored 19, Clemon Johnson managed 10 points and nine rebounds, and Frank Edwards rang up his best professional performance, packing nine points, three assists, two steals and some hellacious defense and fast-breaking into 15 minutes.

"I know it's early, I know there's still a long way to go, but, yes, this could be the best Sixers' team ever," Katz, the team owner, said earlier in the day. "One big difference obviously is that the 1967 team won it all, and we haven't reached that goal yet."

But they could get there. With 27 regular-season games remaining, the Sixers can clinch the Atlantic Division title with any combination of 20 victories and Boston losses. They need 22 wins to produce the best record in league history (the Lakers won 69 in '71–72).

The players say it will only become a realistic goal if they get close. But last night, they applied pressurized clamps to the Bulls, holding them scoreless from 5:28 until 2:08 of the final period, and for more than four minutes with a single field goal. The Sixers might have been able to win even more convincingly, but inexplicably missed seven of their last 12 free throws.

"I'm enjoying it (the record-breaking start) very much," said Billy Cunningham. "It makes coaching, and life, a lot easier. But the important thing is, I've seen us grow as a club as well as win. Our only goal right now is to improve, to be healthy mentally and physically going into the playoffs. And we have to remember there's still a long way to go."

But with Malone, they now have the dimension of being able to survive a serious injury.

"It's tough when you're missing the Doc," said Moses, who contributed 12 points and eight rebounds in the fourth quarter. "But there are a lot of great players here, and we all tried to make up the difference. I can't do it myself, no one player can. Even when they were up on us, I knew we could make a run at them, shut 'em down. When it gets to be the fourth quarter, just 12 minutes left, if you don't do it then, it's over."

"I thought we played a hell of a game," said Paul Westhead, the Bulls' embattled coach. "It wasn't because we caught Philly playing poorly, (but) we faltered at the end. We couldn't keep up the pace late in the game. We turned the ball over, let them run on us at will after we contained their break for 40 minutes.

"It's difficult for a club like us. You've seen us play some bad games, and we need to win when we work hard enough to get one."

Reggie Theus flashed All-Star credentials against the Sixers for the first time, scoring 26 points, handing out 10 assists and taking seven rebounds before fouling out with 4:30 remaining. Orlando Woolridge and rookie forward Rod Higgins each scored 18, Dave Corzine, David Greenwood and Olberding combined for 30 rebounds, and rookie guard Quintin Dailey also scored 14 before fouling out.

"A game like this," said Bobby Jones, "involves a lot of work, because all of a sudden you can't count on one guy (Erving) to score any time you need the points. You've gotta work harder for everything, buckle down. Without Julius, it was gonna get worse unless we began to work at it."

Now you know why Katz went out and bartered for Clemon and Reggie Johnson at the trade deadline. With Erving out, Reggie became the first small forward off the bench, and Clemon emerged as a tower of strength on a frontline with Malone.

"I haven't been here very long," Clemon said, "but it's obvious that with Julius there's a tendency to let him do his thing, things only he can do. Without him, we realized we all had to do a little more, especially since Chicago wasn't just here to make an appearance. They came to win.

"With Moses and I in the lineup at the same time, though, it gave us a larger look, especially when the Bulls were rotating guys in and out. They had fresh people coming in, but sometimes they were smaller or lighter, and we were able to use our bulk to our advantage.

"Good teams, though, excel in close situations, and when Doc got hurt it brought home to me exactly why they had gotten Reggie and I in the first place."

They are now holding an eight-game lead on Boston, their best divisional advantage against anyone since 1978, and have yet to lose back-to-back games. No team in league history has ever survived an entire season without losing two straight.

"I thought," said Cunningham, "we were tested, and that we responded."

It is a measure of their season to point out how infrequently Billy has had to say that.

The view from the top is staggering.

76ERS TOAST OF THE EAST

Philadelphia Daily News
March 31, 1983

THE CAPTAIN SYMBOLICALLY passed the paper cups around, offering 11 other guys a sip of something incredibly sweet, a taste of what they could become.

They had told us all season that the only goal of any significance was the NBA championship, but they clinched the Atlantic Division and Eastern Conference titles last night, and the captain knew that the time was right.

The 76ers beat the feisty Atlanta Hawks, 120–113, in the Spectrum, clinching the division for the first time since 1977–78, winning 60 regular-season games for the fourth time in their history, emerging from the inevitable valley of the October-to-June grind.

Afterward, some of the players drank, some did not, but all of them accepted the toast, its meaning as well as its limitations.

"That's something for inside the locker room, among ourselves," Andrew Toney said. "Sure, there's champagne, but who said we drank it? Who said it's a celebration? We just feel thankful and fortunate to have won this many, but we ain't gonna stop now. We know what we want, and we know we have to go out and get it."

What they want is their first playoff championship since 1966–67. What they would like, en route, is the best regular-season record, guaranteeing them the home court advantage in any series.

The captain, meanwhile, scored a team-high 26 points, then filled his own cup and lots of others. Julius Erving is the only player remaining from the '77–78 team that last won a divisional title, in Billy Cunningham's first, frenetic season as Gene Shue's 11th-hour replacement.

"The last few years," Erving said, "we always put off celebrating. With a veteran team—Caldwell Jones, Darryl Dawkins, Steve Mix and the rest—that was the way to go. We told ourselves the only time to celebrate was when we achieved the ultimate.

"But now the faces are younger, newer. For them, it's their first taste of a crown."

It's worth celebrating, but not over-celebrating.

"I can remember other years when we felt we had to almost wear blinders, to look straight ahead, to avoid any distractions, to meet the status that was being demanded of us. This time, the owner (Harold Katz) made a gesture, and we appreciate it."

The team had been away, as had the captain. Erving had missed eight games with a sprained right wrist, and didn't return until Tuesday night's shambles of a loss in Chicago. The team had dropped three out of five, and had gone seven straight without shooting 50 percent from the floor.

That left the Hawks, struggling to earn a playoff berth of their own, as the unfortunate sacrifice. The Sixers went over 100 points for the first time in four games, and rang up their highest total in their last seven, unfurling some of the terrific slamming and jamming that had been momentarily missing from their repertoire.

Not that Doctor J was taking credit for the turnaround. Maurice Cheeks scored 24 points and handed out a game-high nine assists, Moses Malone had 23 points and 10 rebounds, and Toney and Bobby Jones scored 15 each. The aggregate effort obliterated a superlative 36-point, 12-rebound performance by the Hawks' Dan Roundfield.

"Even when I was sitting and watching," Erving said, "I never felt it was necessary to really turn anything around. We hadn't gone completely in the opposite direction. I know I was a lot less concerned than Billy, but he's the coach and I'm the eternal optimist. All we did tonight was remind ourselves that we can play big games, that we can get back to where we were. To beat a good team, and Atlanta's in that category, reinstates the faith."

Cunningham has spent months staring ahead, steely-eyed, his concentration focused on a singular goal. What did he think about champagne with 10 regular-season games remaining?

"I thought they deserved it," he replied. "This is a good group, able to keep things in proper perspective. They know what they've achieved. For one thing, they know they won't have to play in a mini-series. Now we have to see if it carries over, if they come back to work Friday the same way.

"When we didn't have Doc, when we didn't have Bobby Jones (for two games), we changed our style. We didn't run as much, and when we did run, we weren't nearly as effective. You don't want it to go on like that, but I knew we'd be back."

That seemed to be the majority opinion, even through the eyes of the Hawks, who are playing without injured George Johnson and Eddie Johnson, with Johnny Davis learning the nuances of being a lead guard, and Rudy Macklin plugging in doggedly as a starter.

"The biorhythms of a pro basketball team are no different than the biorhythms of anybody in any profession," suggested Fred Carter, the ex-Sixer who coached the Hawks in the second half, after Kevin Loughery was ejected.

"Tonight, they looked as good as they ever looked. They lost three out of five and maybe some people began to worry, but a stretch like that is inevitable. Nobody could keep playing forever at the level they were playing. And if there has to be a valley, they're better off going through it now than a few weeks from now."

Did somebody say the Sixers were like night and day? Tuesday night, after a tough loss, Cunningham snarled that his team would practice every available day from then until the end of the season. After last night's win, he gave them today off.

"If we had played the way we did last night (in Chicago) or the way we played against New Jersey last week, we'd have gotten beaten a lot worse than we did in those games," Billy said.

"Now, our goals are to improve as a team, to add some things as we go along, and to keep a close eye on each individual, to be sure they're mentally and physically healthy. More than anything, I want them in the right frame of mind.

"I don't want us to get into an attitude that we're just playing (the rest of the games). We have to be playing to win. What I saw tonight, I saw for the first time in a while, and I'm not gonna let it slip away. We've just had a whale of a year. I feel better than I did the other night. A lot better."

Clint Richardson felt better, too. He's the third guard and the player rep, in that order, but the ongoing labor negotiations had been weighing him down, muddling his concentration. When Cunningham went to him in the second half, the coach said, 'Do you feel like playing?'

"I was glad he said it, 'cause I knew he was right," Clint said. "I've been thinking about the possibility of a strike, I had a lot of information to deliver to the guys, and I tried to pick the stuff to tell them. I kept what I felt the bad stuff was to myself, because I didn't want to disrupt what we had going.

"If this was the summer, I could have handled it easier. But we were talking about walking out, and we all knew that wouldn't be good. Not for us, for the city, for the league, for the whole sport, but we'd do it if we had to. I feel like I've almost had to be an ambassador. The training I've gotten the last month or so, maybe someday I'll be able to run for public office."

The mood brightened when Richardson learned that the owners and Player Association had met in New York yesterday, and that they might meet again today, before the Board of Governors meeting at the Waldorf Astoria.

"It sounds hopeful, it sounds positive," Clint said. "I'll feel better when we know for sure, though. We're proud of what we've done, but we want a chance to go after those championship rings. We haven't worked this hard just to get this far and be satisfied."

They toasted themselves, swallowed hard and waited for word from New York.

"All we did," Moses Malone said, "was take a taste. We'll save the rest for later."

LAKERS PLAY PAT HAND TO SECURE LIFE OF RILEY

Philadelphia Daily News
May 24, 1983

THE KID WAS FROM KENTUCKY, a tough, gritty 6-3 inside player.

He struggled through his senior season with back trouble, ignoring the pain, winking at the circumstances.

He was the first draft choice of an NBA expansion team, selected by a coach who never had seen him play in person, but who was projecting him as a pro guard.

In a way, each was ahead of his time, but Pat Riley and Jack McMahon shared the experience, absorbed its lessons and its consequences and went on to other, more formidable things.

Riley is the Los Angeles Lakers' coach, hustling after his second consecutive NBA playoff championship. McMahon is the 76ers' veteran assistant coach and talent scout, taking a gentle overview of the development of the two best teams in basketball.

"San Diego, the 1967–68 season," McMahon recalled. "The league had added us and Seattle. I had made a decision to go with youthful guys who had a chance to get better, The SuperSonics chose to go with older, more established players.

"There wasn't a lot of time to prepare for the draft, but I saw a 6-3 guy jumping center at a school like Kentucky, a guy who had a disc problem in his back but didn't let it stop him. I had had back trouble of my own, so I could appreciate what he was doing. I had a bad disc, I had surgery. He had one, he played ball. That told me this was a tough guy."

Riley played nine seasons, worked as a radio-TV analyst, then became Paul Westhead's assistant with the Lakers. When Westhead was fired, Riley gravitated to the position.

"I had no illusions at the time," Pat said. "I was there to stick my finger in the dam, prevent the flood from getting any worse. We won 14 out of 15, and I'm still here.

"All I tried to do was create a positive environment, learn on the job. We won at the beginning because we had great players, and I felt no pressure because everybody had blamed the players for what had gone on to that point anyway."

When he asked players to accept roles, it was nothing he hadn't done himself. When he suggested they remain tolerant, that there might be times to suppress their own egos in the best interests of the team, he was drawing on experience.

Riley's first day of practice as an NBA player was unforgettable.

Pat Riley, the San Diego Rockets' first-round pick, was working in the backcourt against veteran John Barnhill.

"I brought the ball up three times, had it stolen, had it stripped, kicked it away once," Pat said. "Jack called me over and said, 'That's the worst five minutes of basketball I've ever seen.'

"I couldn't argue. Before camp, he was telling the media I'd be the league's next star."

Riley wasn't a star on that team, but who was?

"I had John Block and Don Kojis," McMahon said. "One broke his right arm, the other broke his left arm. I said, 'Between the two of you I have one player.'

"I had Toby Kimball, but he was working at about 60 percent, with a bad knee. We couldn't score 100 points. Dave Gambee, Henry Finkel, Johnny Green, John McGlocklin, Jim Barnett, Barnhill.

"It was a long season, but I was always proud of the fact that, seven years later, seven of those guys were still in the league, so I knew I had made some good choices. I had Hambone Williams on that club, too. He was about 28. We took him off the street. Later, he got a championship ring with Boston."

There is a philosophy that suggests that great players, or coaches who have begun their careers with excellent teams, rarely ever understand the challenge of surviving with less natural resources.

"That year with the Rockets," Riley said, "we lost every night, but we loved each other, we shared the pain. After a while, reality sets in, you don't expect to win all the games, so you settle for playing hard and accepting whatever comes.

"We were overmatched, and we knew it, but there was no dissension or bitterness. We were ragamuffins, but we had a hell of a time. We beat the Sixers one night, and it made our season. They had Wilt, they had won 15 in a row, we had lost 16 in a row, and we beat 'em. Talk about your major upsets."

The kid had played in college for Adolph Rupp.

"He came to practice every day in starched Army fatigues, worked like a drill sergeant," Riley said of his college coach. "I got used to it.

"In San Diego, Jack was open, loose, I realized it was OK for a coach to smile."

"The image of Pat Riley," McMahon said, laughing, "was there even then. He had an apartment in a complex with a lot of singles, had a closetful of clothes I couldn't believe, had a Corvette, back when it was really prestigious to have a Corvette."

McMahon has conducted much of the talent hunt that produced Andrew Toney, Maurice Cheeks, Clint Richardson, Frank Edwards and others. His days of being a head coach are, by his choice, over, and he is content to watch the young lions attack the profession.

He knows the Sixers-Lakers championship series also includes two of the sport's best coaches. He has seen them grow into their jobs, shed their hesitancy, emerge as personalities.

"You can't be at war with your ego," Riley said. "When you play in this league as a reserve, you learn to hold it in, to control it.

"Maybe that helps me now, I can't say for sure. But I've played on expansion teams, worked as an assistant, worked in radio-TV. I have an appreciation for the life, for its demands."

He is California sharp, California tan, California calm, back in the championship series again.

He played those nine years and never dazzled anybody, but Jack McMahon says the record book doesn't tell you everything.

"He's organized, prepared, gets his guys to play hard every night," McMahon said. "Wins and losses are sometimes dictated by things you can't control, but you can control that much. He may have played for Kentucky, he may be from California now, but he's a New Yorker (Riley grew up in Schenectady) at heart. The one thing you can say about Pat Riley is, he knows the game."

MIND GAMES

Philadelphia Daily News
May 24, 1983

WHEN THE LOS ANGELES LAKERS first trekked into their Center City hotel headquarters last Saturday, there were scouting films to be watched, written reports to be read and a brunch designed to help ease the pain.

"We had something to eat," coach Pat Riley recalled yesterday, "but we also put some tape down on the floor and walked guys through some things."

Is this any way to dive into an NBA championship series? Or is it the only way? Is this the best-of-seven series in which matchups are more critical than ever? Or less critical than ever?

Is this the time of the year when Moses Malone acknowledges Kareem Abdul-Jabbar as the greatest player of all time and beats him anyway? Or is it the time of the year when 76ers owner Harold Katz reminds us that this is why he got Malone in the first place?

Is this when Magic Johnson unfurls his special skill and personality to lead the Lakers to their third championship in four seasons? Or is this finally when Julius Erving, Andrew Toney, Maurice Cheeks and Bobby Jones soar with Moses?

The Sixers, after Sunday's 113–107 victory in the Spectrum, need three more wins to earn their first title since 1966–67, their first in four trips to the finals with Erving.

It is as close as that, and as far away.

"It's as far away as . . . Well, I haven't even thought about when we have to go to LA," coach Billy Cunningham said. "My only concern is Thursday (Game 2, at 9 p.m., on national television)."

The Sixers won the opener for the first time against the Lakers, in part because life on the open court tends to refresh them, in part because LA came in weary after winning the Western title late last Friday night in San Antonio.

The remainder of the games will be the direct result of intensified laboratory experimenting. Nothing drastic, just enough sophisticated adjusting to probe and search for weaknesses.

"If jet lag was a problem for us, it was obvious in the fourth quarter Sunday," Lakers assistant Dave Wohl said. "We didn't want to go five-on-five with them, challenging their strong half-court defense, giving them an opportunity to double on Kareem.

"What we really wanted to do was push it up the floor, but after a while the Sixers would do that, score and then—despite what our intentions were—we'd walk it up. You could see guys trying to fight off the tiredness, and that's a sign of a team that's been together, that's experienced a lot of success. Our guys believe they're invincible, that they won't feel it. It's a way of deluding yourselves, and sometimes it works for a while, but eventually reality sets in.

"Our reality now is, we're down one game, but we have four days to rest, prepare. There are two schools of thought about this situation: one says when you have too much free time on the road, you tend to get restless, lose your concentration; the other says it's a positive experience, that you have the time to absorb the things necessary to do your job better. I think we'll accept the latter."

Hey, it might take that long to get the matchups straight. Sometimes Abdul-Jabbar opens against Malone, other times Kurt Rambis draws Moses and Kareem takes Marc Iavaroni. Magic, despite playing guard offensively, slides upcourt to guard Erving, and Jamaal Wilkes glides into the backcourt to challenge Andrew Toney.

And all of that revolves in fascinating directions when Michael Cooper, Dwight Jones and Mark Landsberger come off the bench. And if Bob McAdoo, who has been out with a muscle pull in his thigh, is ready, the X's intermingle even differently with the O's.

"There's not much you can do differently in terms of matchups at the start of the game," Riley said. "The versatility really becomes a factor when you begin to substitute. In effect, the starting matchups are almost academic."

In their six-game series against the Spurs, the obvious pairings had the most dynamic effect on the results. Abdul-Jabbar faced a more stationary Artis Gilmore in the middle, and Magic drew a comparable big guard in George Gervin. In this series, Magic always has been the special consideration because of his flexibility. But now the Lakers have to contend with Malone, the rebounding champion.

"Moses," Riley said, "is a highly efficient player. His consistency in departments that kill you are extraordinary. We're not talking about just an offensive brute.

"There is a power there. Darryl Dawkins gave them that sense of power, but you never knew if it was going to be there every night. With Moses, you know you're getting 25 (points) and 15 (rebounds), or numbers right around there. And he, in turn, is enhanced here. Peer pressure makes them all better.

"Gilmore stayed in more of a stationary post, trying to beat Kareem to spots, using force against force. But he doesn't have the maneuverability Moses has."

Malone scored a game-high 27 points Sunday and swept 18 rebounds, his best total in 10 playoff appearances this season. He accepts the challenge of Abdul-Jabbar, winces at the constant collapsing zones, and wonders openly about the value of trying to stop him with the shorter, slower Landsberger.

"It's getting tougher and tougher every series," Moses said. "But now they're banging below my knees, too, and I gotta adjust. I don't know why they got Landsberger on me. He can't check me. But LA knows what they gotta do."

Malone has focused more specifically on Abdul-Jabbar, whether or not they always play directly against each other.

"He's 36, but you can't put a man's age at the top," Moses said. "Kareem's the best player of all time, he's there to win, same as we are. And now, the referees are not gonna make too many calls, so you gotta prepare for everything. That's OK, that gives me a chance to do a little banging, too."

Riley indicated he is considering alternatives to deal with Toney but is reluctant to use Magic there, dragging a key rebounder away from the boards. He seems more concerned with fast-break efficiency and an opportunity to win Game 2.

"We wanted to win the first one," Pat said. "Clint Richardson hit it right on the button when he said it was essential for them to win the first one. Had they lost, it would've been a psychological coup for us.

"We came out of the loss confident, and when you do that, it's a plus. Sometimes that doesn't happen, sometimes you lose and you're shaken. What beat us was our play in the open court. By our statistics, we converted on 17 of 39 fast breaks; they scored on 19 of 25. That's a hell of an efficiency percentage for them."

The Spurs beat the Lakers four out of five during the regular season but were unable to win a best-of-seven series. The Sixers turned back the Lakers in their two games during the season, but that's not a factor now, either.

"San Antonio's record against us meant nothing at this point," Wohl said. "It's one thing to play a team, move on to the next city, play again, and so on. When you're down to one opponent, playing a series, the whole focus changes. The same thing holds true now with us and the Sixers."

The goals are the same and yet very different. The Lakers want back-to-back titles; the Sixers want their first since 1967. The Lakers want to defend their turf; the Sixers want to justify their acquisition of Malone.

"To me, the big difference between now and the last two times we faced the Lakers," Richardson said, "is Moses. Plus, we have a year of experience together, we've been there before, we're tired of going to the finals and losing. Boston used to go every year and win. We'd like to be able to experience that feeling."

If McAdoo is unable to play, the Sixers finally might be able to counterbalance the Lakers' flexibility with strength and versatility of their own. If those are the circumstances, Philadelphia will win in six games.

If McAdoo is in a position to contribute, the remainder of this series will be tougher and closer, and the Sixers will win in seven.

You could look it up. That's the one game Harold Katz got Moses for in the first place.

TONEY'S JUMPER ISN'T SHOT

Philadelphia Daily News
April 1, 1983

WITH JUST FOUR, count 'em, four games remaining in the NBA season, where have all the 76ers' jump shots been?

Julius Erving's has been on a sabbatical while Dr. J regains strength and flexibility in his right wrist. Marc Iavaroni's has grown weary and reluctant, perhaps even approaching burnout.

Reggie Johnson's has been on the bench, gathering dust and rust. Clint Richardson's is just coming back, having been uncomfortably locked in labor negotiations.

Wherever Andrew Toney's has been, it came back yesterday, flooding through the Spectrum hoops, a seemingly endless series of grenades exploding on the playoff hopes of the New York Knicks.

Wherever it had been, send some others for the same treatment. Toney buried 16 of 22 shots from the floor, including two three-pointers, finishing with 40 points—his second-best total this season—in a strong 113–97 victory.

The reeling Knicks, who have dropped eight of their last 12 games, have four remaining and are locked in an emotional struggle with Washington and Atlanta for the two remaining playoff berths in the Eastern Conference.

The Sixers (64–14), who already had locked up the best record in either conference, became the fifth team in history to win more than 63, doing it on an afternoon when feisty Maurice Cheeks made six steals, his second-best total, and otherwise-relentless Moses Malone tumbled to season lows in shots (seven) and field goals (two) and went without an offensive rebound for the first time. To Malone's credit, he still managed 16 points, 12 rebounds and four blocks and matched his season high of five assists. He also turned New York center Bill Cartwright, the seventh-best percentage shooter in the league, into an ineffectual 1-for-10.

But if the Knicks already felt as if they were hanging on by their fingernails, Toney was the one driving them over the edge. Andrew would rather take the shot than talk about it, but he comfortably handled both situations yesterday.

"I felt I had it going pretty much the way I like to," he said. "The last several games, I knew I wasn't playing the way I really wanted to, but I understand there are times when I can't perform to my own expectations.

"But I try to just let it flow and see what happens. I never get depressed if my shot's not dropping. You shouldn't dwell on yesterday. I always believe the next one will be a better day.

"Today, I wanted to be aggressive on offense. I was gonna start out by dropping it in to Moses. If they double-teamed him, I was gonna take the shot, and if they came back out to shade me, I was gonna drop it inside again.

"I wanted to get other guys involved, take my shots when they were there, or when plays were breaking down. You can't worry if you miss a few. I have no fear of missing. No fear of taking them, either."

The Sixers, despite all of their success, had shot 50 percent just once in 13 games. If the effort still was there, the crispness wasn't. They still were willing, but they couldn't always locate the way. This time, Toney torched the barriers.

"We can't play great all 82 games," Andrew said. "What we have to do is work hard, concentrate. If we do, things will come back to where they were. We only have a few left, so it's time to pick up the concentration, the aggressiveness, the intensity and the awareness, things that might slip away from time to time over the long season. Get to this point, we've gotta regroup a little. But I'm sure we're (going) in that direction now."

There is a rhythm and back-breaking explosiveness to Toney's game. It's not a Dr. J skywalk, or the bruising inside style of Malone. It's a fireworks display that eventually withers even the most dogged opponent.

"We've seen him do it so many times, we know there's a rhythm involved," assistant coach Matt Guokas said. "Today, he was in it. That doesn't surprise me. What does is when he gets out of it.

"You know the shots aren't going to fall every night, that he can't be an offensive machine every night, but in the first few minutes of a game, you can tell if everything is moving properly, if his timing is good. His confidence level is incredible. Even when they're not dropping, he believes the next one will. Every great shooter thinks that way, but Andrew even more so.

"It's funny, but we never worry about his shooting. We watch other things, like if he's getting out on the fast break, if he's advancing the ball, being alert defensively, rotating when he's supposed to. The big games, we never concern ourselves with his points."

When Billy Cunningham shrieks at his precocious guard, he insists the scene might not be what it seems.

"The only time I get upset with him," the Sixers' coach said, "is when he passes up shots he should be taking. He's a money player. I'm not concerned about him (performing) in the playoffs."

The stream of jumpers comes and goes, and Toney does not pause to question the tendencies.

"If I knew why," Andrew said, "I'd try to correct it (when they're not falling). Other people have opinions. They could be wrong, they could be right. If you worry about changing this, changing that, you'd have a problem.

"I don't worry. I've been that way all my life. When it comes around, take advantage of it, but keep it at a sound level, try not to get too excited. I've been here a few years now, I know the ins and outs, overs and unders."

"Sometimes," Bobby Jones said, "I see him take the ball inside, in a crowd, against a Marvin Webster or a Bill Cartwright—7-footers—and I say, 'Where's he gonna go with that one?' But he gets it down, and then I know he's 'on.' We're talking about a very strong-willed person. He won't let a game or two get him down."

The Sixers have games left against Atlanta (tomorrow night) and Washington (Wednesday), then face a final weekend in New Jersey and Boston. That represents some potential rubble, which—Erving suggested—is why yesterday's convincing victory was important.

"The Knicks are one of the teams we could see after the mini-series," he said. "But the way we played today is not the way we want to play in the playoffs, relying on one guy to score 40. What was important was that our fast break was alive, back and in color. If that continues to happen, then I'd feel comfortable going into the postseason. I don't buy people saying we've struggled recently. It's been a difficult time of the season, maybe a natural reaction.

"What I liked about Andrew's game was, he reminded people of his firepower. To see him shooting, taking his opportunities, not hesitating, that's a key. But I never really worried about him. I always thought he could get a shot any time he wanted. That hasn't changed."

SIX SHOTS: Bernard King shot a tough 14-for-27 and led the Knicks with 29 points. They were within eight with 5:24 left, before Andrew Toney converted two free throws, threw a terrific fast-break outlet to Bobby Jones, then drilled jumpers from 15 and 18 feet and one final grenade from 27 feet that swelled the Sixers' advantage to 21 with 1:50 to go. "We had them in good position the last six minutes," Knicks coach Hubie Brown said, "which is why you have to give Toney even more accolades. He just proved again why he's one of the great streak shooters—and scorers. He wore out everybody we put on him." . . . The Sixers need a crowd of 16,151 against the Bullets Wednesday to break their home attendance record of 644,456, set in 1977–78. Even with three dates remaining, the league road record of 632,944 is out of reach, but they realistically could complete their 41 dates away from home with more than 620,000.

THE PROMISED LAND

Philadelphia Daily News
June 1, 1983

INGLEWOOD, CALIF.—HE SAT IN the visiting locker room in the Forum last June and wept, the only time in his career he could remember crying after a basketball game.

He asked only to become stronger, and he did. If anyone had the slightest doubt, Doctor J still can fly.

He soared three majestic times in the final 2:02 here last night, on a flight plan that brought the 76ers their first NBA championship since 1967.

They reached a height they never had been able to reach, and when they did, they buried the defending champion Los Angeles Lakers, 115–108.

They didn't just win, they swept, becoming the first team since Golden State defeated the Washington Bullets in 1975 to blow through the finals.

They also are the first team in NBA history to lose only one game in the postseason.

"I wanted this team to be remembered," said coach Billy Cunningham, "and now they will be. The players did it."

The players had been here before. They were in the finals for the fourth time since 1977, and in each previous attempt, they had been turned back in six games. Doctor J, among others, had no ring.

Now they do.

"I'm glad we played Los Angeles," said Erving, who scored 21 points, handed out six assists and made the most dramatic steal of his career with 59 seconds remaining, scoring on a breakaway and foul shot that gave his team a 109–107 advantage.

"In my 12 pro seasons, there was only one time I cried after a game, and that was right here last season after the sixth game and the Lakers had the championship. Nothing has ever affected me that way, not even now.

"I'm standing here, feeling so strong, so purposeful, so good because I know—we all know—we came the long way, the hard way. As sweet as this is, I can't take it for granted. I love the moment, but the feelings I have are more than anyone could expect.

"I have nothing but respect and admiration for the people in this room, who stayed together, did what had to be done. Whatever criticism we heard during the season, whatever doubts anyone had, the ones who were with us, were with us."

They had lost to Portland in six games in '77 after building a 2–0 lead. They had lost to LA in the Spectrum in six games in '80, when Magic Johnson filled in for center Kareem Abdul-Jabbar in the clincher. And they had lost again to the Lakers last season.

"We saw the flip side first, and it made a difference this time. This team took six years to do this, and even though the characters changed along the way, we still did it better than anyone."

They were down 16 points in the first half, and trailed by 14 at intermission. But they had been behind in each of the four games against LA.

This time, they were down 11 to start the final quarter. But Erving had said all along, "This was our time," and he held up his end of the bargain. The Sixers scored 22 of the evening's final 30 points, creating a spectacular havoc.

With 2:02 remaining, Erving flicked the ball away from Abdul-Jabbar, raced the length of the court and dunked. He scored again on a breakaway at 0:59, then drilled an 18-foot jumper at 0:24 to give the Sixers a three-point lead.

"The jumper . . . there wasn't time to drive, there wasn't time to swing the ball, so I let it fly. It found its way to the hoop. I didn't find that shot. It found me."

They will be remembered for their weaponry, for their versatility, for their depth and for their consummate approach to the five-man concept of the sport.

Moses Malone, who was the unanimous winner of Sport Magazine's MVP trophy, scored 24 points and tore down 23 rebounds, his best performance off the boards in the postseason. Andrew Toney converted 11 of 12 free throws, scored 23 and handed out a team-high nine assists. Maurice Cheeks shot 7-for-10 and scored 20, and Bobby Jones stormed through 25 minutes, shooting 6-for-7, scoring 13 points and making four steals.

"I thought this was a picture-book ending," Cunningham said. "Doc has worked so hard and has come so close, and now it is ours. I can't think of anything else but to enjoy this.

"Tonight was typical of this team all through the playoffs. To come into the locker room at halftime, down the way we were, and have the ability to overcome it, is special. This is all special. These are special people.

"We played 13 in the postseason and won 12. That's something to remember this team by."

The Lakers got 28 points from Kareem Abdul-Jabbar, 27 points and 13 assists from Magic Johnson, and 21 points from Jamaal Wilkes, but they played without starting guard Norman Nixon (shoulder separation) and backup forward-center Bob McAdoo (aggravated thigh injury), and even though they finished with a 43–41 rebounding advantage, none of their players had more than seven.

"My hand goes to Doctor J and Billy," said Pat Riley, the Lakers' coach. "They really deserved the championship. There's no doubt in my mind that Philly had it all going for them. They really had the incentive. They were in control and had confidence. They're a great, great team . . . one of the great teams of all time. By beating us four straight, they deserve to be the champions. Julius cleaned all those skeletons out."

Riley, Johnson, Nixon and owner Jerry Buss were among the Lakers' contingent to visit the Philadelphia locker room.

"When Harold Katz (the Sixers' owner) went after Moses, I felt it was the right thing for his team," Buss said. "Nothing that has happened would make me change my mind now. Getting Malone didn't help us, but it certainly helped them. This could develop into an interesting series."

The players rocked the locker room, emptying bottles of Paul Masson and Cordon Rouge champagne that were sent by Shelly Margolis, a neighbor of Cunningham's.

"Nothing I have ever experienced," said Clemon Johnson, "was ever this nice. We are on top. No other basketball team in the world is better than we are."

Even Bobby Jones permitted himself a whole lot of high fives.

"This is a team in the best sense of the word," Jones said. "We do what we have to do every night. They ran out of things they could do to stop us."

Malone, meanwhile, had picked up a magnum of Cordon Rouge.

"Let me have some of this, man," he said, splashing more than he consumed.

"I'm so tired, I don't know what to say, except that I feel great. When I wake up tomorrow, I'll feel better.

"I just told myself I had to control the boards down the stretch, and that if I did, we would win. This is the first time I've ever felt this tired.

"I feel a sense of pride. For the players, for the fans, for Doc, for Billy, for the general manager (Pat Williams), for the owner, for the mayor of Philadelphia. But especially for Doc.

"I remember seeing Doc back in the ABA, saw him win two titles there. When I came to this team, it was to win a title with him. I want to be remembered a long time from now as a guy who played on a championship team with Doc."

And what, somebody asked Malone, did he think the Lakers were feeling?

"The Lakers," he said, "will worry about us next season, too. They might want to put us in a summer league game."

Malone was his own man in Houston, insulating himself from the public. That didn't change in Philadelphia through the season and the playoffs. Will it now? Will he finally let us get to know him?

"Gonna be hard," he said. "I'm gonna go to the parade (Thursday), jump up on a float, ride a float, jump on a plane and go home. Moses will be gone. But feeling good. For me, for Doc, for everybody. For the whole city of Philadelphia."

Philadelphia Daily News sportswriter Phil Jasner (*right*) with son, Andy (*left*), photographed at the 1996 NBA Finals. The pair were the first father-son duo to cover both the NBA Finals and the NBA All-Star Game together. (Courtesy of Jasner Family Collection)

Abe Jasner
Business Accountant
Pricing Branch
Father

Born on Philadelphia's waterfront in 1909, Abe Jasner grew up in the heart of the Depression. This might account for his interest in monies, credits, accounting business and the stretching of the dollar.

Abe is known as "Mr. Federal" to his associates at the Wynnefield Credit Union where he is currently treasurer and member of the board of directors.

In 1957, Temple Israel honored him as its "Man of the Year." Through the years, Abe, along with his wife, have been active in many community organizations. He served as officer and director of Temple Israel of Wynnefield and its Men's Club. During the War he was a Post Air-Raid Warden in charge of a group of wardens.

At the Agency, he served as an Officer and Director of the Philadelphia Signal Corps Federal Credit Union from 1956-61. He worked in various activities within the government, including War Assets Administration, Federal Security Agency, Army Audit Agency and Army Signal Corps.

USAEMA'S PROUD PARENTS
by Ted DiRenzo

This is the second in a series of articles spotlighting the outstanding accomplishments of a USAEMA employee and the outstanding accomplishments of one or more of their children. If you know of other USAEMA "PROUD PARENTS" forward information to Ted DiRenzo, USAEMA Information Officer, Room 240.

For a while, Abe attended University of Pennsylvania Wharton School Evening Division and later earned a Certificate of Proficiency in Accounting from the Evening School of Commerce at Temple University.

Jasner's wife Molly is a teacher in the Philadelphia Public School System.

They are both proud parents of their only boy — Philip, age 21, presently a student Sports Director of WRTI-FM and Sports Columnist at Temple University.

Philip Jasner
Temple University Sports Director
Sports Columnist
Son

During this summer Philip Jasner, age 21, is working as a Senior Counsellor at Frontier Day Camp in Bucks County, Pa. In the fall, he goes back to Temple as a major in the University's Department of Journalism.

During his early days at Overbrook High School, his interest in sports earned him the job as Sports Editor of the school paper, the Beacon, as well as sports columnist with the Suburban Jewish World. As a Senior, he was named Sports Editor of the Yearbook and Student Advisor to the Beacon.

Before reaching his senior year, he took a fling at the exciting job of sportscasting. He entered the Junior Sportscaster's Contest,
(Continued on page 5)

Albert Jasner (left) Treasurer of the Wynnefield Credit Union, checks the ledger with Harry Kelnar, member of the credit committee.

(L. to R.) Byrum Saam, Phil Jasner, Gene Kelley and Claude Hering (Phillies-Atlantic Refining Co. Jr. Sportscasters Contest, 1959). Place, pre-game banquet before finals at Drake Hotel.

Abe Jasner and Phil Jasner in Temple News. (Courtesy of Jasner Family Collection)

Daily News sportswriter Phil Jasner shoots against Joe Bryant (Kobe's dad) during the "76 Days of Fun" event in August 1977. (Courtesy of Sam Psoras/*Philadelphia Daily News*)

Phil Jasner with Julius Erving, handing over an award during Hall of Fame weekend. (Courtesy of Jasner Family Collection)

Philadelphia Daily News sportswriter Phil Jasner with former Sixers All-Star Julius Erving. (Courtesy of Jasner Family Collection)

Philadelphia Daily News sportswriter Phil Jasner seen here with former Sixers All-Star forward Charles Barkley. (Courtesy of Jasner Family Collection)

Philadelphia Daily News sportswriter Phil Jasner and his son, Andy, during the weekend after receiving the Curt Gowdy Media Award at the Basketball Hall of Fame in Springfield, Mass., September 9, 2004. (Courtesy of Jasner Family Collection)

Phil Jasner with Dikembe Mutombo receiving the J. Walter Kennedy Citizenship Award during the 2000–2001 season. (Courtesy of Jasner Family Collection)

LEFT: Phil Jasner's acceptance speech after receiving the Curt Gowdy Media Award at the Basketball Hall of Fame in Springfield, Mass., September 9, 2004. (Courtesy of Steven M. Falk/*Philadelphia Daily News*)

FACING PAGE, TOP: Phil Jasner, Sixers beat reporter for the *Philadelphia Daily News*, was named to the Basketball Hall of Fame with the Curt Gowdy Media Award in Springfield, Mass. Jasner with the president and CEO of the Basketball Hall of Fame John Doleva after the presentation. (Courtesy of Steven M. Falk/*Philadelphia Daily News*, September 9, 2004)

FACING PAGE, BOTTOM: Phil Jasner jokes with Hall of Famers, Julius Erving, left, and Billy Cunningham during the Curt Gowdy Media Award ceremony at the Basketball Hall of Fame in Springfield, Mass., September 9, 2004. (Courtesy of Steven M. Falk/*Philadelphia Daily News*)

Allen Iverson paid tribute to Phil Jasner's memory on the occasion of the announcement of Iverson's acceptance into the Basketball Hall of Fame in 2016. (Courtesy of Yong Kim/ *Philadelphia Daily News*)

A headshot of award-winning *Philadelphia Daily News* Sportswriter Phil Jasner, who was inducted into the Naismith Basketball Hall of Fame in 2004. (Courtesy of *Daily News* File Photo)

CHAPTER 7

. . . . . .

THE SIXERS BETWEEN FINALS RUNS:
OCTOBER 1983–2000

Introduction by Earl Cureton

P hil made you feel comfortable. He was always thoughtful and I felt like I could talk to him about anything at any time. I knew I could trust him. It didn't matter what was going on: I felt comfortable with Phil and that was something that occurred from the beginning when I first met him. If he needed a minute of my time, I gave it to him. I wasn't the highest priority on the team at the time and I was fortunate to have met Phil. We became such great friends. He had such high respect for me and I really appreciated that. He just had this way of making you feel so comfortable. We had a great relationship from the very beginning.

I remember one particular story when I was in Houston. I was out of the league for a couple of years and I made a comeback and was signed by the Rockets. We ended up winning a championship in 1994 with Hakeem Olajuwon and everyone. I was a bench player but was able to win a championship. I remember standing in the tunnel after we won and there was Phil with his curly hair and a huge smile. He was genuinely happy for me. Dick Harter was there and was an assistant with the Knicks. Phil looks at him and says, "See, how about Earl?" Dick smiled and said, "You're right. Look, Earl is still fighting. He's still here." Phil was happy for me and I could see that so clearly as a friend. It made me feel so good. My friendship with Phil started with the Sixers and developed over the years. Every time I saw him, like the day when we won the title with the Rockets, it was special. We would talk about what was going on. You knew how genuine he was as a person.

From the early days, Phil always had a smile on his face. You could see how much he loved his job. The respect he had for us made us want to help him. I wasn't a star in the league, but Phil treated me like a star. As a young player, that meant so much. He valued my opinion and what I thought. Phil always remembered everyone. It wasn't just about one guy. It was about team. There have been a lot of reporters

I've dealt with over the years. There's only one Phil Jasner. There will only ever be one Phil Jasner. The relationship we had was special. I think about Phil all the time, especially when I talk to my teammates from the 1982–1983 championship with the Sixers. Phil was a big part of that with how he went about his business and did his job.

Phil was a great man. He covered the team and had a job to do yet treated all of us with such respect. The relationship that we built lasted all the years beyond my time in Philadelphia. I will always cherish the time I was able to spend with Phil. Every time we caught up in the years that followed, it was great catching up. He was the best.

EARL CURETON *played for seven NBA teams and overseas as well in a long career from 1980–1997. He won two championships—with the Philadelphia 76ers in 1982–1983 and again with the Houston Rockets in 1993–1994.*

· · · · · ·

SIXERS RING IN SEASON

Philadelphia Daily News
October 29, 1983

THE GUYS ON THE PICKET LINE will have to examine the tapes of the 76ers and Washington Bullets and decide whether opening night in the Spectrum should be classified as a celebration or a training film. There haven't been this many gaps in a performance since the last time Leon Spinks smiled.

The Sixers began defense of their NBA championship by winning, 117–114, but what was supposed to be a curtain call turned out to be a wake-up call. What was supposed to be a dream come true turned out to be just another nightmare.

If any of the participants had any innocence left, they lost it last night. Hey, guys, in the major leagues you're supposed to bite the bullet, not cough it up. The Sixers blew a six-point lead, the Washington Bullets blew their cool, and a substitute referee who has been here several times before—as a player and as an official—blew an opportunity to establish himself under the most difficult of circumstances.

You want spectacles? Stop by when the Celtics are here. You want murals? Check in during the playoffs, preferably in the later rounds. You want the hugger-mugger of a first-nighter? Glad you stopped by.

The Bullets' Jeff Ruland, on the verge of emerging as an absolute star, scored six points in 42 seconds to force a 114–114 tie with 12 seconds remaining. But Ruland also said something to Bernie Fryer, and Bobby Jones calmly dropped in the free throw after the technical foul.

The Bullets deftly played for the steal, and Darrel Garretson called a foul on Ricky Sobers at 0:03, and Sobers—having fouled out—had to be led away screaming by Ruland. Andrew Toney converted two free throws, Frank Johnson rimmed a beat-the-buzzer three-point jumper, and the Sixers scurried for safety.

While the regular staff of referees, involved in a bitter labor dispute, walked the picket line outside the Spectrum, everybody else walked a tightrope. Including Billy Cunningham, who had said he was protesting the game with 8:42 remaining, after what appeared to be a mysterious call by Fryer.

Once Commissioner Larry O'Brien handed out the championship rings, they could barely settle on last night's adventurous facts.

"I thought we did a good job coming back," said Bullets coach Gene Shue. "We tied the score and I was ecstatic. We were in a huddle, and I looked up when I heard Zink (public address announcer Dave Zinkoff) say 'Sixers will shoot the technical,' I asked Jeff what happened, and all he said was, he thought he was fouled. I think it was a poor time to call a (technical) foul. The last 12 seconds? Let's play, and see who wins."

Let the opening night impression show that the days of McFilthy and McNasty may be over. Ruland and Rick Mahorn played hard, aggressive, effective ball, teaming for 41 points, 20 rebounds, seven assists, 17-for-22 shooting and 10 personals. The rules and built-in controls of the sport aside, the game shouldn't have been decided by something somebody said.

"After the basket, I ran down the court and said (to Fryer) 'Please call the foul. I was hit in the eye.' I repeated it three times. I had had an altercation with him earlier in the game, and he said (then) 'Get away from me.'

"I don't know if he thinks he has 25 years in the league or what, but I didn't think it was against the rules to question the officials. I'd like to see the strike settled. I've said a lot worse things. It was a tough game to lose. Especially that way."

The Sixers won mostly because they had been able to maintain a modest advantage (never more than six points) through the fourth quarter, and because they still have more talent and depth than the swiftly developing Bullets.

Down the stretch, they won in spite of themselves, and in spite of Ruland's 12 points and seven rebounds in the final period.

"I think we have to feel fortunate," said Cunningham. "Considering all the hoopla, the rings and everything, we have to be pleased. We scored 117 against the Bullets, and I don't remember the last time we even scored 100 on them."

Maybe all Billy could recall was the six the Sixers managed in their final meeting last season. They twice went over 100 against Washington last season, and scored 95 or more in each of the other three games.

But the new, improved Bullets were willing, if not particularly adept at racing the ball up the floor. They did get 28 points from Frank Johnson, but were only able to generate nine points from 19 fast breaks. Meanwhile, the Sixers were beating them 41–36 off the boards and shooting 13 more free throws (the Bullets were 22-for-29, the Sixers 33-for-42).

Andrew Toney and Moses Malone produced 27 points each, and Malone—last season's MVP and rebounding champion—swept 19 rebounds. Julius Erving contributed 23 points, five rebounds, five assists and a game-high four blocks, and very nearly flicked away Johnson's final, desperate home-run try.

"I blanked out the (pregame) ceremony and tried to get my game back in order," Malone said. "The last 10 years, the first game has always been one of my weakest. I need time to get my concentration going, get the feel of the ball. Every year, they change the balls. Maybe if we had gotten the rings a week after we won the championship, we'd have had all summer to look at 'em, and we'd have been all right tonight."

Maybe. In other outposts of the locker room, guys were stirring other notions, other potions.

"I just thought it was a typical Washington game," Erving said. "Our guys showed what we're made of, yet showed a lot of imperfection, letting them come back. We haven't heard the last of it, and at the same time we're not going to dwell on it. We've got a flight (to Indianapolis) in the morning, another game (against the Pacers) tomorrow night (tonight). I'm just glad we're moving on 1–0 instead of 0–1.

"The way we played tonight, practice (Friday) was like that, too. We can play better, we probably can play worse, and hopefully it'll get better before it gets worse. For all intents and purposes, though, we should deal with winning or losing, and leave the intricacies of how it happened for more private moments. I'm not going to come in and feel bad about how we played when we've won. It's fruitless. It takes all the fun out of it."

The people in the stands know they have seen better, the guys on the picket line, if they're being honest, know they have seen worse. The ones restlessly shuffling their feet are the players, who aren't sure what's coming next.

Did they, somebody wondered, ever think they'd miss the referees?

"I thought that," replied Bobby Jones, "all along."

SIX SHOTS: The Sixers drew 16,167, 1,754 below the reduced 17,921 sellout figure. Last year's opener against New Jersey sold out at 18,482.

76ERS RECORD OWN THRILLER

Philadelphia Daily News
December 5, 1983

BOSTON—BILLY CUNNINGHAM IS REACHING for the unreachable. He wants what never can be, knowing that in the fierce cauldron of the chase the 76ers can earn a place in basketball history.

"Some of the people in this (locker) room may not be talking to me at the end of the season," the 76ers' coach said after last night's 121–114 overtime victory over the Celtics in the Boston Garden.

"Why? Because I'm going to push 'em. It's my job to do that. And I'm not knocking our record, or the character of the men involved. But I'm after perfection. You surely have to shoot for something. Should I say that because we won the championship (last season), we don't have to do anything now?

"No. I'm going to push 'em."

The Celtics own 14 championship banners; the Sixers have won one since 1967. No team has won back-to-back titles since 1968 and '69, when Boston did.

The Sixers (14–4) pushed aside the memory of Saturday night's ragged loss to shorthanded Washington in Landover, Md., then gruffly pushed aside all the logic that said they would not win last night.

They won a regular season game here for the second time in 13 attempts since wondrous Larry Bird (22 points, 11 rebounds, 13 assists) joined the Celtics, hung onto first place in the NBA's Atlantic Division and avoided the ignominy of back-to-back losses, something that happened only twice in their remarkable drive to the 1982–83 title.

They became the first team in 13 games to beat the Celtics (13–6) after being behind going into the fourth quarter, ended the Celtics' winning streak at four, improved their record to 3–0 in OT and forced the extra period after being behind by three points with 26 seconds remaining.

From that point, the teams lifted the sport to an excruciating level of artistry and drama.

"Our team responds to being driven," Julius Erving said afterward. "But Billy knows us, too. We won't be treated like we're a bunch of rookies. We're a veteran team."

The Sixers exhausted their last time-out at 0:26 and set up a sidecourt out-of-bounds play designed to get the ball to Andrew Toney in three-point range.

Toney pulled the trigger, but the ball fell off the rim, where Moses Malone slapped it to Bobby Jones, who sent it flashing back to Toney for another home run try.

This one, from slightly to the right of the key, swished, tying the score at 98.

"I thought the first one was a good shot," Toney said. "I squared up, shot straight, thought it was in. It didn't float or anything, but it didn't go in. The second one felt the same way, but it dropped. I just wish I could take a few like that when it's not a desperation situation. I think I can make them."

The Celtics used a time-out at 0:13 and generated enough motion to get Bird free for a jumper at the left of the foul line that gave the Celtics a seemingly crushing two-point advantage at 0:06.

But Malone whistled a spectacular length-of-the-court inbounds pass to Erving, who caught the ball in stride, waited for the racing Bird to pass him, then turned and hit a 17-footer from the right side to tie it again.

"It looked awfully good for us when Larry made his shot," said Celtics coach K. C. Jones. "There was no breakdown in our defense, either. Moses made a great pass, Doc (Erving) hit the shot. I was hoping it'd miss. It had fingers. It just seemed to stick to the rim and then rolled in.

"But it was their man-to-man defensive pressure that really beat us. 'Turnover' was the title of the game. They created scoring situations for themselves with tough, tough defense. We were ahead, got down, came back, got down again. We thought we had it, and then Doc threw one in. I've been in the league a few years, though. It's all part of the game."

The Celtics used their remaining 20-second time-out, but had to take the ball the length of the floor. Erving smacked away Bird's inbounds pass to Kevin McHale.

There were four ties in the five-minute overtime before Bobby Jones— who turned in an incredible performance with 19 points, on 7-for-11 shooting, seven steals and no turnovers in 31 grinding minutes—hit a jumper with 1:25 left to put the Sixers up, 110–108.

Maurice Cheeks followed by flicking the ball away from the Celtics' Robert Parish in the post and going coast-to-coast for a layup, drawing a foul from Bird.

Cheeks converted the free throw for a five-point advantage (113–108), and Malone stripped Parish again. This time, Erving dropped in two free throws.

"What do I take from this game?" Cunningham said. "I take our ability to do things when we have to, but I by no means underestimate the Celtics. They're a fantastic team, like we are. We've played them twice now, won by a point in Philadelphia, won in overtime here. They could just as easily win the next four.

"But I'm going to drive our guys. It's not going to be a problem for me anymore. I'll be on 'em all the time. When they walk out of a huddle, they're going to know the play, and they're going to run it. Every guy is going to know what we're doing, or I'm going to use somebody else."

He proved that last night by using fifth guard Sedale Threatt for 12 minutes, sending him in as a replacement for Toney with 9:50 remaining in regulation. Cunningham yanked Malone—the league's defending MVP and rebounding champion—with 7:32 to go, and didn't send him back until 3:18.

"From about four minutes to go in the first half, I was very pleased," Cunningham said. "The only thing we weren't doing was limiting them to one shot. Later, we began to make the extra pass, and it was a big factor in our comeback. When you're a good team, if you do the things that made you good, you can come back. We have a great ability to rise to occasions. When we have to go out and extend ourselves, we can do it."

But they've done it sporadically through the first 18 games of the season, which is why Cunningham has adopted the most demanding stance of his career.

Will his team respond?

"I don't have a choice," said Erving, who finished with 20 points in 41 minutes, "unless I want to change addresses, and I don't want to do that.

"It's nice to break through early, to win one here. We've always tried to do it, and haven't had much success, at least during the regular season. One big thing is, by winning, we stay in first place. If we lose, Boston's in first."

He didn't hit his game-saving jumper off any preconceived play.

"There wasn't any time for that," he said. "But that's what you love about the game. You can't predict what will happen, you can't be absolutely sure of anything. One of the most beautiful things about the sport is the unpredictable element.

"The shot I made just flowed, the way so much of the game did. That's when you move away from playing the game on paper to playing it on the court. I was fortunate that I was able to catch the ball and shoot it without taking a dribble. I knew Larry was coming, but even as he flew by I knew there were still a couple of ticks on the clock. I didn't have to rush. I got a good shot, got a sweet roll."

What about the wisdom of reaching for the unreachable?

"You can never reach perfection," Erving said, "but we can get closer than we've been. I understand Billy. Billy wants perfection. Billy wants to go undefeated. And that's not going to happen. But you can shoot for it. Why not?"

Cunningham cracked the whip and got game highs of 29 points and 14 rebounds from Malone, who shot 12-for-21. The 6-10 center, who did not attempt a free throw Saturday night for the first time in his career with the Sixers, dropped in five of seven from the foul line.

Malone wouldn't talk about Cunningham's approach, but Toney did.

"Billy's been on me all the time anyway, so nothing's really different," Toney said. "He's trying to drive us in the right direction, to be the best we possibly can be. It's hard to argue with that.

"We're not playing as good as we want, but it's early. We'll be in the best of shape at the end of the season, when it's the most important, but we also don't want to fall into a slump of any kind. One way to avoid that is to play as hard as you can.

"I like to win 'em all, but I don't count 'em, I just play 'em and see what happens. This is just one more win, we have to take it in stride, go home and get ready for Denver on Wednesday. That's the way the season is."

ZINKOFF DEAD AT 75, HAD A NAME FOR EVERYTHING

Philadelphia Daily News
December 24, 1985

MARINA DEL REY, CALIF.—There was "Two for Shue." "Wali, by golly." "Gola goal." "Dipper dunk."

Later, there was "Errrrrrrrving." And "Malone alone."

There were even a couple worth trying at least once. "Cannon aid," when Larry Cannon got credit for an assist. And "A basket of Pickles," when Bill "Pickles" Kennedy scored for the old Warriors.

There were the kosher salamis Dave Zinkoff used as gifts, as calling cards.

And even the occasional glitches. Albert King would become "Al," Bernard King, "Bernie," Mike Gminski, "Minski," Sidney Moncrief, "Sid."

Zink seemed to have a name for everything, even if he didn't always remember yours.

He couldn't run, couldn't jump, probably didn't know an X from an O, but he became part of the fabric of athletics in Philadelphia.

He died yesterday at 75, in Hahnemann Hospital, a week after undergoing open heart surgery.

"He lived a remarkable life," said Pat Williams, the 76ers' general manager. "His is an irreplaceable loss. There was only one. An institution has ended. I find it comparable to William Penn tumbling off the top of City Hall, to the shutting down of a soft pretzel factory.

"It's a time to mourn, but it also becomes a time to celebrate a remarkable, unusual man. He packed more into his 75 years than others could pack into 200 years. He met kings, he met presidents. And anyone who met him for the first time had an instant friend. He had a voice that impacted millions."

Zink was the public address announcer for the Warriors, and later, the Sixers. He was at the microphone for the first Sugar Bowl, and he stayed close to Temple University, his alma mater, doing as many games as his schedule and his strength would permit. He never scored a point, never fired a shot, but he is already in the Owls' Hall of Fame. He was inducted the same day as entertainer Bill Cosby, and he asked Julius and Turquoise Erving to share his moment.

His strength? It always had seemed boundless. Fitz Dixon, the former owner of the Sixers, had let Zinkoff go, apparently believing his time had come and gone. Harold Katz, the day he purchased the team, brought Zinkoff back.

I was a senior in high school when I met Zink for the first time. Met him? I scrambled down from the rafters of Convention Hall to show him the lucky number in my program, and he rewarded me with two tickets to a future game. I came down with the chicken pox shortly afterward, and had to trade in the tickets, but that is another story, one my mother and father still like to tell.

My wife, our son and I lunched with Zink and Al (the Temple sports information director) and Ruth Shrier years later in Atlantic City, and our son was fascinated by the things Zink put into one cup of tea. Enough to start a fire. Or put one out.

"Never fear," he would say, prancing into a crowded room, "the Zink is here."

Ask him how he was feeling, and the answer was always the same. "Neverrrrrrr betterrrrr," he would say.

The late Eddie Gottlieb was his mentor, the Shriers became his guardian angels, but the events at which he worked remained secondary to what the man was really about.

He knew high drama when he saw it. He knew when to turn up the volume, when to let his voice trail off, allowing the crowd to create a wall of noise. He could become bleating, nasal, pitching: "The Celtics call tiiiime." He could whisper that Billie Jean King was about to take center court in a women's tennis tournament. When the referees might need to stop play, he could shriek, "Hold it, hold it, hold it."

Or he could choose his moment ever so carefully and tell an unsuspecting audience that a car in the parking lot had "its lights on, its motor running . . . and its doors locked."

"He had a servant's heart," Pat Williams said. "There was never a cause he wasn't involved in, a group for which he would not make an appearance. He was Jewish, but at the same time he had the qualities of a year-round Santa Claus. When you think about it, he'll take his place in the sports history of the city with Julius, Wilt Chamberlain, Mike Schmidt, Bobby Clarke. He wasn't a player, but he's right there with them."

The Sixers once staged a Zink-A-Like contest in which Daily News reporter Gene Seymour finished an unabashed second. Later, when Seymour celebrated a birthday, reporter Maria Gallagher brought Zink to the party.

And when NBA writers had to telephone league publicist Alex Sachare at home, they frequently would get an answering machine tape of Zink explaining that Alex was not at home, but that, at the sound of the beep, to begin their message "immmmmmmmmmmmmmmediately."

When Zink first became ill this season, Dan Baker—the public address voice of the Eagles and Phillies—filled in, saying it was "like pinch-hitting for Babe Ruth," that he was merely "minding the store until the rightful owner returned."

Ron Dick, who works in the Sixers' offices, found Zink nodding off in the Spectrum press room one night and quickly went for help. Zink was hospitalized, Dick filled in for a game at the mike and said he felt "honored."

When Jim Wise, a young radio guy from Atlantic City, was hired, he said he knew he was replacing a legend.

"I feel uncomfortable about that," Wise said.

Zink loved center stage, had abiding respect for the microphone and what he could accomplish with it. He had emigrated from Russia and, inexplicably, became a public address announcer, something his father never wanted him to be.

He knew publicly when he saw it.

"If you could look up and ask Dave now what he was thinking," Pat Williams said, "he'd say, 'I can't wait to read about this. Save me the clips.'"

They're here, Zink. They're here.

THE FIRST SKYWALKER

Philadelphia Daily News
April 16, 1987

THERE WAS A TIME when Julius Erving truly believed he could fly. One time.

"An All-Star Game, between NBA and ABA guys, the summer of '72, I think," Erving said. "Out in Nassau (Long Island). The NBA had Wilt Chamberlain, Oscar Robertson, Walt Frazier, Dave DeBusschere, the best players. I was there, with Artis Gilmore, Dan Issel, Willie Wise.

"I was coming down on the break, Oscar was back on defense, Clyde (Frazier) was hurrying to catch up. Anyway, I picked the ball up on the dead run to avoid Clyde's hands . . . I took off.

"When I did, I could see Oscar in front of me, backpedaling, backpedaling, backpedaling. I was in the air, flying; he was still backpedaling.

"I got to the basket, I don't think I dribbled more than once after I crossed midcourt. I was stretching it out . . . ended up dunking. Oscar, though, was still backpedaling, so when the ball came through the net, it fell right into his hands. The place just turned out.

"Definitely a skywalk. That might have been the one time in my life I felt like I was flying."

It is not a story that has grown with the re-telling. It is not a toy of the imagination.

"I know, I was there," said Ray Wilson, the gentle man who coached Erving at Roosevelt High in Long Island, who today directs the Erving Group, overseeing many of Erving's business and charitable interests.

"Julius and I have never discussed it, but I would have said that was the one time I thought he could fly.

"I remember him leaving the ground, and I thought, 'He's not going to make it, he's not going to get there.' The last thing I wanted was for Julius to be in any way embarrassed. But he just continued. The ball fell in Oscar's hands and I said, 'What do we have here?'"

What indeed?

If Erving was not the sport's first skywalker, he was the one who brought the move home as an art form. Not simply dunking, but seemingly walking on air, striding across clouds, hovering, contorting, remaining aloft—inexplicably—even after others who had risen to challenge had dropped helplessly back down to ground level.

Skywalking.

Creating a moment.

It is there, in front of you, and then it is gone, and all you can do is glance to either side, to be sure everyone else saw what you saw.

But it is nearly time, after 16 professional seasons, to leave. The skywalker's jersey can be sent to the Hall of Fame, his bronze statue can be erected outside the Spectrum, his banner can hang in the rafters of the building.

His game should be left in a heliport, on a jetway, perhaps in a space station. Somewhere above, where it always was played.

"The one thing that was different about him was that you weren't expecting it," said John Kerr, the Chicago Bulls' television analyst who, as a vice president of the ABA's Virginia Squires, signed Erving to his first pro contract. "You see Michael Jordan, Dominique Wilkins today, you're primed for what's coming. You're anticipating it, excited about it. But in those days, nobody knew this man. You'd be watching, and then 'Whoooosh,' he was gone. It got to the point where I'd go to practice and the games wondering when I'd hear the first sonic boom.

"Could he fly? Sure. At least a little."

Who was first? The list includes the obligatory playground legends: Jackie Jackson, Helicopter Knowles, Earl Manigault and other nameless, faceless athletes lost in the obscurity, the biting circumstance of the parks and playgrounds of the inner city. It was their game, their special contribution, and they probably never knew.

Among the pros, there was Elgin Baylor, using almost mystical body control; Johnny Green, wide-eyed and awe-struck when he first saw others reach for the sky; Connie Hawkins, swooping majestically long before it was fashionable.

And there was Doc.

Julius Winfield Erving, born Feb. 22, 1950, in East Meadows, N.Y. Don Ryan, the volunteer Biddy League coach, opened the first door to opportunity at the Salvation Army youth center in Hempstead.

"When he first came to the center, he was 11," Ryan recalled. "If someone had said then he would become a Doctor, I'd have said a medical doctor. He was so intense, so serious.

"It was my second year coaching. Today, we run and press, score about 80 points a game. Back then, we played a tight 1-2-2 zone, walked it up, worked for a good shot, averaged about 40. He got 11 a game, a good percentage.

"Even then, I can remember him jumping over people. He had gotten hurt when he was 8, got taken to Nassau County Medical Center. He laughs now, says people were always suspicious that the doctors put springs in his legs.

"I had an assistant at the time, Marcel Coulon, who would tell me, 'Don't rush him, the years will go by all too quickly.' He was right."

Julius Erving became Doctor J, then simply Doc. He didn't just play 16 seasons, he danced, he flew to save jobs, to preserve dignity in a doomed ABA. When he came to the NBA in 1976, it was to a league that, despite its established presence, was struggling to locate an identity as a sport, as an entertainment medium.

Fly, Doc. Fly.

"I don't fly," Erving said. "I'm able to jump high. I've been able to do that since elementary school. It's a matter of getting the most out of your talents.

"You jump, your purpose is to escape the defense, to jump over someone to take a shot. If you can, then you've done what you set out to do. In running, open-court situations, sometimes you commit to the air and you don't have exactly in mind what you want to do. So you buy time while you're up there.

"Maybe you make the decision out of necessity, as opposed to having to make it before you act. Maybe that helps create the effect of staying in the air a little longer. Maybe you really are up there a little longer, but I think it has more to do with one's creative abilities. You're up there, you think, 'By the time I do make my mind up, I hope I'm still up here.'"

Each skywalk is a matter of seconds, yet can be broken down into marvelous sequence. It is a move made for slow-motion, stop-action cameras. Perhaps that is also how it happens, unfurling frame by frame in the camera of the mind's eye.

"Sometimes," Erving said, "you're up there waiting for an opening.

Because of my coordination, I've been able to have a range time—it's not as if I have to take a shot at the height of my jump. I can take it at the beginning, in the middle, at the end, anywhere in between."

WHY HIM? Why has Erving been able to do what others have only dreamed of doing?

Is there a medical reason? Something that might show up on an X-ray? In a battery of tests? In an examination of an ink blot?

"I would think it has to start with the genes," said Dr. Jack Jeffers, the Sixers' ophthalmologist. "That doesn't mean Mom and Dad were skywalkers, but two genes came together, and what he was given he has been able to use.

"After that, he developed it to the maximum, combined it with great flexibility, good size (6-6), large hands, large feet, plus the skills of the sport.

"One difference could be the development of fast-twitch and slow-twitch fibres in the muscles. He developed the tendons and ligaments, the joint movement, synchronized them, almost into a fantasy.

"But if I could pin that down medically, I'd be asked to make one, then make a better one. And you can't. The M.D. in this case is God."

"You see the fast-twitch fibre development in sprinters," said Dave Berman, the team podiatrist. "But even knowing about such a thing, I find myself wondering why he can do things, why somebody like Moses Malone can hardly get off the ground, yet has a level of stamina others can't match."

"The physiology of the muscles is a fascinating study," said Stanley Lorber, the team's internist. "Julius has an ability to elongate his muscles, to stretch them to their maximum, to create a spring far greater than normal. Ballet dancers can do it. Broad jumpers. You look at a football player, with tight muscle groups, they can't jump much at all.

"There are probably some metabolic factors, too. Complicated, intricate stuff. The best thing to say is, Julius has it."

Or does he?

"Why can he when others can't?" said Mike Clancy, the team orthopedist. "I have no idea. I'm not being facetious, but nobody has proven any of the theories about fast-twitch and slow-twitch, why a player can levitate.

"Who knows why? The fans sit in the stands and wonder; I wonder, too. I don't know that Doc's muscles are any bigger than anyone else's. Maybe in Russia, you could biopsy the players, do the studies, find something, develop it."

The skywalks, even unexplained, leave people breathless. The residue is what has helped to create the legend of Doctor J.

"When he comes to the hospital to visit patients, I tell myself I have to be dignified, very professional," Jeffers said. "But, really, I'm like everybody else. Inside me, there's a 10-year-old going bonkers."

ERVING HAS INITIATED and he has imitated. Every original, in effect, starts by taking something from someone else.

"I think of Baylor, Hawkins, Green, I think of the guys I found the most exciting to watch," Erving said. "Even some small players, shooting the fadeaway jump shot. When I was in high school, I got the chance to see Charlie Scott play in college. He had a turnaround fadeaway jumper, literally jumping away from a defender to get a shot off.

"I remember Tiny Archibald able to get himself in the air in order to get a pass off. Guy Rodgers could get in the air to make a pass and, if the defense didn't react, could keep the ball and make the layup. I put Lenny

Wilkens in that group, too. It wasn't just a matter of size, either. Proportionately, the smaller guys might jump higher, just not play over the rim.

"That was where I learned about hang time. Those guys did their share of skywalking. When I began to do things, I was just a bigger person doing in the air what they had done. I'd finish with a dunk instead of a layup.

"I watched and I learned and I borrowed. The finger roll from Wilt, dunks from Bill Russell, body control from Baylor, the set shot from Larry Costello. Scott's fadeaway, Hal Greer's jumper. You take some of each, then bring some things of your own.

"I used to spend hours just throwing up shots, hundreds of ways. Right-handed, left-handed, checking spots on the backboard, the spins, the rolls. In the games, you have options, going up, over, around, under guys. I realized you could make your own space if you understood the angles."

THE SKYWALKERS ARE a small fraternity. They share the sensation of flight, the wonder, the splendor.

When Erving thunderdunked over the Los Angeles Lakers' Michael Cooper, the other skywalkers reveled in it. When Erving wrapped around ex-Laker Mark Landsberger, going from one side of the backboard to the other, they celebrated.

Each time. Every time.

"There's no better feeling in the world than when you go walking in the air and there are 12,000 or 14,000 people in the stands and they're screaming because you're flying," said Atlanta's Dominique Wilkins. "It's the greatest thing there is.

"Doc was the first I ever saw do more than just dunk. A lot of guys can dunk, but nobody could skywalk like Doctor J. The first time I tried, I messed it up quite a bit. In fact, I almost hurt myself. It gave me something to work on."

"He set the standards in creativity for players like myself," said Chicago's Michael Jordan. "He was the first to carry the label. He opened the way for others. No one focused on it until he began to do it. Creative dunking.

"How do you do it? I don't know, I can't explain it. Some have it, some don't. And everybody has his own way. I go up, I spread my legs on the way down. I don't know why, really, except maybe to keep my balance.

"The one where Doc runs from three-quarter court, gets to the foul line, maybe 2 inches over and then goes to the basket . . . I do it, but I dribble the ball all the way. Doc doesn't. He just runs. I pump the ball in the air, he doesn't.

"I've heard people say there are some dunks that are impossible. To me, everything can be done, eventually, by somebody. I've watched Doc, he finds his way in, gets there, does what he has to do, gets out. But each time, it's new.

"You look at film afterward, you're in awe of what you've just done. I've looked at tape of the dunking contest at the All-Star Game, and it's totally different in slow-motion. It looks . . . beautiful."

Doc dared. Dared to try. Dared to be great. Took the chances. Accepted the risks.

"Fastbreak," Chicago coach Doug Collins remembers, reconstructing a moment from his own career with the Sixers. "I'm in the middle, Doc's on one side, George McGinnis the other. I look one way, pass the other, to Doc. But as I do (Bulls' guard) Wilbur Holland gets in position to take a charge.

"Doc takes the pass in stride, sees Wilbur, just scissors over him. Wilbur wants to fall down, but he knows he hasn't been hit.

"Another time, in practice, Doc stood along the baseline, out of bounds, leaped out, reached across and dunked. I've never seen anybody else do that. Never.

"There were times I'd hear guys say, 'He took off too soon.' I knew he hadn't. I had seen him too much. It's funny, you could take all the people in the world and work on their vertical leap, most would improve, at least a little. But none of them would be able to jump like he can.

"What I've always found unbelievable is, kids identify with a fantasy. They don't identify with Larry Bird shooting 500 shots. They say that's work, that's boring. It's amazing, they identify with the skywalk, the thing they're least likely ever to be able to do."

THERE ARE THOSE who say, if you never saw Doc with the Virginia Squires, in 1971, at the beginning, then you never saw him.

"I went from Virginia to New York (to the Nets)," Erving said, "and the Nets did have a national audience. They wrote about us in the New York papers, that got us worldwide coverage. People knew who I was. If more people had seen me then, that would have affected them, not me. I didn't have any anxiety about exposure.

"There are people who say if you didn't see me in practice, then you never saw me. The truth is, I did things in practice I never did in games. When we'd scrimmage, we'd be far less calculating, make greater use of our instincts. That's why you see great stuff in summer leagues, when guys are out there barnstorming.

"One year, I did a summer camp with Mychal Thompson (now with the Los Angeles Lakers). Jack Ramsay was there. We had played Jack's team (Portland) in the playoff finals in 1977, I had scored 40 in the last game. Did he know me?

"Anyway, we played a pickup game at camp, and after 20 minutes Jack walked over and said, 'I didn't know you could do all those things.' Six games we had played for the NBA championship, and here, in a pickup game, he's saying that? He had seen me play, and yet he hadn't.

"Another time, I played a game in Lexington, scored 41, got the bucket that sent it into overtime, made the winning bucket in overtime. Adolph Rupp (then the University of Kentucky coach) was there. He said, 'I've never seen a player like you.' He was a purist and I was into my high-wire act, but that's what he said. Does that mean that anybody who didn't see me in that game never really saw me?

"Everything is in the eye of the beholder. In 1980–81, Billy (then-Sixers' coach Billy Cunningham) went on record saying I was playing the best ball I had ever played. And he had seen me.

"In my own mind, my three years with the Nets were the most enjoyable, some of the years with the Sixers were my best as an all-around player, learning about winning, about mastering my craft. I decided to dedicate myself to that after my 30th birthday. I knew I wasn't going to run faster, jump higher or shoot straighter, but I wanted to get better.

"And I did."

THEY REMEMBER WHEN.

"My playground was the 'Playground of Stars,'" said Cecil Watkins, now director of community programs for the NBA. "P.S. No. 127, out near LaGuardia Airport.

"I was involved in his first New York-Philadelphia tournament. He was the MVP in his age group, in the Singer Bowl, where the Tennis Center is now. I remember Don Ryan called from the Salvation Army youth center, said he had two or three kids who would make my eyes light up. I was tough about the tournament, though. Made it an invitational, said you needed a powerhouse to get in. Doc's team won it.

"I smile, though, when people ask if Doc could really fly. I think of flying, I think of the Rucker tournaments, up at 125th Street, with people watching from rooftops, hanging out windows, or standing along the side, faces pressed against the fence. I remember one day, all you heard were ooohs and ahhhs. It wasn't even that he skywalked, it was the way he did it.

"That's always been the difference. I've seen leapers, jumpers, scoopers, hangers, but Julius has a certain control. I saw Connie Hawkins, saw him as a creator, a guy who made things happen. Julius didn't just make things happen. He did them."

Watkins says he knew, from the start, what he was seeing.

"People say I have a gift for that," Watkins said. "That I can look at players at a young age and know what they will be. I saw Julius, traveling from Long Island into the city, to prove a point. To come where the action was. I refereed his first game. It was for kids 12 and 13. I wanted to check his age.

"But just because you see something in a kid doesn't mean he'll be a success. I remember Joe Hammond, all-playground, but never did anything in the pros. Couldn't make the adjustment. I thought Lloyd Daniels, the kid recruited by Nevada-Las Vegas, would be the next Doc, the closest I had seen. Then I read that he got arrested.

"It reminded me that you need people behind you. A mentor. The ones that fall by the wayside latch on to the wrong people. The ones that make it find a shelter."

"JUST AFTER HE signed with Virginia, he went to the Rucker, the league of legends, outdoors, to get in shape," Don Ryan said, the memories flooding back.

"I remember I paid a kid a couple of dollars to get me a seat. The neighborhood stars, with Knowles, Hammond, Manigault, against a team sponsored by the New York Daily News, with Charlie Scott, Ollie Taylor, Manny Leaks. Two overtimes. Best pro game I ever saw, because there were no inhibitions. Scott would toss up alley oops, Doc would come out of nowhere to catch them, jam them.

"I used to say, 'Clear the runway, fasten your seatbelt.' That day, somebody took a shot from half-court at the buzzer. Doc was on his way up the court, caught the shot on the run, kept going, dunked. It was a good thing it was halftime, because they needed that much time to get the people back in their seats.

"I was convinced Doc landed in the same playground only because that was where the basket was."

"YOU GO 15 FEET in the air, that's pretty close to flying, isn't it?" said Kevin Loughery.

Loughery coached Erving with the Nets, and now coaches the Washington Bullets. Loughery saw the young star carry the ABA, then launch a new career in the NBA. Now he is seeing Erving at 37, taking one last, charming lap around the league. A victory tour if there ever was one.

"The thing about him was, he was never finished," Loughery said. "Others would come down, he'd still be up, handling a basketball like it was a softball. Always had something left. He never surprised me in a game, but he did in practice.

"One memory I have is coaching my first game in the ABA. We're holding for the last shot of the first half against Indiana, and he took off from the right baseline. Darnell Hillman, Dan Roundfield, George McGinnis came to meet him. Two of them ended up sprawled on the floor. Doc dunked.

"That's one thing people tend to overlook about him: his strength. He has the strength of a guy 250 or 260, but he's closer to 210, 220."

Doug Collins likes to explain the midair maneuvers by saying Erving uses his off-hand as an airbrake. Bob Bass, a charter ABA coach and now the general manager of the San Antonio Spurs, insists he has seen Erving back up in mid-skywalk. Isiah Thomas says Erving simply stops in the air.

"He changes direction," said Thomas, the Detroit lead guard. "I watch Jordan now . . . one of those dunks at the All-Star Game, he was laying down in the air, if that's possible. I began to wonder: If there had been no rim to catch him, would he have just kept on going for a while?

"But the most amazing thing I ever saw Doc do was in Lansing, Mich., doing a camp. It's the summer, it's hot, but he had fresh legs that day. I swear it looked like he went from the top of the key to the basket, moving the ball back and forth, like he was walking on air.

"I don't want this to come out wrong, but sometimes the people who watch our game don't know what they're watching. Players do unreal things. But that's the beauty of it. They just do it. They don't stop and think about what they're going to do. You do that, too often the play is gone."

"So many times, you say to yourself, 'I wonder what that feels like?'" Bass said. "It's crazy, sometimes you wake up at night because you were dreaming you could. I swear. It's happened to me."

EVERYBODY NOTICES, even those assigned to notice other things.

"You tend to notice things more when you first see a player, especially when he shows a move you haven't seen before, or it's something you feel couldn't have been done," said Darrel Garretson, the NBA's chief of officials. "Sometimes you call a walk or a goaltend because you're surprised. I remember, early on, I saw Erving wrap around the basket, come out on the other side. I was the lead official, there was a tendency to want to make a call. But what?

"I saw him in Pauley Pavilion, in an all-star game of some kind when he was in the ABA. I remember the look on (then-UCLA coach) John Wooden's face. Doc went up, held the rim, pulled himself to the hoop and jammed. John didn't like that kind of stuff in his gym. Me, I just hoped he never tried that in a game. You never want to take away a poster shot."

"Doc's the one who helped me learn to hold the whistle, because you never knew what was coming," said Jess Kersey, an official in both the ABA and NBA. "In the ABA, I saw him jam on Artis Gilmore. He went up on the right side, Artis went up with him, didn't give him room. Doc brings the ball down, changes hands, jams with his left. I said 'How?' I had the whistle. I was waiting for contact. There was none."

"I saw Doc with the Squires against the Nets," recalled Bob Ryan, the Boston Globe basketball writer. "I remember (then-Squires coach) Al Bianchi saying, 'The difference is, if you ask 'J' for change, you get four quarters, not 90 cents.'

"I saw him in college, too. First time was in Roberts Center, at Boston College. He had 26 points, 18 rebounds, didn't look good. I said, 'If this is an off-night, I want to see a real night.' Looking back, I feel he must have held something back in the Yankee Conference. There was no dunking, a lot of zones, the desire couldn't have been the same.

"My brilliant prediction, though, was that this guy, Julius Erving, would be a great rebounder."

JULIUS ERVING refused to be restricted.

"I thought I knew his limitations," said Ray Wilson, "but I never really did. He would never allow himself to be restricted by limitations placed on him by others, anyway. If he had allowed that, he'd still be trying to get off the floor.

"I still look forward to watching him play, to seeing something I've never seen before. I get that feeling of my heart going up into my mouth, waiting, anticipating."

The Doctor sees with all-encompassing eyes. He sees past Jordan launching 35 shots a night. He sees past Wilkins shooting when he should be passing, passing when he should be rolling inside. He takes a muted view of the high-fives splotched through every sequence, wondering what all the premature, misplaced celebration is about.

"I don't watch guys taking 35 shots," Erving said. "I averaged 31 points one year, didn't take that many shots. The longer I played, the more I streamlined my game. Go directly to the basket. Fake left, go right. Fake right, go left. Lean, twist, turn . . . There's a whole lot you can do when you're young. If you're going to be here a long time, you have to modify.

"Michael, Dominique, they're attractions. But Michael's team wins 50 percent of the time, Dominique's team wins more, but I have to watch them from a professional standpoint or I might lean toward being critical. If I were coaching these guys, if I was interested in winning a championship, I'd have to have them make a lot of adjustments.

That's probably why I won't coach."

ERVING SAYS he never planned this career. He says he didn't choose it, it chose him.

"Bill Russell said once, 'How come these good teams keep following you around? What's the deal?'

"People would say I created the merger, but I don't want that on my shoulders. All I was, was a factor.

"Same with elevating the level of the game. I just did things guys my size hadn't done. I'd leave my feet before deciding what I was going to do, and the purists would cringe. I told myself, 'If you jump high enough, you've got time to think about what you're going to do.'

"I've always looked at things I do as things others are capable of doing. Something you see, get an image of, then try. Maybe 10 percent of the time, you do something you just dreamed up or were forced into. Maybe 1 percent of the time, I might say, 'I don't know where that came from.'

"But in another way, I'm a purist, too. I'm result-oriented. All the celebrating about a shot, a steal, an individual play . . . an individual play is usually the result of everybody being in sync. Acknowledge a good pass, that's purposeful, team-oriented. But the celebration should be after the game is won."

Doc's flight plans are designed to win, not to excite.

Don't ask why it happened, or how, or how often. Accept it as an art form, as an era in the evolution of a sport.

Julius Erving could fly.

I know that is what I will tell my grandchildren.

MOSES CARVES THE BEEF

Philadelphia Daily News
March 29, 1984

MOSES MALONE WOULDN'T CONTRIBUTE to this story. Maybe he thinks it's enough that he gives at the office.

The only message he left last night was the one etched in the box score of the 76ers' sleepy-eyed 109–103 victory over the Washington Bullets.

Malone scored 22 points, swept 22 rebounds, yanking down a season-high 16 off the defensive boards. He got to the foul line eight times and made them all, and found enough cutters to hand out a season-high five assists.

You think that doesn't speak volumes? In capital letters? In italics? In the universal language of the sport?

You think the Bullets didn't file out of the Spectrum feeling as if they had just been lectured? The Beef Brothers had extracted their pound of flesh—Greg Ballard scored 27 points, Jeff Ruland 22 and Rick Mahorn 14, but they had an aggregate total of 20 rebounds, two less than Malone, who emerged leaner and meaner. He is the NBA's Player of the Week, has shed 15 pounds, has restricted his diet and is generally feeling better. If you want any more than that, you're on your own.

"I won't have any comment the rest of the year," he said.

The rest of the Sixers were too bone-weary to concentrate on anything tougher than a day off before facing Dallas here tomorrow night. They've won 11 of their last 13, seem solidly entrenched as the No. 3 seed in the Eastern playoff picture and have an outside shot at slipping past Los Angeles for the league's second best record.

"Everybody's tired this time of the year," said Maurice Cheeks. "I'm no exception. A lot of it is mental, a lot of it is physical. We're still fighting for the second best record, so we can have the home court advantage for as long as possible. If we were really in a race right now, we could overcome the way we feel.

"You feel it more on the road. At home, the crowd can pick you up. This is a hard time, when you're winding down, with 10 games to play, but still having to get ready for the playoffs. Three or four days off would be nice, but I'll be ready to play any time there's a game, whether something's at stake or not."

What's at stake seems to be the delicate tuning of a team that has dedicated itself to becoming the first in 15 years to win back-to-back championships, at the same time protecting itself against fatigue and injury.

That's why coach Billy Cunningham was so encouraged by his Bantam Backcourt—rookie Sedale Threatt and recently signed Wes Matthews. Threatt had eight points and three assists in 21 minutes, hit four of his six shots and didn't turn the ball over. Matthews generated six points, seven assists and two steals in 16 minutes.

"It's a time of the year when you have to be on guard mentally," suggested Marc Iavaroni, after the Sixers improved their record to 46–26. "It's sort of a limbo area between the end of the regular season and the start of the playoffs, a time when you still have to strive to improve. When you reach this point, half the battle is timing. The idea is to be at your best going into the postseason. It requires what I'd call a reserved cockiness, a belief that you can do just that, and it becomes a challenge in itself. If we face the challenge, get good results, the next thing we know the playoffs will be starting and we'll have gotten something out of it."

Jack McMahon shrugged off Tuesday night's loss in Atlanta as an aberration, an affair not worth remembering.

"The Atlanta game, I didn't even look at the box score," the assistant coach said. "It's just something that happens once in a while, but doesn't really mean anything.

"We may have looked tired tonight, we might not have played our best game, but at stages when we had to, we had the ability to turn it on. The last four minutes, when we won, we got into it defensively, we made things happen.

"Maybe we're resigned to the spot we're in, second place behind Boston in the (Atlantic) division. Maybe there's some truth to the idea that we never have an easy game with Washington. What I liked, though, was the way we jumped on 'em when we had to. That kind of defense was the sign of our championship year, and it reminded me that at money time that aggressive, intense attitude is still there. It's such a long season, it's hard to show it every night, all the time."

Malone has been showing it as much as anyone. He has generated 15 or more rebounds in five consecutive games and has strung together performances of 27 against Boston, 16 against Atlanta and 22 last night.

"We have endurance other teams don't have," said Bobby Jones. "Tonight we did what we had to do in spurts. It's a time of the season when I look for things to motivate me. I wanted 100 steals and 100 blocks this year. I've got the steals, I need a few (three) to get 100 blocks. Statistics aren't usually important to me, but they can be valuable as something to get me going."

"We've moved," said Julius Erving, "into strategy time. That's when you play to win, but don't kill yourself."

In what hopefully won't be remembered as the Silent Spring of Moses Malone, the 76ers apparently will wait for the playoffs to deliver their next thunderclap.

SIX SHOTS: General manager Pat Williams represented the Sixers at the Board of Governors meeting Tuesday in Dallas. "There were really no major issues on the docket, so it became a workshop session with the new commissioner (David Stern)," Williams said. "He strongly believes in stressing the selling of the product, on the local and national levels, and that's an issue the league has never concentrated heavily on at the ownership level. David obviously will be a roll-up-his-sleeves type of leader, and he can afford to do that because Larry O'Brien passed him the torch with all the crisis fires put out."

THE PROMISED LAND

Philadelphia Daily News
May 13, 1998

HAROLD KATZ SEES KEVIN GARNETT, of the Minnesota Timberwolves, holding a six-year contract extension worth $21 million a season and smiles. If Garnett, who has completed two seasons in the NBA and has never won a playoff series, is worth that in today's bloated NBA market, what would Moses Malone have been worth to the 76ers in 1982–83?

"I look at Garnett, and you tell me if that's insanity," said Katz, the former owner of the Sixers. "Moses, one of the great scorers and rebounders of all time, vs. a kid who has played two years who's getting 10 times the money? If Garnett is worth $21 million today, then Moses would have to be worth $42 million, because Moses would say he's twice as good. And he'd be right, too."

As it was, Katz signed the 6-10 Malone to a six-year contract worth $13.2 million in the summer of 1982. It was, at the time, a staggering amount of money, but to Katz, Malone represented the final piece that would propel his team to a championship.

No major team in the city has won a title since, and as the 15th anniversary approaches later this month, one enduring memory comes floating back from the first day of that season's training camp at Franklin & Marshall College.

Malone stopped during a drill, turned to the owner and said— depending on whose memory is being tested—either "Don't worry, we'll win about 70" or "Don't worry, we're going to win it." The specifics don't matter as much as the reality: Malone led the league in rebounding with an average of 15.3 and finished fifth in scoring at 24.5. Teaming with Julius Erving, Maurice Cheeks, Andrew Toney and Bobby Jones, he drove the Sixers to a record of 65–17. They lost just one postseason game, to Milwaukee in the Eastern Conference finals, then swept the Los Angeles Lakers, 4–0, in the championship round.

They were 12–1 in the playoffs. Malone was the perfect fit, so dominant and relentless on the boards that backup guard Franklin Edwards nicknamed him "Chairman."

It has been two seasons since Katz, who purchased the franchise from F. Eugene Dixon in 1981 for about $12 million, sold it to the Comcast Corp. for about $147 million. Katz insists he does not miss the involvement, but just as surely he never has forgotten the euphoria that came with winning a title. Amazingly, though, other than visiting the Comcast

SportsNet television studios in the CoreStates Center, he never has seen the inside of the team's new arena.

He loves the game as much as ever but did not attend one anywhere this season.

"I really thought I would have missed it, and the first year I probably did," Katz said from his home in South Florida, where he is occupied in various business dealings. "But I really don't. The athlete has changed so much . . . Today, I'm not the right guy. I can't take the way athletes have become.

"We had guys who would run through brick walls, who played through injuries. We didn't say they had to play hurt, they did it for their teammates. Today I hear, 'I don't want to jeopardize my career,' and that's from guys with four years left on guaranteed contracts. We never heard that.

"When our guys lost, they felt it, they showed it. The last few years, it's been more, 'I want to win, but it's not the worst thing in the world not to.' Take away Michael Jordan, Scottie Pippen, Karl Malone, the average athlete today isn't like Bobby Jones, Cheeks, Erving."

But if Katz believes he no longer is the right guy to own a team, he clearly was the perfect guy in '81. The Sixers had been to the finals in 1977 and 1980 and would go again in 1982, each time losing in six games, once to Portland, twice to the Lakers. Katz reacted by trading away Lionel Hollins and Darryl Dawkins, then signing Houston free agent Malone to an offer sheet. Since the rules at the time called for compensation, he gave the Rockets the popular Caldwell Jones and a first-round draft choice.

But he had exactly what he wanted.

Billy Cunningham, the Sixers' coach, was in Pinehurst, N.C., having just completed nine holes of golf with friends when he received a telephone message. Katz wanted him in New York that evening, at the Grand Hyatt Hotel. They were signing Malone.

"I left my clubs at the 10th tee, grabbed a quick shower and drove to the airport in Raleigh-Durham," Cunningham recalled, chuckling. "I caught a flight to Newark [N.J.], found a cab and asked the driver what he would charge to drive me to the Hyatt. The price was $70, which I couldn't see.

"I took a bus, paid $8. I got up to the suite, met Moses. Then Harold told me he was paying him $13.2 million. I said, 'I have good news. I just saved you $62.'"

Katz's timing was impeccable. The Rockets were in the process of being sold from Gavin Maloof to Charlie Thomas, and neither seemed prepared to pay Malone $13.2 million. The Sixers had gone as far as they could with Dawkins and Caldwell Jones.

"There was no sense in us changing unless we could get the final piece, and that clearly was Moses," Katz said. "What struck me was, Moses wanted to win. I felt he could swallow his ego a little and still score, and

Julius and Bobby Jones only thought about winning. Our guys could fit in with anyone. Not to take away anything from the players we had, but Moses made us special."

Still, it was a wrenching time for Cunningham, who loved the work ethic of Caldwell Jones. Cunningham recalls it as "a valuable lesson."

"I learned from that point on not to get too emotionally involved with my players," said Cunningham, who now splits his time between South Florida and the Philadelphia suburbs. "I had to keep the goal of improving the team ahead of everything else."

The Sixers of that era had offered the fans slogans such as "We Owe You One" and "The Seats You'll Never Sit In," but they weren't able to fulfill their promises until Malone arrived.

"We had everything else," said Erving, who had won two championships with the New York Nets in the American Basketball Association. "We had the physical talent and intelligence and the intangibles, like hustle, desire, enthusiasm, love and leadership. We had stars and we had guys who were willing to follow.

"When we got Moses, our focus was very clear about what we had been put together to do, particularly after not having been able to do it in the past. There was an overriding need, a passion to really close the deal. Actually, there was a fear of not doing it, because the window of opportunity was going to close. It was our time."

But not even Erving, the unforgettable Doctor J, was ready to assume the Sixers would win.

"The three previous times we had been to the finals, we had lost 4–2," he said from his office in Orlando, where he is a vice president with the NBA's Magic and the parent, RDV Enterprises. "When we got Moses, did I know he would be the difference between it being 4–2 them or us? I couldn't look at getting him as a guarantee."

"We were down about 15 in the second half of Game 4 in the finals," Erving recalled. "We got in a timeout huddle in the [Great Western] Forum and Billy looked at Moses and said, 'If you get every defensive rebound, we can win.' I don't remember exactly what Moses said, but it was like, 'Yeah, I can do that.' And he did."

Yet, in the locker room afterward, Malone deferred to Erving.

"It was Doc's game," Malone said. "Doc's game."

Championships, Erving said, do not come easily.

"Look at the NBA," he said. "We're up to 29 teams, but over the last nine seasons the championship has come to just three—Detroit, Houston and Chicago.

"I don't find it a statistical oddity that a city could go 15 years without a title. Look at Chicago before Jordan. The Bulls had won none.

"The truth is, it wasn't as if it was our turn to win. Nothing is promised. You've got to be really good and you've got to be lucky."

It wasn't just that the team was good. The whole organization was.

Erving, Malone and Cunningham were named among the Top 50 players in the league's history. Cheeks, now an assistant coach with the Sixers, and Bobby Jones were acknowledged as two of the most dynamic defensive- and team-oriented players of their time. It is widely believed that had Toney's career not been cut short by foot injuries, he would have been a prime candidate for the Top 50, too.

Cunningham (Miami) and general manager Pat Williams (Orlando) became architects of expansion franchises, assistant general manager John Nash became a general manager with the Sixers, Washington and New Jersey. Assistant coach Matt Guokas became a successful head coach and a respected TV analyst. The late Jack McMahon was recognized as a superscout. The rookie video specialist, John Gabriel, is now the general manager of the Magic.

Role players? Clint Richardson and Edwards were regarded as one of the best backup backcourts in the league. Gangly Earl Cureton was a helpful soldier off the bench. Free agent Marc Iavaroni had been imported as a starting forward, allowing Bobby Jones to remain comfortable and effective as a sixth man. Clemon Johnson and Reggie Johnson were acquired during the season. Mark McNamara was the wide-eyed, first-round draft choice.

"We weren't the most talented team," said Cureton, now the coach of the Camden Power in the United States Basketball League, "but we were the best team. And we had a coach who was a perfectionist."

Lucky? In '82–83, the Lakers lost James Worthy and Bob McAdoo to injuries, then saw Norm Nixon hurt during the playoffs. But that should in no way minimize what the Sixers accomplished. In 1980, the Sixers might have believed they had caught a break when Lakers center Kareem Abdul-Jabbar missed Game 6 of the finals with a migraine. Instead, they were crushed at home by spectacular rookie Earvin "Magic" Johnson.

When the Sixers visited the White House in June, President Reagan said "I think coach [Pat] Riley of the Lakers put it best when he likened your playoff style to 'controlled fury.' And he should know, since he was on the receiving end."

"I remember how that season began as if it were last night," said Nash, now the general manager of the Nets. "Harold brought his people together for dinner in town at Jimmy's Milan, talked about toughness, about rebounding, about his concern for Dawkins not being able to be consistent. He mentioned Truck Robinson, Kareem, Dan Issel as possibilities. And every once in a while, he brought up Moses."

When Williams left on a prearranged tour of China, Katz instructed Nash to move Dawkins. Nash, after also speaking with Utah, finalized a deal with New Jersey for $700,000 and a first-round pick.

When a reporter reached the traveling Erving at a hotel in Hong Kong, Erving said that without the hulking Dawkins, the Sixers of he, Caldwell Jones and Bobby Jones would be "the all-skinny team."

Williams, returning from his tour, stepped off a flight in New York to headlines of his team acquiring Malone.

"All the stuff you talk about at high school banquets, all the necessary characteristics, we had it," said Williams, now a senior vice president with the Magic.

"We were up, 3–0, in LA," said Richardson, who now lives and works in the Seattle area, "and Billy came in and said we could win the title or we could make history."

Cunningham, who worked so relentlessly during the playoffs that he lost more than 15 pounds, had been startled at the end of the regular season when he asked Malone what he was expecting in the playoffs.

Malone's response became a battle cry: "Fo', fo' and fo'."

He was very nearly right on the mark. They swept New York, lost once to the Bucks, then swept the Lakers, taking the last two at the Forum in Inglewood, Calif.

"We could easily have been the first team ever to have won 70," Katz said. "But Billy sat out his starters down the stretch, gave them their rest.

"He was on [a mission], and conveyed that to them. There was no second place that would have been good enough. He never said it, but it was common knowledge among all of us."

Funny the things you remember.

On the flight to Philadelphia the morning after winning the title, McMahon quietly instructed the flight attendant in the first-class section that any time he held up four fingers, she was to bring four liquor miniatures: two for him, two for Cunningham. It became an animated trip.

"But before Game 4, what I remember is, Moses couldn't exhale," Cunningham said. "He had taken an elbow the previous game. All I was thinking was, 'We've come this far, we're so close. Oh, no.'"

In the final weeks of the regular season, Cunningham had experienced similar agonizing moments. Malone was playing on a bad knee and sore tendons. There had been some atrophy in his leg. When Malone winced, so did the coach.

Not to worry.

"What I remember, watching the games now, is that we had no security guards, no bouncers as we went through the season," Richardson said.

These were the days before charter flights. The Sixers flew commercially, enduring wake-up calls at dawn and screeching fans in airports.

At the time, Richardson said: "Those wake-up calls are getting to be a tradition by now. At 5:15, you feel like it's the middle of the night, you wonder what time people who work 9 to 5 get up. Then you remember that all it takes is two solid hours of effort to make up for everything else, and you go do your job."

Today, Richardson understands as well as anyone that it was more than worth it.

"We all enjoyed playing there, we weren't trying to go elsewhere," he said. "We were special, a family. If any team has a unique place in Philadelphia history, it should be us."

BIG GUY'S ONE FOR THE AGES

Philadelphia Daily News
October 29, 1996

LOS ANGELES—WILT CHAMBERLAIN WANTS to set the record straight.

On what he believes was a misconstrued interpretation of his statement that he has slept with 20,000 women.

On today's NBA players, including Michael Jordan.

On his past, present and future, including celebrating his 60th birthday.

He will touch on those subjects and others in his next book, titled, *Who's Running the Asylum,* due to be released in about a month. And he talked about many of the subjects during an introspective, three-hour interview with the Daily News last week at his Los Angeles mansion, high on a hill that offers a panoramic view of the San Fernando Valley.

Chamberlain, who won championships with the 1966–67 76ers and the 1971–72 Los Angeles Lakers, who forced the sport to change several of its rules, will be in New York today for the announcement of the 50 greatest players in the league's history.

Make no mistake: Even though the list will not be in any order or relative to position, Wilt has to be one of the names right at the top.

Today's news conference will mark the start of the celebration of the league's 50th season. Chamberlain, who burst on the national basketball scene as a rising star at Overbrook High, celebrated his 60th birthday Aug. 21.

But let's get to the issue of the women, because, despite Chamberlain having some important things to say on other subjects, that's what people remember most of all from his last book.

"I regret the context in which people chose to take it," he said, lounging in a soft, deep leather chair. "It's like saying you saw 'Casablanca' a thousand times. You mean you saw it a lot. I used 20,000 as a figure of speech. If I had been bragging, I'd have mentioned some names.

"But it was a chapter titled 'Sex Rules the World.' I called my relationships 'encounters,' because that's what they were. Not conquests, the way some people like to say. And, listen, men don't conquer women; it's usually the other way around. If it comes down to a matter of conquests, then I'm the most conquered man around.

"I'm sorry if I did an injustice to my women friends. I've always had the ultimate respect for women. I grew up with six sisters and a mother like no other. I would never demean the character of women. Anything I've done with women has been a thing of mutuality."

Chamberlain, who never has married, said, people read the start of the chapter but somehow didn't finish.

"A few pages later, I said if you think sleeping with 1,000 different women is special, (sleeping with) one woman 1,000 times is what's really happening. I'd say that on talk shows, and no one heard me. And I did over 550 talk shows. I wasn't there to promote promiscuity. I've never believed in infidelity.

"I've fostered women's groups. I think when Magic Johnson's situation (testing positive for HIV, the virus that leads to AIDS) surfaced, people began pointing fingers. I believe we need to be more careful, more caring.

"People knew 20,000 was a fictitious number, a number used to make a statement. But I know what happens. They say, 'You're Wilt. It might be true.'"

He isn't ready to divulge all the subjects he touches in *Who's Running the Asylum*. When asked about Lower Merion High's Kobe Bryant becoming the first guard to make the jump directly to the pros, he said, "Read the book."

But he was more than willing to discuss Jordan, the most dominant player of the current era; to be critical of the players who go through entire careers dependent on sheer talent rather than developing a knowledge of the game; and to chide the NBA for having been lax in attempts to make the public aware of the players who helped build the sport.

His opinions, his directness and his career are all as legendary as the home in which he has lived for more than 25 years. It includes a 2,200-pound front door, a master bedroom with a triangular fish pond with a fountain in the center, surrounded by electronic lighting, plus a grouping of sheep-skin rugs and a mirrored ceiling above a bed that seemed bigger than mere king-size.

"I built the house, decorated it, helped design it, wanted to feel it was mine," he said. "If a professional decorator does it, then it's theirs. I like to make my own mistakes in things I can afford to make a mistake in. I'll ask for help in areas where I'm a novice.

"In terms of the book, as egotistical as I am, that ego helps me voice my opinions. I'm not a middle-of-the-road guy. I talk to people in positions of authority, some of things they say are amazing, but they'd never say those things for print.

"Some things need to be said, and I'll say them in the book. And it's not just big-mouth Wilt popping off. I'm trying to be constructive.

"I'll give you an example: Some people called me last year about (San Antonio Spurs center) David Robinson being soft. They were looking for me to tell them what they already wanted to say. David's a very intelligent man who was raised to make his statements with his mind more than his body. He gets (criticized) because he's not out there with the same attitude a few other people have. But that's his MO. To try and change that in a person is a no-no. Recognize what you've bought; don't buy it and then try to make it something it isn't."

He gets asked a lot about Jordan, because Jordan has won four championships and has led the league in scoring eight times. Chamberlain won the scoring title seven times.

Amazingly, it has been 23 years since Chamberlain's last season in the league, but his legend has only grown. He was inducted into the Basketball Hall of Fame in 1978, was named to the league's 35th Anniversary Team in 1980.

The litany of his other records is incredible: He is the all-time leader in rebounds (23,924) and rebounding average (22.9), and recorded 118 games of 50 points or more, including 100 against the New York Knicks on March 2, 1962, in Hershey. He has accounted for 15 of the top 20 scoring and 12 of the top 20 rebounding performances in the league's history. He was the field goal percentage leader nine times, the Most Valuable Player four times, All-NBA first team seven times, All-Defensive first team twice. In 1961–62 with the Philadelphia Warriors, in 80 regulation games plus 10 overtime periods, he averaged an astounding 48.5 minutes (games are 48 minutes long), all but eight minutes of the season.

"Jordan is the most visible player of the present, I'm the most visible player of the past," Chamberlain said. "I just don't see how (broadcaster and former center) Bill Walton has the right to say Michael's the greatest player ever. He can only say it's his opinion of the players he's seen. He saw me three or four years with the Lakers, that's all.

"And, believe me, Michael is deserving of all the accolades he gets. He's also very fortunate that his abilities are appreciated. Some players aren't appreciated. Me? I'd say I'm in that category. I'm about the only guy for whom the rules were changed to stop my abilities—widening the lane, changing the rules on free throws, disallowing inbounds passes over the top of the backboard.

"The rules that have been changed (more recently) have aided Michael's abilities: no hand-checking for one. Zone defenses aid him. When they widened the lane, the idea was to get me farther away from the basket. So I averaged 50 points a game (50.4 in '61–62). I used to catch inbounds passes over the top and dunk them. In high school, we'd intentionally miss free throws to the left. I'd catch them and dunk.

"But after a while, everything is about numbers. As I've walked through the corridors of life, fathers and grandfathers grab their kids, point to me and say, 'He scored 100 in one game.' Nobody talks about the other things. I understand. If Michael didn't lead the league in scoring eight times, I don't care how great he is defensively, he wouldn't be the Michael Jordan he is. And I like his defensive game better than his offense—he's a sensational defender.

"He knows. That's why he continues to lead the league in scoring, why he scores just enough to do it . . . Otherwise, he'd be scoring 23 or 24 a game. That's why Kareem (Abdul-Jabbar) stayed out there as long as he did (20 seasons), so his number (38,287, the all-time record) would be greater than mine (31,419, second place). Averaging 50 in a season kicks 100 in one game in the butt. Averaging 48.5 minutes is a helluva number, the most staggering."

At 60, Chamberlain has mellowed. But not as much as you might think. When he turned 50, he said he was "doing just fine, my man." Now, he says it's "more of the same."

"Age," he said thoughtfully, "is more than a number. It can represent a whole lot less and it can be non-descriptive. What one has done is what's important. I have a friend, a former player, who always says, 'Hey, big fella, we're in our last quarter.' I tell him I'm hoping to have a little more than a quarter. But he meant a quarter of really true productivity.

"Many people allow themselves to cease being productive, truly functional. Do that, it doesn't even count. I've always been an achiever, had goals, pushed myself. I've enjoyed having the spirit, the willing body to do things. At 60, I can cite some problems, but they're minimal and we all have them. I can still do anything physically that I want to do. That's a real plus for a guy who has taken this body through major battles, ones with resistance.

"Most of the things I've done haven't been good for the body. The things I've done tend to break down the body—the triple jump, the long jump, volleyball, basketball. My workouts build the body back up. Doctors would always talk about keeping the cardiovascular system strong, but now they want older people to build muscle. Many older people can't get themselves out of a chair.

"But 60 is a strange number. You're reaching that geriatric stage, that Social Security age. People say, 'You can't be 60.' If they didn't know the number, they wouldn't think that way."

But 60 he is. And happy to be there.

"I never thought I'd get to be 60," he said. "In truth, bigger people don't live as long, and I thought I used up most of my life in my early living. I never anticipated living a great length of time. To me, anything long meant past 40 or 50."

But 60 is also old enough to allow Chamberlain to offer a perspective on the growth of the NBA, on changes in the game. He retired after the 1972–73 season and says he hasn't attended "more than five games" since, but that he watches as many as he can. His bedroom system include two huge TV sets and three dishes.

"When you're young and you're faster, stronger and jump higher than anyone, at the lower levels of the game you can be far above your contemporaries," he said. "At that point, you're depending on talent rather than knowledge.

"I compare Larry Bird and Dominique Wilkins. Dominique is gifted, can jump to the moon. Yet there's Bird, seemingly slower, can't jump more than 4 or 5 inches. Apparently, Bird had something Dominique doesn't have. But my favorites in recent years have been Bird, Magic, Jordan and Sir Charles (Barkley). They could play in any era and rebound, pass, score, run the complete game.

"Too many guys have become specialists. We've limited some of them to doing just the part they can do. Jordan became a full-fledged star after he left North Carolina. A great coach like (Georgetown's) John Thompson had Patrick Ewing play like Bill Russell, but Ewing comes to the pros and you find out he has, like, one of the greatest (shooting) touches in the game. Where was that touch in college?"

Chamberlain seems to be enjoying the league's concept of a 50th anniversary, but questions whether it's enough.

"Basketball has been totally good to me, and I've reciprocated," he said. "No organization in sports has done more to elevate men of color, to give them a chance to prove themselves worthy in all endeavors, than the NBA, and they're to be applauded for that.

"But they've forgotten the people who started it, people like Danny Biasone (who invented the 24-second clock), like Walter Brown (the former owner of the Boston Celtics). I understand the media is out there to sell today's game, the same way Oldsmobile is trying to sell today's model, not the 1956 one. But the league and the media need to pay more attention to those who have come before. I'm putting the knock on the league for that a little in the book."

What about the differences between the players of Chamberlain's era and now?

"Some of the problems today are not the fault of the kids," he said. "When I was in high school, did that stop me from working? I was a bellhop at Kutsher's (in the Catskills). I remember one day, Red Auerbach wanted (the high school kids) to practice at 3 p.m. I said, 'Hey Red, at 3, I'm servicing the mahjong games.' I'm not intentionally picking out one guy, but how many jobs has Shaquille O'Neal ever had? Today's young players don't know what it means to be out there in the workforce.

"Again, I understand. A family sees a chance for a kid to make millions of dollars. Our parents said having a paper route was part of the deal.

That's why I see young guys—like Kenny Anderson—with talent but not the work ethic.

"Every tall black kid is compared to Wilt, not Bill Russell. Am I the standard? Yet when they want to talk about standards, the media goes to other doggone places. Along comes Shaquille O'Neal. He plays as differently from me as I did from Bird. I resent people not understanding that I was skinny, weighed 100 pounds less than Shaq when I came in, but I was breaking records, doing incredible things."

Chamberlain said his greatest accomplishment has been "to acquire the friends I have . . . I'm loaded with friends," that his current challenge is to try to do more charitable work, to help worthy causes as much with his time as with his finances. In fact, the proceeds from the book have been targeted for several charities Chamberlain supports.

His "happiest days" were at Overbrook, his favorite teams were the '66–67 and '67–68 Sixers and "my Narberth summer league team when I was a kid, when Guy Rodgers and Hal Lear were substitutes because we had the great Sonny Lloyd and John Chaney, and Claude Gross, who became my bother-in-law, and Bob Gainey."

"If I could have taken that Narberth team with me," he said, "I think we could've beaten anybody."

He does not worry about having won just two rings in the NBA.

"I lost a lot of seventh games (in playoff series), maybe by a total of eight to 10 points," he said. "But if I had five more rings today, would I have been any different as a player?"

Over his career, he lost five seventh games by a total of 21 points and won four by a total of 59. But his point was well taken.

"If Jordan, with his four rings, didn't have them, would he be different?" Chamberlain said. "And sometimes what I did or what Jordan did wasn't the issue. If John Paxson hadn't hit that shot one year, would the Bulls have won? Michael didn't have anything to do with that shot dropping, but he did win a ring."

At 60, he enjoys his celebrity, cherishes his privacy. He says he will not use a car phone, a car fax system or a cell phone and hates call-waiting.

"I wouldn't be caught dead with that," he said, laughing. "It means the person you were speaking with first becomes last, because of the interruptions.

"The new car I just purchased has one of those phones that's voice-activated, has a fax. I like the car, so I bought it, but I also know I paid for some things I'll never use.

"My home phone rings constantly, but I don't always pick it up. Sometimes I just leave the message machine on. I've had the same number for more than 25 years, but you get me when you get me, when I'm ready to be gotten."

Even at 60, Wilt Chamberlain remains a striking, commanding figure. In the most crowded of rooms, it would be virtually impossible to miss him.

"Young people stop and ask, 'Are you a player?'" he said. "I say no. They say, 'Were you?' I say it depends on who you ask."

When Chamberlain was 50, teams such as the Sixers, the New Jersey Nets, the Lakers were still calling, wondering whether he would consider coming out of retirement.

He believed he could have played, but knew he would not be happy with the regimentation of the pro life. That is why, he said, he did not pursue his dream of becoming an Olympic volleyball player. He still lifts weights and trains regularly in a workout area adjacent to the master bedroom.

He appears to be very much at peace with himself, high on a hill, just off one of LA's seemingly endless ribbons of freeways. Close enough to the action to still do whatever he wants, just far enough away to achieve the serenity he has always cherished.

Regrets? Sure.

"Who could live a life without regrets?" he said, somewhat startled.

"Somebody once said, 'There's a lot I would like to have done, but most of what I've done, I'm glad I did.'"

CHAPTER 8

. . . . . .

THE DREAM TEAM

Introduction by Charles Barkley

The biggest thing to me with Phil was that he wasn't going to be like everyone else. He was always fair. Always. That's the biggest compliment I can pay to him about how he went about his job. He had a job to do and he always did it in the most professional way. He was fair in every way. Things can easily get out of whack, but he never made anything personal. Number one, he was a nice man. But beyond that, he was so professional and I always appreciated that, especially when things got off track. It was never personal. I couldn't say that about everyone in the Philadelphia media. Phil was always fair. Phil was always professional. I understand it more now than I did then, but his fairness meant so much to me.

In a sports city with the Eagles, Phillies, Flyers, Sixers, Villanova, St. Joe's, and so much more, there weren't always stories written that were fair. Phil's stories were always fair and professional. He checked everything. If he wrote something critical, it was at least fair with all the facts checked. Again, like I said, I appreciated that very much. As far as the other sports, I couldn't always say that. With the Sixers specifically, I could always say that. With Phil writing the story, you knew it would be detailed and accurate. He would never put something out there that wasn't accurate.

I'll tell you a story. Before the 1986 draft, Phil called me at six in the morning. It was quite a long conversation and it was early in the morning, so you can imagine how I was feeling. I was tired. I answered the phone and Phil says, "Charles, the Sixers are trading the number one pick in the draft. What do you think?" I said, "They're trading the pick, which should have been Brad Daugherty? We're trading Moses (Malone) and getting Jeff Ruland? Then in a separate deal, we're getting Roy Hinson?" Phil said, "That's what is going to happen. Do you have a reaction?" First off, it's six in the morning and Phil is calling my private phone number. I didn't just give that out to anyone. But I trusted Phil. To be honest, I thought it was a practical joke because the trade seemed so crazy. I thought, "There's no way we can be doing this. It doesn't make any sense." Phil said, "This is what I'm hearing is going to happen." I mean, think about it—it's that early in the morning so it has to be a joke. How can we make such a trade like this? Once I thought some more, I knew it wasn't a joke and Phil was on top of the story. I trusted him enough to know that he wouldn't call unless it was very important. That was Phil. He was so hard-working and professional and even though I was a young player, I trusted him. Can you imagine the young stars today just giving their cell phone numbers out to reporters? It's a different world. I would trust Phil just as much today as I did then.

I miss reporters like Phil because first off, there aren't many. He did his job at the highest level. So many reporters today—I'll call it click-bait—put stuff out there without checking anything. I appreciated Phil's work ethic and how he went about his business every day. He just wanted to do his job. There would be times that critical stories would have to be written. But the facts were always there with reaction from both sides. I have the utmost respect for how he went about his business. That's all you can ask. I miss him. Phil was such a nice man and a great reporter.

CHARLES BARKLEY *was the No. 5 overall pick by the Sixers in the 1984 NBA draft from Auburn. Barkley played eight seasons for the Sixers and later competed for the Phoenix Suns and Houston Rockets. He was also a member of the 1992 U.S. Olympic Basketball "Dream" Team. Barkley was an 11-time NBA All-Star and currently serves as a highly successful NBA analyst for Turner Sports.*

. . . . . .

PRACTICE FOR DREAM TEAM?

Philadelphia Daily News
August 3, 1992

BADALONA, SPAIN—BEFORE DAWN BROKE across Philadelphia this morning, the Dream Team was on the practice floor.

The practice floor.

"We need a practice," Magic Johnson said last night, shortly after the U.S. Olympic basketball team beat Spain, 122–81, to complete its preliminary round with a 5–0 record and a berth against Puerto Rico in tomorrow night's quarterfinals.

Just remember, it was 4:30 in the afternoon Philadelphia time when the Dream Team began dismantling the host squad, but it was 10:30 at night in Spain. The late, late show at the Palau d'Esports arena.

Don't get the idea that these guys agreed to an especially early wake-up call, but this morning's workout will be the first since their opening victory over Angola.

Whatever Johnson saw that led him to believe the team needed an additional workout wasn't evident in the box score, other than Michael Jordan shooting 5-for-16 and finishing with 11 points. The Dream Team hammered Spain on the glass, 45–25, and committed just nine turnovers.

Most of the players felt a practice was necessary.

"One player was adamant against it," said Jordan, refusing to identify the player.

Despite an evening in which the Dream Team rang up the third-highest total in U.S. Olympic history and matched a U.S. record with its fifth consecutive performance of 100 points or more, some felt a practice was in order.

"I asked for it," Johnson said after testing his healing right knee during the first 9 minutes and 8 seconds of the second half. He failed to score.

Johnson had sat out the previous two games with a pulled muscle behind his knee. The team's other point guard, John Stockton, who had missed the first four games while recovering from a broken bone in his right leg, played 6:24.

"I said it in front of them," Johnson said. "I don't hold anything back. We're there, but not quite. We're missing balls we should catch and (missing) layups we should make.

"We're here to win the gold. . . . I'm not going to let us slip. My job is to make sure we're ready. When we practice and practice hard, we're ready for anybody."

But even Johnson isn't always ready for Charles Barkley's antics. Barkley drew a foul with 3:53 left, and drew whistles—the European version of boos—when he stepped across prone Spanish player Enrique Andreu and dropped the ball next to him.

For the record, when the game ended, Barkley left the court with his arm draped around Andreu.

"Charles is Charles," Johnson said. "There's nothing you can do about it. He's going to make his statements and speak his mind, do what he wants to do.

"Of course, what he does (reflects) on us. People look at him and think, 'They're all like that.' There's nothing you can do but hope he doesn't go overboard."

Barkley scored 20 points and mixed in six rebounds, four assists and a spectacular over-the-head assist to a trailing Scottie Pippen for a one-handed slam.

Afterward, Barkley didn't appear interested in being as entertaining as he has been since the first game, and grumbled about having to practice.

The whistling?

"I've been whistled at and booed by better teams in better places," he said.

Barkley was asked about a banner in Spanish that, loosely translated, read, 'Go Spain, They Are Common, They Are Human.'

"The person that wrote that," Barkley said, "didn't graduate from high school."

What the Dream Team seemed to want, though, was a workout for the common good.

"Our intensity level was down a bit," Jordan said. "We've played a lot of games that are basically meaningless. Now the games begin.

"It's been like playing an 82-game season to get ready for the playoffs. Now we've positioned ourselves for the playoffs and it's time to go."

WILL BARKLEY LISTEN, OR PLAY UGLY AMERICAN ROLE?

Philadelphia Daily News
July 27, 1992

BADALONA, SPAIN—CHARLES BARKLEY, who insists on portraying himself as the Ugly American, has done it again. In his first game at the Olympics. For a reason that seemed perfectly clear to him, but to no one else.

Angola, the African nation that absorbed a 116–48 beating yesterday against the United States in the opening game for both teams, didn't like it. Barkley's teammates didn't like it, and told him so. The people in the Palau d'Esports didn't like it, either.

The concept of the Ugly American just got a little uglier.

This was a game in which the Angolans never had a chance, not even if they had played six against four, or even seven against three. The Dream Team almost effortlessly unfurled runs of 31–0 and 46–1 in the first half and left their opponent without an assist for the first 33 minutes.

So why, with 7:39 left in the first half, did Barkley insist on drilling heretofore unknown Herlander Coimbra? Why did he shove David Dias, another Angolan? Why, on a second-half fast-break, did he insist on trying to flip the ball off the glass to set up a failed attempt at a just-for-the-hell-of-it dunk?

Barkley, predictably, wondered why anyone even would ask. He placed the questions in the same category as those about why the NBA players were not living in the athletes' village, and why they even were participating in the Olympics in the first place.

The elbow to Coimbra's sternum?

"He hit me [earlier], I hit him," Barkley said. "You guys don't understand that. It's a ghetto thing."

Whatever ghetto Barkley was talking about is likely to pale in comparison to the troubles the Angolans have seen. Their country has been ripped apart by a long-standing civil war that was settled with a cease-fire a year ago. They rebuild one painful day at a time. Their players work part-time, or go to school, or both. They scrimped and saved just to make it to the Olympics.

"Somebody hits me, I'm going to hit him back," Barkley repeated. "You [media] guys bitch and complain. If we lose the gold medal, you'll bitch and complain. You never complained about Steffi Graf and Jim Courier [competing in the Olympics as tennis professionals], so quit complaining about us.

"I don't understand why we're taking heat. Typical Americans. If they don't like it, turn the bleeping television off. . . . Magic [Johnson] and

Michael [Jordan] shouldn't stay with the other athletes, that's just the way it is."

The Dream Teamers appreciated Barkley's performance, which included team-highs of 24 points (10-for-13 shooting) and six rebounds. They enjoy the entertainment value of his strident one-liners. They laugh with him, not at him. But they don't want to see him cross the line into unnecessary mayhem. They don't want to lose whatever good graces they still have left.

Is Barkley listening? Does he want to listen? Will it matter?

"There wasn't a need [for the elbow]," Jordan said. "I think it sends a mixed message. We were dominating. It wasn't needed; it's not going to help."

Forward Karl Malone also voiced his displeasure.

"We're not here to baby-sit Charles," Malone said. "We just need to go out and play and not rub things in people's faces. I don't think we need to be degrading people."

Jordan and several teammates tried to counsel Barkley afterward, to let him know they needed his bark and bite, but not his spite.

"I think he took it that he did something wrong, that he could get thrown out," Jordan said. "If Charles quits doing what he does, we'll get cheers instead of whistles [the European version of boos].

"Charles is his own person. You can try and calm him down, but he's [still] his own person. We all have spoken to Charles. Charles knows his limits. He's going to take [his behavior] to a point and not exceed it. He's not a crazy individual."

BIRD STEALS SHOW

Philadelphia Daily News
July 30, 1992

BADALONA, SPAIN—THIS WAS A POSTCARD from the past, a reminder of the purity Larry Bird brought to basketball.

This was Bird fending off continuing problems with his lower back to offer a 21-minute glimpse of what he once was.

This was Bird knocking down seven of 11 shots (4-for-4 from two-point range, 3-for-7 from beyond the three-point arc) and scoring a team-high 19 points in the Dream Team's 111–68 blowout of Germany, a win that raised its Olympic record to 3–0 before tomorrow night's game against Brazil.

This was a taste of Larry Legend. Maybe we will be permitted more tastes with Boston in the NBA next season, maybe we won't, but if Bird has decided on whether he will play, he won't say. If he's even leaning toward one decision, he won't say.

"The way I play here does not affect anything," he said. "We're just trying to win the gold medal.

"Every day, I feel better and better, but I still can't sit for long periods of time . . . (Last night), I felt the best I've felt."

There was the soft, feathery shot, the one that almost floats into the basket.

There was the seemingly effortless three-point range.

There was the vision of the floor that only a special few have ever had, an ability both learned and instinctive to always know where the other nine players on the court are and what they're doing.

This was Bird, the 6-9 forward, taking his game to the perimeter and lofting shots that land like knives in a defense's heart. This was Bird, at 35, still seeing seams where others see only roadblocks.

"He's talking about retirement," Dream Team coach Chuck Daly said. "I don't know."

A vague Bird rumor somehow came floating out of the baseball venue, which Bird visited Tuesday night to watch the United States beat Italy. Did Bird tell a U.S. baseball player he was going home?

"Everybody was talking, there were people throwing questions at me in English and Spanish. There were 10 people asking for autographs at a time," Bird said. "It was total chaos.

"You guys can write whatever you want. I'm going to be here 'til the end of the gold-medal round and go home with the gold medal . . .

"I'm (on the team) for one reason, to shoot the ball, make the outside shot. This is really the first time I've faced a zone. I wanted to get on a roll, because if Chris (Mullin) is on one side and I'm on the other, no one can stop us."

The Dream Team, as it has all through the Tournament of the Americas in Portland and the Olympics so far, did whatever it wanted last night. Play-by-play? Hansi Gnad, a 1987 draft choice of the the 76ers, scored the game's first two points, the Dream Team scored 16 of the next 17. Case quickly closed.

Whether there was any historic value—Bird's final days?—is a question still unanswered.

"He looked like the old Larry Bird to me," said the Dream Team's Clyde Drexler. "He was making big shots, running well. We've seen it in spots, but tonight even Larry was blushing. He knew he was 'on.'

"This is just my opinion; from a competitor's perspective, he looks as if he's coming back (rather than retiring). I think he's coming back, but that's just me. He loves the game, you can see that. But I think his health will answer the question. I haven't asked him.

"I think we saw a healthy Bird in this game, the way he was contributing. But he's capable of contributing even if he's not 100 percent. When we see it, we get as excited as the fans."

BARKLEY ALMOST AT PEAK OF PERFECTION

Philadelphia Daily News
August 1, 1992

BADALONA, SPAIN—PEAK?

"What does peak mean?" Charles Barkley wanted to know after the United States basketball team beat Brazil last night, 127–83.

Peak?

"We just play hard for 40 minutes," Barkley said, shrugging. "I don't know what the perfect game is."

Here's a thought: If Barkley wasn't perfect last night, he was breathlessly close.

A 12-for-14 finish from the field.

Thirty points.

Eight rebounds.

Four steals.

A defensive blanket on Brazilian legend Oscar Schmidt.

A proud salute to the section of Palau d'Esports arena where he believed most U.S. fans were sitting.

Barkley threw his arms up in exultation toward the crowd after a three-point play that gave the Dream Team an 81–48 advantage.

"Just having fun," he said. "I'm on spring break."

Some fun. U.S. Olympic teams are now 8–0 in Olympic competition against Brazil. Last night's 44-point U.S. win was the second-highest margin of victory over Brazil ever, topped only by a 62-point decision in the 1956 Games at Melbourne, Australia.

"Playing with the (76ers) last season was like being Brazil (in this game)," Barkley said, alluding to both teams' futile efforts. "I'm happy to have USA (on my uniform)."

By winning its fourth straight preliminary game—Spain remains tomorrow night—the United States has won Pool A and faces Puerto Rico in a medal-round game Tuesday. Puerto Rico is the No. 4 team in Pool B.

"What ticks me off the most is, it's not that these other teams are bad, this is just a great, great, great team," Barkley said. "Our team's just awesome in every aspect . . .

"There's not an adjective you can use (to describe us). I get amazed playing and watching. People said we couldn't play together. People said we couldn't play against a zone. We solved that problem. People said we had too many egos. We solved that problem."

With Magic Johnson (strained muscle behind his right knee) and John Stockton (fracture of the right fibula) unavailable, U.S. coach Chuck Daly started Barkley, Clyde Drexler and David Robinson up front and—surprise, surprise—assigned Barkley to Schmidt.

Check Schmidt's line. With Barkley and Scottie Pippen sharing the job, Schmidt struggled through a 2-for-10 first half. He finished with 24 points, shooting 8-for-25 from the field, but none that mattered competitively.

"They (the Brazilian team) said that they were going to be our worst nightmare, and that made us mad," Barkley said, referring to comments made during the Tournament of the Americas at Portland in June.

Or maybe the Brazilians were misunderstood. That's certainly a concept with which Barkley should be able to identify.

"I was very understood," said Brazilian guard Marcel de Souza, the source of the supposedly grievous comment. "I also said a lot of good things about them."

It didn't matter what de Souza originally said. It mattered that the Dream Team seized it as one more motivational force.

"We certainly remembered them saying we played too much golf and weren't taking (the qualifying tournament) seriously," Pippen said. "We're taking it seriously enough to beat teams by 50 points."

Can the Brazilians, or any country, catch up? And if so, how many years will it take?

"A hundred, a lifetime, never," Pippen said. "We can still pick 10 more (NBA) teams to come over here and do this."

They can pick all the teams they want, but can they pick a uniform to wear on the medal awards stand?

Michael Jordan, a Nike client, first said he wouldn't wear the official uniform supplied by Reebok, a direct competitor of Nike. Then he hedged. Then Nike officials said they were suggesting that their clients (six on the U.S. roster) wear the Reebok uniform. Then USA Basketball president Dave Gavitt said he is trying to get things straightened out.

"The whole situation is ridiculous, personally," said Barkley, a Nike guy. "We came to represent the U.S., that's all. I blame Nike. I blame Reebok, it's all ridiculous . . .

"It's been blown out of proportion. The Olympics are about sport, not what column I'm writing for USA Today, not what I'm going to wear. We're here to prove we're far and away the best team.

"We're the only ones having fun. Everybody else is bitching."

Schmidt seemed to grasp that as well as anyone.

"They play at a different velocity," Schmidt said. "They play at 33 (RPM); we play at 45."

THEY REFUSE TO JUST DO IT

Philadelphia Daily News
July 30, 1992

BADALONA, SPAIN—WILL MICHAEL JORDAN acquiesce to the Olympic dress code? Will he challenge the system when it's time to accept the gold medal in basketball? Will he transform the award ceremony into a platform of controversy?

Questions, questions, questions. Will Jordan, who earns an estimated $20 million through his six-year contract with Nike, wear the official Olympic warm-up suit, may[be] (gulp) Reebok? Will any of the other five Dream Teamers (Charles Barkley, David Robinson, Chris Mullin, Scottie Pippen and John Stockton) under contract to Nike?

They will if they want to be presented with their medals, USA press chief Mike Moran said.

"This is a U.S. Olympic Committee rule," Moran said. "Every athlete who wins a medal wears (the Reebok suit) at the ceremony. If an athlete doesn't wear it, he won't go on the medal stand."

Medal winners wore a warm-up suit designed by Levi Strauss at the 1984 and 1988 Olympiads. Reebok earned the corporate contract this time with a higher bid. The USOC's deal with Reebok is believed to be worth some $4 million. It calls for all medal winners to wear that company's warm-up suit when they step on the award stand.

"Would (wearing the suit) endanger a contract (with another company)?" Moran said. "That's beyond belief.

"With the money from this contract (and other sponsors), 1,500 athletes get supportive checks from the USOC, $75 million in grants go to our governing bodies. The Reebok money makes it possible for (Olympic figure skater) Kristi Yamaguchi to pay for coaching, for ice time. It pays for bullets for the modern pentathlon team.

"An athlete who refuses is snubbing his nose at the rest of the athletes . . . No athlete ever has (refused)."

But these athletes very definitely are thinking about it.

"I might wear it and put something over (the Reebok logo)," Barkley said yesterday, after the U.S. basketball team's 111–68 victory over Germany. "It's the games that are important, not stuff like that.

"As far as Michael, I don't think anybody who ever won a gold medal was earning $20 million from Nike."

And if the players can't step on to the award platform without wearing Reebok's apparel?

"We'll get back to the U.S. a lot quicker," Barkley said. "They can ship my medal to Bala Cynwyd, by way of Phoenix. If Reebok or whoever gets upset by four or five (medal winners) out of 600, that's a joke to even discuss . . . I think they should leave (the logo) off our (award ceremony) uniforms. I don't think people in Des Moines are going to care."

Karl Malone cares. Patrick Ewing cares. Malone, under contract to LA Gear, and Ewing, who wears his own brand of shoe, also both said they will not wear the Reebok uniform.

This is bigger than Nike vs. Reebok.

Jordan said he hasn't made a decision, but in the July 22 issue of Sports Illustrated he is quoted as saying, "there is no way in the world I am wearing a suit made by Reebok."

"We've got to win the gold medal first, I'll make the decision then," he said last night after delivering a game-high 12 assists plus 15 points and four steals as the starting point guard in place of the injured Magic Johnson.

"I signed the (standard USOC agreement) everyone has to sign. But once you win the gold, they can't take it away from you. A gold is a gold. I've been on the stand (in 1984). I know what it means.

". . . I signed, but I X'd out (rule) No. 14 (which presumably deals with the awards ceremony uniform). I agree, except for rule No. 14. I didn't get it (returned) . . . No one has ever come to me personally and said, 'You better have Reebok on.' I haven't gone to anyone and said I'm not going to wear it. If everyone wants to wear Reebok, that's their decision.

"Some want to, some don't. I'm probably the head honcho in not (wanting to). My contract with Nike is more lucrative than my contract with Reebok, by far. (He has no contract with Reebok.)

"It's like asking you to leave your dad. I won't do that."

Is that a no?

LITHUANIA GETS WHAT IT EXPECTED

Philadelphia Daily News
August 7, 1992

BADALONA, SPAIN—LITHUANIA MOVED the basketball frantically. Not crisply. Not with a lot of purpose. Just frantically.

The Lithuanians tried desperately to get somebody open. Tried to set enough screens to get somebody a clear shot.

None of it worked. In Badalona Dreamland, against the United States, against the Dream Team, it just doesn't.

Not that this came as any great shock to the Lithuanians. In a 127–76 loss to the Dream Team, they got just about what they expected, a lopsided defeat and a berth against the Unified Team in tomorrow's bronze-medal game.

"This means a medal to these guys," said Donn Nelson, the Golden State Warriors assistant who is assisting the Lithuanians. "It doesn't matter what medal. To them, they're all gold."

Lithuania's perception of gold has to do with its culture, its dramatic separation from the Soviet Union, its breathtaking desire to put together a competitive team on short notice. The Dream Team, on the other hand, is going for the Olympic gold against Croatia tomorrow night.

"I'm so glad we're down to one game," said Charles Barkley, who, with 13 points, was one of nine Dream Teamers in double figures. "I'm counting the seconds and the hours.

"I miss America. I miss crime and murder. I miss Philadelphia. There hasn't been a brutal stabbing or anything here the last 24 hours. I've missed it."

But Barkley wasn't in so much of a hurry that he hadn't noticed the U.S. women's team's stunning Wednesday semifinal loss to the Unified Team.

"That lets you know right there how really big a deal it is for these teams to beat someone from the U.S.," Barkley said. "It was a wake-up call for us. We talked about it (Wednesday), we talked about it (yesterday)."

As capable as the Dream Teamers have been on the court, they have been almost more adept at finding ways to motivate themselves for opponents over which they already have an almost unimaginable advantage.

Last night, they focused on Lithuanian guard Sarunas Marciulionis (6-for-17, 20 points, seven turnovers) and 7-3 center Arvidas Sabonis (4-for-17, 11 points). Collectively, the Lithuanians shot 26-for-76 (34.2 percent).

"They pushed me away like I was there," said Lithuania's Arturas Karnishovas, the Seton Hall forward. "My coach said, 'You are like a girl.' I say to him, 'There are a lot of bigger guys than me they push around in the NBA.'"

Sorry, Magic Johnson said, The Dream Dream Team just needed the competition. Don't mention that, though, to Scottie Pippen, who injured his right hand in the first half and was taken for X-rays after the game (the results were not immediately available). And definitely don't mention it to assistant coach Lenny Wilkens, who suffered an Achilles' tendon injury in a pickup game against some of the security people who have squired around the U.S. traveling party.

"They're a dangerous team, so we had to pick up our intensity, play better defense," said Johnson, who had 14 points and eight assists. "And offensively, we played very well."

There was Michael Jordan—a disturbing 1-for-11 in Tuesday night's quarterfinal victory over Puerto Rico—knocking down nine of 18 shots and scoring a game-high 21 points. There was Karl Malone rumbling inside for 18, David Robinson, celebrating his birthday with 13 and Patrick Ewing, Clyde Drexler, Larry Bird and Chris Mullin, contributing 10 each.

"I told Michael that we didn't need him to be Michael Jordan (last night), we needed him to be Air Jordan," Johnson said. "Now, we have one game left and we'll be just where we want to be.

". . . Now we have to play even better. We can't worry about the last game. I don't predict scores. We're just trying to win. It doesn't matter if you win by 50 or by one."

Or by 51, as they did last night. The only thing missing was "Sweet Georgia Brown." In the first half, the Dream Team seemed modestly ahead at 14–8, then ripped off 20 straight points. Whatever game plan the Lithuanians might have had became a moot point. The Dreamers were wailing.

"If they stop one guy, they can't stop the next guy," Bird said. "We have the ability to get (the ball) off the boards, get it up (the court) quick, play defense when we have to. It's pretty amazing. We can go 5, 10 minutes and we're up 20."

Still, the Dream Team had a remarkable handle on the motivational factor. Last night, Bird said the players were "scared" about the game. Scared?

"This was a game we were a little leery about," Bird said. "We knew the Lithuanians were capable of scoring, (so) we didn't take them lightly."

The Lithuanians, showing perfect perspective, took the game not as a challenge but as a prelude to the bronze-medal game.

"The bronze here means twice as much as the gold in 1988 (when four members of the current Lithuanian team and four members of the Unified Team were playing for the champion Soviet Union)," Nelson said.

"In '88, these players had no other choice. Now they're playing for a cause they believe in. Less than a year ago, they wouldn't have guessed they'd even have a team. To compete against NBA players, to share a photograph (with them) afterward is a success in itself. It's one of the fruits of Lithuanian freedom."

CHAPTER 9

. . . . . .

IVERSON AND THE 2001 FINALS RUN

Introduction by Allen Iverson

I thought he was fair. I thought he was fair and he was thankful and he was credible of me when I deserved it. Looking back on it and being so young, I didn't understand it that way then because I thought Phil was my friend, and he was but he had a job to do. Get what I'm saying? That's where I didn't understand it, and I didn't get it until I got older. I realized somebody can care about you, but doing their job is doing their job. They've got to do their job. It was like one of the earth-moving moments of my life when he passed because it bothered me as far as all the spats that we had. And I really loved him. That's why he was able to hurt me because I thought that he cared about me. That was a problem that I had to deal with after his passing. I'd rather have had a conversation with him to tell him how much I really loved him. Outside of the business of what we're doing, I wanted to tell him I loved him.

He was with me every day. Always with me. And we laughed together. And we were mad at each other at times. It always was like that. If he wrote something that pissed me off, I flipped out. We were always cool with each other. The only reason that I flipped out is because I couldn't believe he would say anything negative about me. He was being a professional, but I was too young to understand. That's why I was mad. He was just doing his job. That's all. I was so much of a hothead that when I felt like somebody did me wrong, I didn't want to talk. And his whole thing was, he was doing his job and reporting what he had to report, what was going on. I didn't understand that because I was so young and didn't understand he had a job to do. It wasn't a friendship. He had to report what he had to report. I had to play. Because I knew I was wrong with how I felt. Maybe some of the things he said were malicious and shouldn't have been said, but whatever . . . him speaking on what needed to be spoken on during the times that were going on, I know now that he was supposed to do that. But I just didn't like it because I thought he was my guy. I didn't understand it.

I just liked him. I just liked the guy. I don't remember the actual fallout the first time. I always just liked him. I always liked him. I always liked him. When he would say, "Can I get a minute of your time?" I'd tell him, "I'm finished doing the interviews, Phil, but I like you so much that I'll stay this long." My family was waiting on me, but I would give him the feature. I would give him what he wanted because I liked him. I don't know what it was. You knew him. You knew what type of guy he was. People would just gravitate to him because he was that type of guy. I would just do what he wanted. Our fallout was because I liked him and I thought he said something against me that I didn't like. In hindsight and in the aftermath of all of this, he was right at the time. Get what I'm saying?

It might have been the smallest thing. That's why I don't even remember the little spats. It might have been the smallest thing . . . Not you. All the other media people that's in the city, yeah, maybe them. But not you. That's why I don't even remember it because it hurt so bad and it could have been the smallest thing in the world.

When I come here, every time I come here, I think of him. I know that he would be proud of my accomplishments, of me being a Hall of Famer. I know he would say, "I'm proud of you." I know he would say that to me. He would have been there. He would have been there. He would have been there. He would have been there. He would have been there. He would have been there. He would have been there. I know it. I know he would have been there. And he would have been proud. I know it. I know it. I know he's sitting up there with God and he's sending me more blessings and he's being there for me up there. I know it. He was great. He was great. In his field, he was A1. In his field, he was the best, A1. I can never take that from him. I would never try to take that from him. No way in hell. No way. No way. No way. I loved the man.

ALLEN IVERSON *was an 11-time NBA All-Star who led the Sixers to the Finals in 2000–2001 before falling to the Los Angeles Lakers in five games. Iverson was named Rookie of the Year in 1996–1997 and the 2000–2001 Most Valuable Player of the league. Iverson was recently inducted into the Naismith Memorial Basketball Hall of Fame. Iverson spent 12 seasons with the Sixers with stops in Denver, Detroit, and Memphis. He scored more than 24,000 points in his illustrious career.*

. . . . . .

SWEEP THIS!

Philadelphia Daily News
June 7, 2001

LOS ANGELES—THE 76ERS PROBABLY don't see the enormity of it all. They never have.

They know themselves as no one else does. Only they know what's really left in their tank. Only they know how much of what's on the drawing board they truly can accomplish.

This was a performance that came from deep inside a reservoir only they believe they have. They did not come to die. They came to do what they do best, to sneer in the face of long odds, to smirk at their disbelievers.

They did exactly that last night, shocking the defending champion Los Angeles Lakers in overtime, 107–101, in the opener of the best-of-seven NBA Finals, snapping LA's 19-game win streak. They did it with Allen Iverson scoring 48 points in 52 of a possible 53 minutes, coming within shouting distance of the 51 scored against the Lakers by Golden State's Sleepy Floyd in 1987, the most ever scored against LA in the postseason.

Iverson did it on 18-for-41 shooting from the floor.

"We wanted him to have to take 40 shots to get 40 points—he did it anyway," said Lakers coach Phil Jackson.

So many people said it couldn't be done, that the Sixers—the so-called junior varsity from the terribly overmatched East—could not possibly have the answers to turn back the seemingly immovable Lakers.

But the Sixers, three days removed from a draining Game 7 victory over Milwaukee that secured the Eastern title, had the Lakers literally tied in knots. And, as always, Iverson was in the eye of the storm, raining in 41 in regulation, lobbing in perimeter jumpers, raging to the basket despite the presence of the Lakers' immense Shaquille O'Neal.

"We've got heart," Iverson said. "We're going to play with that first, play with the talent second."

After the game, it was learned that Sixers guard Aaron McKie had suffered a chip fracture in his right ankle.

"He'll play," said general manager Billy King.

So, what else is new?

Iverson scored 38 of his points in the first 29 minutes, then added just three through regulation. O'Neal had the same 41 points at that stage. No surprise, then, that the score was 94–94 as they careened into overtime.

Amazingly, the Sixers had their chances to win before the start of the five-minute extra period. Even at 94–94, the Lakers' Kobe Bryant missed a shot and Robert Horry missed a follow-up.

The Sixers' Eric Snow pulled down the rebound at 1:12. When Iverson missed, the Sixers' Aaron McKie corralled the offensive rebound, setting the stage for a drive by Snow. When O'Neal went for the block, the Sixers' Dikembe Mutombo was able to snatch the rebound and draw a foul from Horry. But Mutombo missed two free throws.

There was yet another chance coming their way. Bryant turned the ball over as he tried to weave through traffic with 18.9 seconds remaining.

But Lakers backcourt sub Tyronn Lue relentlessly shadowed Iverson, forcing Snow to throw up an off-balance runner as the fourth quarter ended.

The Lakers scored the first five points of overtime, but the Sixers rallied. Iverson nailed a three with 1:19 left to put them ahead, 101–99, then scored from the corner for a 103–99 lead with 48.2 seconds left. After Bryant scored, Snow locked it up with a runner at 10.5 seconds.

So much for all the predictions of a Lakers sweep.

"They're a great team," Sixers coach Larry Brown said of the Lakers. "Shaquille O'Neal is as good as it gets. So many guys came off and contributed [for them]. They should be the favorite. They are the best team. I think we recognize that. The biggest thing about us is, we're just going to try and compete.

"Nobody's crazy picking those guys. They've got a coach who has won championships every season he's decided to coach. They have two of the best players in our game, the most dominant player. They should be the favorite. Our guys just try hard. This is unexpected, but it's kind of neat."

More than a foot shorter and roughly half the weight of the 7-1, 330-pound O'Neal, Iverson went where no one his size should be able to go in the land of the giants. When Jackson was asked whether he had seen anything about Iverson in the videotapes of previous games, he said, "Things I don't want to talk about."

"Basically that he's got the ability to get off shots in a league where athletes basically pride themselves on how many shots they can get off in a ballgame, because they can," Jackson said, expanding on his response. "Here's a young guy that's as slight or small as almost anybody we've had in this league . . . and he's not only able to get off shots but lead the league in scoring. How he does it, I'm still in a quandary about."

There were other quandaries, too. Bryant also went 52 minutes, but had 15 points on 7-for-22 shooting. Derek Fisher, the Lakers' starting point guard who had emerged as a perimeter force, was 0-for-4 and scoreless.

In the end, the Lakers lost for the first time since April 1. They had won their final eight games of the regular season and came into the Finals 11–0 in the postseason.

"No one really gave us a chance," Snow said. "Even with this win, no one has given us a chance. But we believe in ourselves, and we have to keep doing what we've been doing and just play hard."

Brown had his own dilemma. He could plan and scheme, but the Sixers could not contain O'Neal, the self-proclaimed most-dominant player in the league. Shaq erupted for 18 points in the third quarter, doing enough damage around the basket to see Sixers backup center Matt Geiger foul out in 13 minutes and Mutombo try and survive with five fouls midway through the fourth quarter.

Perhaps the 10 days off the Lakers had between sweeping San Antonio and opening the best-of-seven Finals were a factor. But if they needed time to shake off the rust, they eventually began rolling as—what else?—a pure Shaq Diesel. Down 73–58 against the stunning work of the Sixers, they scored 19 of the final 25 points of the third quarter.

The Lakers trailed only 79–77 as the fourth period opened, almost as if they suddenly remembered they were playing not only for the championship but for a place in history. Having swept through the first three series of the postseason, they were attempting to become the first team to go through undefeated. At the same time, the Sixers seemed to be wondering why a place in history couldn't be for them?

"Whatever they have to give me is enough," Brown said. "I know they'll try."

The Sixers—the ultimate underdogs—were picked by two Los Angeles newspapers to be swept out of the series.

"I just thought it was Middle Tennessee vs. North Carolina, one of those games,"

Brown said, smiling. "I was scared to death."

Now, he said, "We're one up, the sweep's not going to happen."

YOTOMBO!

Philadelphia Daily News
February 23, 2001

DIKEMBE MUTOMBO KNEW HE'D probably be traded. The soon-to-be-former Atlanta Hawk even joked about it with the 76ers' Larry Brown, who coached Mutombo's victorious East team in the NBA All-Star Game in Washington 12 days ago.

"He told me he wanted a warm climate," a smiling Brown recalled as snow fell yesterday outside the First Union Center.

What remains to be seen is how toasty a reception the 7-2 Mutombo receives in the same building when he makes his first home appearance in a Sixers uniform Monday against Milwaukee.

By then the Sixers, whose 41–14 record is the best in the NBA, will have played two road games, tonight against Detroit and tomorrow against Charlotte. Those should start to provide an indication whether their bold acquisition of Mutombo, a three-time NBA Defensive Player of the Year, has helped advance their championship dreams or disrupted what has been a marvelous team chemistry.

Continuing a tradition of trades that have upgraded an also-ran into a contender, Brown and Sixers general manager Billy King pulled the trigger on a blockbuster, six-player deal. In addition to Mutombo, the Sixers received third-year forward Roshown McLeod. The Hawks got injured All-Star center Theo Ratliff and forward Toni Kukoc, who earned three championship rings with the Chicago Bulls, as well as seldom-used center Nazr Mohammed and rookie guard Pepe Sanchez.

"I am going to Philadelphia to play with a great player in Allen Iverson, a scoring machine who plays with tremendous energy, and the opportunity to win a championship is certainly there," Mutombo said.

David Falk, Mutombo's agent, said a lot more.

"This is an extremely bold move by Billy King, one of the rising young executives in the league," Falk said. "In an era in which there are very few trades, he and the Sixers have been very aggressive, making a move to go for it all. They already had one of the top three or four offensive performers in Allen Iverson, and now—at least to me—they have the single-best defender and shot-blocker. This really represents a chance to go for it."

Mutombo can become a free agent July 1, but Falk said that was not his client's focus at this point.

"Dikembe's goal was to get to a championship-caliber team in the East, and he's done that," Falk said. "Once he gets acclimated, there's no reason to expect they couldn't come to a deal. But right now, he's focusing on playing. He's only been to the playoffs in five of his 10 years. I'm biased, but I believe he's the best player in the league for what he does."

And if people think this represents a risky move for the Sixers, Falk totally disagrees.

"Not risky," he said. "Bold."

While the general reaction around the league is that the Sixers, who beat out New York, Dallas, Portland and Phoenix for Mutombo's services, took a major step toward the franchise's first NBA title since 1983, local fans—and possibly some of Mutombo's new teammates—might need convincing. Ratliff, who could be out another four to six weeks while recovering from wrist surgery, was rightly hailed as a major contributor to the team's startling rise this season.

"Everybody's talking about not trying to fix something that's going in the right direction," Brown said of the trade, which was consummated less than two days after the Sixers' interest in Mutombo became public. "But when I saw Tyrone Hill sprain his ankle [Wednesday's against Vancouver], the only thing I could think of is that you can't take anything for granted in this league.

"I think the defining moment for us was when we realized we were going to be without Theo for 16, 20 games, or who knows how long?

"This team has been racked with injuries. There's no lock we're getting out of the East. If Tyrone is hurt, I don't know where we'd go. But what I do know is that while Theo is healing, we'll have Mutombo out there, and he might give us a chance to secure home court [advantage throughout the playoffs], which gives us the best chance to move on.

"This is a magical year, in my mind. Pat [Croce, the team president] talks about it all the time. To think about what this team has been able to accomplish, with all the adversity it's been through, has been mind-boggling to me."

Brown said several key players were consulted, and that a single dissenting opinion might have prompted him to kill the trade. But while no one on the team objected, the mood seemed to be more of stunned acceptance than jubilation.

"When something like this happens, a lot of stuff goes through your head," said guard Allen Iverson, the NBA's leading scorer. "Last summer, my future was uncertain here. I found out the hard way that this is a business.

"I feel like coach is going to get a lot of flak over it. Maybe even myself, for some reason. But I have to stick with him. I feel that he did this to better our team. That's what he's been doing since he came to Philadelphia.

"It's rough, but we've got to move on. I told [Brown and King], 'I don't have any problem with us keeping our team as it was, but if anything would make our team better, that's on you. Y'all call the shots.'"

Brown and King have furiously tinkered with the roster since they came to the Sixers in 1997. In their first season together, they sent Jerry Stackhouse, Eric Montross and a second-round draft choice to Detroit for Ratliff, Aaron McKie and a first-round draft choice. That trade helped a team that had been 22–60 improve to 31–51.

The Sixers were 28–22 in the lockout-shortened 1998–99 season, during which Tim Thomas and Scott Williams were swapped to Milwaukee for Hill and Jerald Honeycutt. Then, last season, the Sixers improved to 49–33 in part because of the acquisition of Kukoc as part of a three-team deal in which disgruntled second-year guard Larry Hughes and Billy Owens were sent to Golden State.

Not all of those trades initially were met with enthusiasm in the Sixers' locker room, Iverson noted.

"I was friends with Larry Hughes, Tim Thomas, Vernon Maxwell, Derrick Coleman, Doug Overton. . . . guys I felt I wanted to finish my career with because I was tight with them," Iverson said.

Saying goodbye to players who are your friends, guard Eric Snow said, always is the hardest part of any trade.

"From a personal standpoint, this hurts," Snow said. "Theo and I are very close. But we talk about this all the time. We understand you can be gone at any time."

Snow said he had been taught that lesson when he was a young player with Seattle.

"When a team feels a need to make a change, if they feel a need to get better and it's at your expense, then you're gone," Snow said. "That's how it is. It's unfortunate."

Not even the 41–14 record was enough to stand in the way of the move.

"I guess the decision they had to make is that the regular season doesn't win you games in the playoffs," Snow said. "I guess they thought it was our best opportunity to win in the playoffs. Mutombo is a great center, a great defender. Obviously, he's a dominant force in this league, and has been for quite some time. He still has to come in and fit in, and that's still a question mark."

In the 34-year-old Mutombo, the Sixers get the sort of "character" guy Brown loves, as well as possibly the most intimidating defensive presence in the league. Mutombo leads the NBA in rebounding, with 14.1 per game, and has blocked an astounding 2,571 shots in 10 seasons.

"Anybody who saw the All-Star Game, as great as Allen was, as great as Stephon Marbury was, Mutombo got 22 rebounds in 27 minutes against the best players in the world," Brown said. "He completely changed the complexion of the game."

Iverson, who, like Mutombo, played collegiately at Georgetown, said he expected more of the same from someone for whom he always has had the highest respect.

"I'd be lying if I said this guy couldn't help us win a championship," Iverson said. "I mean, he's a rebounder, he's an intimidator. He can change a game by himself. I think he'll come here and fit right in.

"My feeling is, when he heard about the opportunity to play for us, he saw a team that really has a shot, even without him—and a much better shot with him."

Snow felt the same way.

"I hope you do it to make the team better," he said. "That's why I don't think trades were made in the summer, because they didn't think it would make the team better.

"I would hope that, if you change the team with the best record, that's the outcome."

—Daily News sportswriter Bernard Fernandez contributed to this report.

54! IVERSON EXPLODES, SERIES TIED

Philadelphia Daily News
May 10, 2001

BY THE END of the torturous evening, the kid should have been reduced to a puddle. If he was 5-11, 165 pounds at the start, he should have been no more than maybe 5-8, 140 at the finish. He should have been drained of virtually everything inside him, taking fluids intravenously.

But this was Allen Iverson raw, uncut, uncensored. This was a rap that rocked the 20,870 fans in the frenzied First Union Center last night, that left the Toronto Raptors back on their heels. This was Iverson as a pure energy form, a wisp of electricity careening through the arena, leaving breathtaking plays in his wake. This was Iverson setting a 76ers playoff record with 54 points, unfurling a performance for the ages.

This was Iverson flashing past the record 50 points set by Billy Cunningham on April 1, 1970, against Milwaukee in the NBA's Eastern semifinals. This was Iverson smoking the Raptors with 19 straight points in the fourth quarter en route to a 97–92 victory that evened this semifinal series at 1–1 and set the stage for Games 3 and 4 Friday night and Sunday afternoon in Toronto.

"The fourth quarter, he was just phenomenal," Sixers coach Larry Brown said. "He didn't settle for shots, he took it to the goal. His last field goal was a 12-footer; I commented that that's got to be his mind-set. And he topped it off by deflecting the last inbounds pass."

Who knows where Iverson's flood of energy comes from? His heart? His mind? His fierce determination?

"Life," Iverson said, identifying the source after hitting an incredible 21 of 39 shots from the floor, three of his five three-point attempts and all nine of his free throws in 47 minutes. "Going through the things I've been through, trying to get to this point.

"Poverty. Everything. I feel like God gave me an opportunity to do something positive with my life. A lot of guys from my neighborhood would love to be here. Not to score 54 points, but just to be here, on the bench, part of it. On the injured list.

"People always talk about struggling in basketball. There's no struggling in basketball; there's a lot worse. People go through worse things in life every day. To go 0-for-something? I cherish life a little bit more than that."

The Sixers fell behind by 17 points in their Game 1 loss and didn't wake up until the fourth quarter. Too late. They dropped back by 14 in the second quarter last night, then rode Iverson's magnificent wave.

Eric Snow, with 10, was the only other Sixer to reach double figures, but he went 35 gritty minutes without a turnover. Tyrone Hill swept 10 rebounds, Dikembe Mutombo contributed nine rebounds and five blocks and Jumaine Jones had nine points and five rebounds in a 4-for-4 shooting performance.

But this was pure Iverson. Two weeks from now, 100,000 people (200,000?) might tell you they were in the building. As people were filtering out of the arena, they were wondering whether they had seen anything like this since Michael Jordan.

"He's one of those rare guys," the Sixers' Aaron McKie said. "Raw talent, raw athlete. It's funny how guys always talk about how important it is to get your rest, to be ready. He can be up all day, come in and give you 40 points and be ready to play another 48 minutes.

"Some great players have come through here, but he's definitely different, in a league of his own in how he does things, how he makes things look so easy. He gets that little scoop shot up, and the big guys rarely block it. He uses his speed, he uses the mental part.

"Obviously, he's scored 50 before, but not in a playoff atmosphere like this. This is how stars are born. Some guys are stars in college, get pumped up, come into the league and people are right away passing them the torch. He took it."

Iverson was so dominant, he overshadowed a 28-point performance by the Raptors' Vince Carter that included four triples and a series of magical moves. Antonio Davis supported him with 19 points and 10 rebounds, but Dell Curry and Alvin Williams—the guys who scorched the Sixers in Game 1—were rendered ineffective by a more dedicated defense. Curry, a deadly 7-for-12 in Game 1, was 3-for-10. Williams, 6-for-9 in Game 1, dropped to 6-for-17.

"We're not going to go away," Raptors coach Lenny Wilkens said, knowing his defenders had let Iverson turn the corner and race to sweet spots too many times, but equally knowing this had been a night when Iverson had been a blur.

Sixers backup center Todd MacCulloch, said of Iverson: "I wish I could find that fountain, that source of energy, and take a drink. He's fueled by his passion. He was very upset the last two years, losing in the second round, seeing Indiana end his dream. It was like he wouldn't let that happen tonight. You could see it in him right from the beginning.

"There was one point when [backup center] Matt Geiger told him he had to keep it up, and he already had 40. He was playing as if he had 10. He took the team on his back."

Wilkens, who guided Seattle, Cleveland and Atlanta through some white-hot playoff games, took the high road when someone asked whether Iverson's performance was reminiscent of Jordan.

"Everyone ran into Jordan at that time and none of them beat him," Wilkens said. "This is a little different. If we come down here and we're 0–2, we'd be really upset and a little bit down. We didn't perform as well as we're capable, but we gave it a great effort. We got a split.

"We were right there, even though we didn't cover [Iverson] as well as we're capable; he was incredible. If our execution in a couple of situations had been a little better, who knows? We're not going to go away. We'll be back."

THEIR ANSWER

Philadelphia Daily News
May 12, 2001

TORONTO—HIS EYES WERE GLINTS of steel. In a sea of 20,436 faces in the crowd, Vince Carter saw only the rim. Not the 76ers' George Lynch, who attempted to guard him at the start. Not Aaron McKie, who was next.

Not anyone or anything but the bright orange of the iron. A circle of doom for the opponents.

The white netting below the rim? Probably never noticed. Carter was on his way to a magnificent 50-point performance that included 19-for-29 shooting and 9-for-13 from three-point range. Triples that must have seemed like layups.

To say the Toronto Raptors merely blew out the Sixers, 102–78, would be to terribly understate what happened. In a sense, Carter did to the Sixers what Allen Iverson did to Toronto with his superb 54-point effort Wednesday night in Philadelphia. But what the Raptors did to the Sixers as they took a 2–1 lead in their NBA best-of-seven second-round playoff series was much, much worse.

The Raptors left the Sixers, whether they want to accept it or not, in disarray. When the carnage that included Antonio Davis' 20 points and 14 rebounds and Chris Childs' 16 points and 10 assists was over, Sixers coach Larry Brown spoke just briefly to his team. The players then had what one termed "an extended meeting" in which Iverson, McKie, Eric Snow and Dikembe Mutombo were the primary voices.

The idea, one player said, was "to light a fire, to get in each other's butts." They were furious, not that Carter had scorched them, or that they had shot poorly (35.1 percent from the floor), but that they had been dominated and, worse, outhustled. One ramification could well be a lineup change in tomorrow afternoon's Game 4, with McKie—winner of the league's Sixth Man award—starting at point guard in Snow's place.

Snow, who had 10 points and four assists in 30 minutes, is laboring on a tender right ankle in which a screw was inserted in early January to repair a stress fracture. The current problem appears to be tendinitis in the area surrounding the original injury. He has been unable to key the defense, as he did for much of the season, or to initiate the offense as skillfully.

The ineptitude was contagious. The Sixers rarely threw the ball inside, leaving the 7-2 Mutombo with just three shots. Snow, Tyrone Hill and George Lynch were unable to make the hustle plays that have been their trademark in what, to this point, has been a proud season.

"Was I surprised [by Carter]?" Iverson said, wincing. "That's a dumb question, man.

"I expect him to come out and play. I expect him to have a good game, at home, in front of his crowd, the series tied, 1-up. He had a good game last game, and the game before that. You can't shut anybody like that down.

"If he's the type of player to turn it off and on like that, then, damn, I'm scared to see what he's going to do the next game. 'Iverson had a big game, I'm going to have a big game'? You don't approach it like that. If I scored five the last game, think he would've tried to score less than that?"

Iverson had 23 points in 45 minutes, but played uphill all night.

Carter was everywhere, contributing six rebounds, seven assists, four blocks and a steal against a single turnover in 45 minutes of a night on center stage as worthy of a place in history as Iverson's effort Wednesday. Carter set league playoff records by draining eight treys in succession and eight in the first half. He established a Raptors playoff record with 34 points in the first half and franchise and personal playoff bests.

"I think no matter how good we defended, we wouldn't have had an answer for that," Brown said. "The bottom line is, it's not going to be Allen or Vince winning the game, it's going to be the other guys who do the job the best . . . This'll change on Sunday."

Brown, who waited an uncharacteristic 20 minutes before arriving in the postgame interview area, might get a sense of whether the players believe that when they gather for practice today.

"We can't put ourselves in a hole the way we did," Hill said. They fell behind by as many as 19 points in the first half, 21 in the third quarter and 26 in the fourth.

"We're going to be all right, but we're not playing like the old Sixers, not doing the nuts and bolts things," he continued. "We've got to get our minds right. Eric is doing the best he can out there, but he can only move so much. We're used to winning with a low field goal percentage, but we're also used to stopping guys and we're not doing it."

Carter was so strong, the Raptors won with shooting guard Alvin Williams going 2-for-11 from the floor and reserve sniper Dell Curry 1-for-7. Davis' and Childs' statistics notwithstanding, this was Carter, Carter and more Carter.

"Once I hit three or four shots, the rim seemed like it was getting bigger," Carter said.

"Once my shot was falling, I started moving without the ball, trying to get my feet set. When you hit a couple, you get excited, you just want to get it up there."

But he wasn't out there to show his three-point skills or to match Iverson's previous performance.

"I just try hard every day I step on the floor just to be an all-around player," Carter said. "Not just getting to the hole and dunking. Not just passing, not just shooting, not just penetrating, but to do it all at one time . . .

"[Iverson] is a great player, and he can do it night in and night out. I'm not going to try and get in a '50' contest; I don't think I'm ready for that yet."

OH DEER! WITH IVERSON HURTING, BUCKS EVEN SERIES

Philadelphia Daily News
May 25, 2001

THE KID MIGHT FINALLY have met his match.

Not anyone in an opposing uniform. Not a defender smothering him. Not a double team designed to steal his opportunities.

Allen Iverson, who has fought all season through injuries and circumstances that would have totally stymied many players, can't play like the Most Valuable Player he is if he can't run.

And make no mistake, the 76ers' star guard could not run during last night's disturbing, 92–78 loss to the Milwaukee Bucks. For the third playoff series in a row, the Sixers have given away the home court advantage, this time waiting until Game 2 instead of doing it in the opener.

This time, it is more meaningful than ever because Games 3 and 4 of the NBA's Eastern Conference finals will be played tomorrow and Monday in Milwaukee's raucous Bradley Center. And if Sixers coach Larry Brown had his way, Iverson would not only sit out today's practice, he also would skip tomorrow's game, allowing precious healing time for the severely bruised left sacroiliac joint injured in Game 7 of the second round against Toronto.

Brown asked Iverson, who shot 5-for-26 last night, to stay home today. After meeting with reporters, Brown had an earnest conversation with Gary Moore, Iverson's personal assistant. But Brown also understood there probably were no words that would keep Iverson away from this afternoon's charter flight.

"I don't think he should've played this game," Brown said. "But I'm not going to take the opportunity away from him. He's the reason we're here. But you can see he just can't play.

"When your star player is struggling, your bench is shorthanded and other players are having difficulty, it's going to be a grind. Allen can't do the things he's capable of doing, and we don't have any time to adjust. We've just got to hope 36 hours [between games] will help, but I'm not confident.

"He told me he wants to travel with the team. It's not my place to ask him not to. This is what he's played for. This has been his dream, to be in the conference finals, with a chance to play for a championship."

If the basket seemed an unreachable goal for Iverson, it was a huge, incredibly friendly target for the Bucks' Ray Allen, who scored a career playoff-high 38 points on 15-for-24 shooting that included draining seven of 11 three-pointers. And with Glenn Robinson scoring 16 points and Sam Cassell contributing 14 points and 11 assists, the Bucks were home free.

Two Allens, two diametrically different perspectives.

"I was making shot after shot," Ray Allen said. "Sam was finding me, and I was telling him, 'Let's keep doing this.' At the same time, Sam was like, 'Don't think about what's going on with the team. You just continue to put the ball in the basket.'

"I didn't think about scoring or where I was scoring from. I didn't want to think about what I was doing. I wanted to make shots.

"I never imagined being able to go out and score knowing I had to chase [Iverson]. We know he's hobbled a little bit, [but] now's the time we definitely have to take advantage of him being disabled at this point. I'm going to try to put him in screens as much as possible.

"He stands funny. He stands like an old man a little. He holds his back, he holds his tailbone as well. I've always applauded his effort because he's a tough guy. A lot of guys through the league, because of an injury like that, would sit down."

Iverson sit down? Frighteningly, Iverson has even considered it. "All through my career I've had some tough injuries," Iverson said somberly. "This ranks up there with one of the toughest, just because it takes away a lot of my speed, my lift on my shot.

"It's kind of frustrating to be settling for jump shots, not being able to go to the basket when I want to. It's a tough time for me to deal with."

Iverson said he would consider sitting if he felt he were hurting the team, but he also said, "I need to start thinking about myself, too."

"It seems like it's getting worse," he said. "It's not getting better. This has been my dream, to be in the Eastern finals, [but] I never had to play this season with an injury like this. The last time I had this injury, I sat out five games.

"Just trying to run, to push off is real hard, when I know nothing's there, [it's] just so weak. I felt like [the Bucks] knew that as well.

"I can't recall too many times when I didn't have any driving layup attempts. I had one where I got my shot blocked and I saw the guy coming. Stuff like that doesn't happen very much.

"I'm hurt at a point where I don't want to be hurt. This is it right now."

As much as his offense was jeopardized, Iverson was equally concerned about his inability to keep up defensively with Allen.

"I can't chase him like I want to," he said. "And I think I'm the best on the team at that. I just couldn't keep up with him. I could see a lot of shots he hit were open shots coming off screens."

If Ray Allen were dealing with a similar injury, and if his coach suggested taking a game off in the Eastern finals, would he?

"I wouldn't do it," Allen said. "At this point in the season, these games mean so much. That's why he's out there playing. He's watched these games . . . he dreamed about being in this situation. He's giving it a shot. I'd do the same thing."

SIXERS START TO REGROUP, BEFORE IT'S TOO LATE

Philadelphia Daily News
April 23, 2001

LITTLE BY LITTLE, the life began seeping back into the 76ers. That, they knew, is what the practice floor and film sessions are for.

Agonizing bit by agonizing bit, they began to look ahead to tomorrow night's Game 2 against the Indiana Pacers rather than Saturday afternoon's inexplicable 79–78 loss.

They stopped thinking about blowing an 18-point lead in the third quarter, or about scoring 26 points in the second half, or about seeing the Pacers' Reggie Miller rise above everyone and nail a 27-foot game-winning three-pointer.

"[Saturday night] I sat in my house and I was thinking about every little thing that we could've done to win," the Sixers' Allen Iverson said. "I thought of all the mistakes and all that did was make me a little bit angry and make [tomorrow] seem that much further away. So I just stopped dwelling on everything and just concentrated on trying to win the next game."

The competitor in Iverson had brought him to say, in the postgame news conference, "Our asses got tight, simple as that."

He didn't apologize yesterday. Because he knew—and his teammates knew—what he meant.

"We've just got to control leads when we have them," he said. "That's all I meant by that. We had a 16-point lead at halftime; you're supposed to, if anything, win by one. We don't lose with a 16-point lead. I learned that in elementary school, high school.

"You're up 16 points at halftime, you're supposed to keep that lead. We didn't keep it, and I felt like our asses got tight. I didn't mean any disrespect to myself, to my teammates, the coaching staff. I just . . . that's how I felt right then, and that's how it felt to me. We had a game right here at home and we let it slip away. It's going to be harder on us, but nothing in life is easy."

They are, unexpectedly, down one game in the best-of-five NBA first-round playoff series. So much for being the No. 1 seed in the East vs. the No. 8 seed.

"As long as you understand you've got to win three games, no problem," Iverson said. "For us to lose our confidence now and get down on each other, it'd be stupid. We played 82 games; to come in and get down after we lose one game, it's crazy, and I think the makeup of the team is a little better than that. We've got a little bit more character than to just throw it away on one game. It's time to go play in Indiana after this game."

SIX SHOTS: The Sixers, who drew a sellout crowd of 20,613 to Saturday's game, averaged a franchise-record 19,651 during the regular season, including 18 capacity crowds, eight more than last season. The average was up 1,189 from last season and up 7,716 from 1995–96, the season before Comcast-Spectacor became the primary owner and Pat Croce was installed as the president. The Sixers finished with the fifth-best home attendance in the league; on the road, they averaged 18,583, second only to the Los Angeles Lakers at 19,628.

SAY CHEESE! SIXERS TOAST BUCKS IN OPENER

Philadelphia Daily News
May 23, 2001

THIS WAS GOING TO BE the tale of the tailbone. You know, the tailbone connected to the Eastern Conference finals, connected to a chance to win a championship. The tailbone connected to the lifeblood of the 76ers.

Close enough. What really hurts Allen Iverson is the left sacroiliac joint, high up on the buttocks, to the side of the tailbone, connected to the hip and the pelvis.

What feels good is an almost eerie ability to play through the kind of pain that necessitated hours of electrical stimulation treatment, ice, ultrasound, gentle massage and stretching, along with moist heat at halftime last night.

What feels the best, Iverson insisted, is knowing the Sixers came away with a 93–85 victory over the Milwaukee Bucks, taking the opener of the NBA's best-of-seven, Eastern Conference finals. Game 2 is tomorrow night, also at the First Union Center.

Iverson has played through injuries all season, including coming back from a slightly separated shoulder in five days and an earlier blow to his tailbone. But maybe nothing like this.

"Allen can be out there with one leg and would play," the Sixers' Aaron McKie said after Iverson shrugged it all off to score 34 points in the full 48 minutes. "That's the kind of individual he is; that's the kind of heart he has. That's the way we grew up, playing the hand you're dealt, whether it's favorable or not."

The hand Iverson was dealt included missing all nine of his shots in the first quarter and seeing the game deadlocked, 19–19. He hit 13 of his remaining 26, handed out a team-high six assists and committed just three turnovers in a remarkable performance that left the sellout crowd of 20,877 in the First Union Center gaping. For the first time in the playoffs this season, the Sixers opened a series with a victory. It would not be an understatement to say they did it the hard way.

"We don't have too much concern about how Allen gets started," said McKie, who put up 23 points of his own. "If we lived and died on how he shot at the start, we'd be in trouble. He can miss nine, and we know he's capable of making the next nine."

Iverson bruised the sacroiliac joint in Sunday's second-round, Game 7 victory over Toronto. Monday, he did virtually nothing at practice. Yesterday, he ran a little during the morning shootaround and walked through the scouting report. Last night?

"I was just out there hurting," Iverson said. "Coach [Larry Brown] asked me before the game how my [buttocks] were feeling. I told him it was worse than the last time I hurt it, when I missed five games. But that didn't have anything to do with some of the shots I missed—easy shots I make with my eyes closed, shots my son would make. And I missed them. That's what you play for all season, to keep playing . . . The game was ugly, but the results were pretty."

The results included center Dikembe Mutombo reaching for 18 rebounds to go with 15 points and four blocks, Tyrone Hill battling his way to 12 rebounds and Jumaine Jones finding his way to eight points and five rebounds in his fourth-ever start. Mutombo contributed seven of his rebounds off the offensive glass, four fewer than the entire Bucks team.

All of that was enough to overcome a 31-point effort by the Bucks' Ray Allen, 20 points from flak-jacket-protected Sam Cassell and 15 from Glenn Robinson. Robinson, who scored 29 in each of the last two games of the Bucks' second-round triumph over Charlotte, shot just 7-for-22 from the floor, missing 13 of his first 17.

"Allen was really hurting," Brown said. "You could see he was really struggling. But we got a great game from Jumaine, a phenomenal game from Dikembe; Aaron was terrific, we got good minutes from Matt Geiger."

Geiger, who appeared in one game in the second round and didn't dress for the last three because of a problem with his right quadriceps, had two points and four rebounds in 12 minutes.

In truth, the No. 1–seeded Sixers needed every one of those performances to overcome the No. 2 Bucks.

"This is a [Bucks] team as talented as anybody in the league, especially from an offensive standpoint," Brown said.

Fortunately, the tailbone was still connected to the . . . well, you get the idea.

"I asked [Allen] before the game how it felt, specifically how it compared with [when he hurt it against] Sacramento," Brown said.

"He said it hurt more, was more numb. And the way he started, it looked like he had no lift . . . The kid has a big heart, as you guys are aware of."

The players are more aware than anyone.

"They say when you get hurt in a game, you can finish it playing on adrenaline," backup center Todd MacCulloch said.

"But you feel it the next day. I asked him as he was coming out of the shower [Sunday] how it felt, and he said, 'Hell, if I can walk, I can play.' To him, if he can hobble, he'll say, 'Let's get it on.'

"He's so dangerous, Milwaukee has to play him like he's healthy. It's like gladiators, a case of not showing weakness when you think you're hurt. He was still out there commanding double-teams and triple-teams."

Backup guard Kevin Ollie saw the situation through similarly appreciative eyes.

"He's done it so many times, I knew he'd play, I knew he'd come out aggressive, playing hard," Ollie said.

"He didn't have any lift, but he made smart decisions. When he does that, it gives everyone else the fortitude to go out there and do what they can.

"He looked hurt, but he still got us crucial points. You worry about him, because he plays with such fearlessness. He's not the bulkiest guy, but he plays with the heart of a lion.

"I felt better when I saw him moving around at the shootaround. It's when he stays in the training room that I worry."

7TH WONDER—SIXERS PASS THE BUCKS; HERE THEY COME, LA

Philadelphia Daily News
June 4, 2001

THEY WERE RAGING BULLS, the 60-year-old coach from New York, the 25-year-old guard from Hampton, Va. The coach who insisted his players do everything the right way, the rebellious kid who said he had his own way.

They could not do it alone, but they had yet to find a way to do it with one another, within the framework of Brown's definition of a team.

The coach seemed in a constant, unspeakable quandary, the kid seemed lost in a maze. His talent was exceptional. All that was missing was the right showcase.

They found each other just before the NBA All-Star break. They grew closer and closer as the season wore on. By the time the playoffs started, they had melded. They were together. The 76ers were together, prepared to go where precious few people truly believed they could.

Last night was a culmination, an outpouring. In their second Game 7 together, Brown, Iverson and the Sixers raced past the Milwaukee Bucks at the First Union Center, 108–91, to win the Eastern Conference championship and advance to the Finals for the first time since 1982–83.

The attempt to climb the final mountain will begin Wednesday night against the defending champion Los Angeles Lakers in the Staples Center. Games 1 and 2 will be played there, with Games 3, 4 and 5 in the best-of-seven series at the First Union Center.

"I'm just so happy we're going," Brown said. "[The Lakers] are the best team. That's why you play the games. It's like David vs. Goliath. That's the way it's going to be. We've got to figure out how to slay a giant. I don't know."

Fittingly, Brown and Iverson are each going to the Finals for the first time. The difference is, Brown has been a coach for 29 years, 18 in the NBA. Iverson is in his fifth season as a pro. Just as fittingly, the two embraced before the tip-off, then again as pandemonium reigned at the final buzzer. Sometime today, the Lakers, their 11–0 record in the postseason, their 19-game winning streak and the imposing figures of Shaquille O'Neal and Kobe Bryant will be something on which to focus. But not late last night.

First, the Sixers literally leaped into one another's arms. Forward Tyrone Hill danced giddily on the press table. A portion of the mob on the court carried Iverson off on their shoulders. In the runway leading to the locker room, Brown and his wife, Shelly, shared an embrace. The fans chanted "Beat LA, beat LA . . ."

Brown scrawled his signature on what has to be his most satisfying season as a pro coach, milking 32 minutes from Eric Snow, playing with two fractures in his right ankle, getting an almost surreal nine minutes from late rookie addition Raja Bell, and a furious, 44-point performance from Iverson. And even as Iverson was draining 17 of 33 shots from the floor, including four three-pointers, center Dikembe Mutombo was doing precisely what he was brought here to do: 23 points, 19 rebounds and seven blocks. At the same time, the ever-steady Aaron McKie was feeding the ball through forests of bodies to accumulate 13 assists.

But in the center of the storm, it was the coach and the kid. Still, in their own ways, bulls, but no longer raging at anyone or anything other than the opponents.

"You know my frustrations during the season and before," Brown said. "But I'm learning more and more about what Allen's made of. There are still some issues I don't understand completely, but I know where his heart is. Whatever else is going on, I know he cares. He has an unbelievable will; I have the same kind of will. In my career, I've had some great things happen to me, but these guys have taken me with them. I look at us, and there are just so many great stories."

These are the Sixers, with 56 victories and the No. 1 playoff seed in the East, riddled by injuries, nearly torn apart before the coach and the kid found one another. It should be, Snow suggested, a movie.

"Will Smith as Allen, Sylvester Stallone as coach," Snow yelped.

Places, everyone. The cameras are rolling.

"I understand pressure where I come from, with what I go through in everyday life," Iverson said. "I don't put pressure on myself when I'm dealing with basketball. I go on the floor with four other guys."

He knew the questions about himself and the coach would be coming, so he took a preemptive strike.

"I heard about, 'Can me and coach co-exist,' a bunch of talk," Iverson said. "All I thought about was, I had the opportunity to change everything around."

The kid led the league in scoring, became the Most Valuable Player. Brown became Coach of the Year. With everyone else riding the wave, Mutombo became the Defensive Player of the Year, McKie won the Sixth Man award.

"Coach and Allen both wanted to win," guard Kevin Ollie said. "They just didn't know how to handle each other until they realized, to win, they needed each other. Both are stubborn, but both sacrificed a little, gave a little, took a little."

There were times it seemed the coach and the kid might never find common ground.

"When it looked bad, though, it was never as bad as it appeared," said backup center Matt Geiger. "When it was good, it wasn't as good as it seemed. That's how it was for a long time, but somewhere along the road it came together. And when it did, it helped the whole team. Really, it was awesome."

BELIEVE IT! IVERSON, MCKIE ELIMINATE TORONTO

Philadelphia Daily News
May 21, 2001

THE GENESIS of the most significant victory in the Allen Iverson/Larry Brown/Pat Croce era stretches all the way back to last season, when the 76ers scrambled, battled and began to discover the elements of being a team.

"Aaron [McKie] and I would talk with Allen a lot, telling him it's not the same on every team," Sixers guard Eric Snow recalled, savoring the memory. "He would always say he had never been around a group of guys like this. Aaron and I had been on other teams. He's only been here.

"We'd say, 'Talk to the guys who have left here,' see what they say. We made a trade in February of this season, and a little later Nazr Mohammed called from Atlanta and said, 'Now I understand what you were talking about.'"

Iverson, already the NBA's scoring champion and Most Valuable Player, has a better grasp than ever of that concept after last night's heart-stopping, 88–87, Game 7 victory over the Toronto Raptors that propelled them into the best-of-seven Eastern Conference finals for the first time since 1984–85.

That was why, every chance he got, Iverson said, "I feel for the first time in my career that I'm really on a team."

That was equally why Brown—the professorial coach—momentarily lowered his guard and fired back at Los Angeles Lakers coach Phil Jackson, who had said it was an insult that his center, Shaquille O'Neal, had been just third in the MVP balloting.

"In spite of what Phil Jackson may think, Shaq would be no more valuable to this team than this little kid," Brown said. "He had to overcome so much. Statements like that in defense of his player really tick me off. But when you win all those championships, I guess you can say what the hell you want."

This was history being etched across the First Union Center, as the Sixers won a best-of-seven series for the first time since 1984–85, as they won a Game 7 in Philadelphia for the first time since 1980–81, as they won a best-of-seven series for the first time in their last seven attempts.

This was the day the Raptors' Vince Carter got his diploma in a morning graduation ceremony at the University of North Carolina, then got taken to school by a Sixers team that has survived on grit, determination and a philosophy that Brown has worked overtime to infuse.

Each time this team has appeared to go as far as it possibly could, it has found a way to go farther.

That the Sixers will be opening the series against the Bucks tomorrow night at home is a marvelous testament to Snow's characterization of their makeup.

They got a remarkable career-high 16 assists from Iverson, who discovered an area in which to excel as he was shooting just 8-for-27 from the floor. They got 17 rebounds from Dikembe Mutombo, including nine off the offensive glass, one more than the entire Raptors roster. They got 16 points from Jumaine Jones, who was making the third-ever start of his two-year career. They had McKie lead the way with 22 points, just the second time in 11 postseason games that Iverson wasn't the team's high scorer.

With it all, they grew wings on the errant flight of the final shot of the day, from the left baseline by Carter with less than two seconds left. And as bedlam erupted on the court and spilled into the locker room, Snow couldn't help but recall all of those conversations, all the way back to last season.

"There's a camaraderie here, a caring," Snow said after contributing 13 points, blocking out the discomfort of tendinitis in his right foot that leaves him limping late in games.

"There's no jealousy. Everybody supports each other. Everybody thinks about one thing, and that's winning. Winning together. It starts with coach Brown and [president] Pat Croce, guys who work hard, who do things the right way. And now we have the best player thinking the same way. When that happens, everybody else just follows suit."

Follow the leader. Iverson, who scored 54 and 52 points in two earlier games in this taut series, struggled mightily with his shot and landed hard on his already-sore tailbone early in the third quarter. He stared into a firestorm of double teams and scanned the floor for open teammates, "not just an open man, a guy open for a shot that he could make."

"I feel so good about this win because I know, I really, really know and believe inside I have a team for the first time in my life," he said. "I have a team I feel we really can win a championship with. I really feel like we've got an opportunity."

From there, Iverson's mind flashed to other words, from another source. "Sonny Hill [a senior adviser to the team] always jokes about our games being ugly," he said. "Yeah, it was an ugly game because of the way I shot. Yeah, it's ugly when we shoot [42.7] percent, but the results are pretty."

The sheer chance of reaching the NBA's equivalent of the Final Four was what nudged Iverson back on the floor after he hurt his tailbone.

"The first time I went to the bench it was hurting so bad, I said to myself, 'After all this time, all year getting hurt, I'm getting hurt in Game 7,'"

Iverson said. "I was thinking about sitting out, it hurt so bad, worse than the last time I fell on it. [Then] I just looked in [his teammates'] faces, and it was bothering me, bothering me. . . .

"As soon as I heard the horn, I just got up and walked toward the table to go back into the game. I never thought about it again 'til right now."

Brown thinks incessantly about the growth of this improbable team. "I've had a lot of terrific years in terms of dealing with kids who have made sacrifices," Brown said, "but this team has overcome more than any team I've ever been involved with."

You could make the argument that, on the day Carter got his diploma, the Sixers graduated.

THAT'S 3! SIXERS POISED TO WRAP IT UP

Philadelphia Daily News
May 17, 2001

THINK ABOUT THE SHEER number.

Fifty-two.

Think about the threes.

Eight.

Think about the only other guy ever to score 50 points or more twice in a single playoff series.

Michael Jordan.

Now think about Allen Iverson, who last night took the Most Valuable Player trophy from NBA commissioner David Stern, then took the Toronto Raptors by storm, triggering the 76ers' stunning, 121–88 victory that gave them a 3–2 advantage in the second round. The Sixers are one victory away from a berth in the Eastern Conference finals.

This was Iverson, who scored 54 points in Game 2 of the series, then watched the Raptors' Vince Carter put up 50 in Game 3, coming back with a superlative performance that overshadowed anything that had gone before.

When Carter scored 50, he said the basket "looked like a lake."

"He said a lake," Iverson said. "To me, it looked like an ocean."

This was Iverson unplugged, dropping in 21 of 32 shots from the floor, draining eight of 14 triples, handing out seven assists, making four steals, placing 52 points in his box score line that virtually defied description.

"It's hard not to watch him," Sixers forward Tyrone Hill said. "Everything he does, everything he touches turns to magic."

The Raptors blinked, and they were down 17–4. They blinked again, and they were down 33–12, at the end of the first quarter. How could they have known that Iverson, with 12 points, was just getting started?

He had 17 in the second quarter, 18 in the third. He had a final five before asking to come out with a little more than four minutes remaining. This was all against an opponent that includes Charles Oakley, who had said Iverson wouldn't get 50 again; against Chris Childs, who had said the Raptors should have swept the series.

Instead, the Sixers are within a victory of winning a best-of-seven series for the first time since 1984–85, which is also the last season in which they reached the conference finals.

Iverson, who somehow simultaneously took in every ounce of the outpouring of emotion from the sellout crowd and yet floated above the adoration, seemed startled that an opposing player would say he wouldn't get 50 again.

"I would never make a comment like that," he said. "I don't know what a person is capable of doing. I can't say that. They might have been trying to boost their team up, or trying to get in my head or something. That's crazy to say somebody won't do something again. You never know, the game just might go that way."

And even though it sometimes seemed as if Iverson were out there alone, there was help all around. There was the ever-steady Aaron McKie getting 19 points and nine assists, Dikembe Mutombo contributing 14 points and nine rebounds. There was Jumaine Jones getting nine points and four rebounds in his first-ever start, filling in for the injured George Lynch. There was Rodney Buford, who barely had played in the postseason, providing 13 minutes as Jones' relief man.

Still, in the midst of it all, there was Iverson, a human storm. Heat lightning. Rolling thunder. Pushing, pushing, then pushing some more.

He is the only player remaining from 1996–97, the season before coach Larry Brown arrived.

"It's been a rough five years for me, up and down, up and down," Iverson said. "But that's life. I cry a whole lot, but I don't whine about too many things. Just because I won the MVP, it doesn't stop right here."

He heard his teammates talking about his magnificent performance, and he attempted to redirect the conversation. "If I had had one point and we won the game," he said, "that would have been the best night. It's been a great ending to the night just to win. I heard the people on TV saying that maybe with the excitement and everything I might not be able to perform, that there might be too much attention.

"I heard all those things. I just felt like I owed it to myself to play the game, to do what got you the MVP; just play basketball, whether the shots go in or not. Just keep playing, play hard."

He made the only two free throws he attempted, meaning his jumper was sweet, his touch was beyond reproach. He was the player even his teammates, who see him every day, sometimes can't help but be amazed with.

Iverson won't get 50 again? The Raptors felt they should have swept? "Some of that is like a slap in the face to us," McKie said. "I guess it was along the lines of Oakley saying something to Carter [to motivate him]. Maybe it was to build up their team's confidence, but it was motivation for us.

"Hopefully, in the next 24 hours, they'll make some more sarcastic comments."

CODA • PROFILING GIANTS

STAR LIGHT STAR BRIGHT

Philadelphia Daily News
May 25, 2006

FOR ALLEN IVERSON, there was never a singular moment, at least one that anyone can universally agree on. His quest to achieve superstardom has been a metamorphosis, an evolution.

Here is Iverson, a barely 6-foot guard weighing in somewhere between 160 and 165 pounds. He has won four scoring titles and has been an MVP in his 10 seasons. In 2000–01, he drove his team to the Finals for the first time in 18 years. He finished this season with the highest scoring average (33.0) of any player who did not win the scoring title since 1969–70, when the league began declaring the winner based on average rather than total points.

But what Iverson hears—even as he says how much he wants to remain—is the bleat that a championship team cannot be built around a player of his size and position, that after a decade of show-stopping seasons, it is time for him to go, that it is time for the Sixers to start fresh. In this arena, superstardom does not necessarily come bathed in adulation and overwhelming success. Seven straight starts in the All-Star Game? Nah, say the cynics. Not hardly enough. A record of 34–48 in his 10th season? Give us more, they say.

As fascinating as the genesis and development of Allen Iverson the superstar has been, it has been equally fascinating trying to determine an exact starting point.

Maybe a surreal sequence in 1997, when he became the league's first rookie to score at least 40 points in five games in succession?

"Those games were when everybody realized he could be really special," says Doug Overton, Iverson's teammate that season and the team's director of player development in 2005–06. "He just caught fire, just took off. But all through that year, he kept doing different things, even though we didn't win a lot of games. What I remember is just the hype, how focused he was. At the time, I don't think we all realized how amazing 40 points in five straight games was; now, he gets 40, it's no big deal. I don't think, at the time, anyone had seen a little guy be that dominating."

But Iverson wasn't Magic Johnson, nine inches taller, bursting into the league in 1979–80, joining Kareem Abdul-Jabbar and James Worthy and winning a championship.

In 1996–97, Iverson's Sixers won 22 games.

In 2000–01, they went to the Finals.

"It takes years to put 'superstar' next to a player's name," says Steve Mix, who had a 13-season career and is now the Sixers' TV analyst. "In the Finals, a superstar is someone who can put his team on his back and carry it. He was the lone offensive player on a defense-oriented team."

So maybe superstardom arrived March 12, 1997, at the Wachovia Center, when he scored 37 points, including a fadeaway 19-foot jumper off a crossover move that staggered Michael Jordan?

"He had Jordan on a yo-yo," said Henry "Que" Gaskins, global vice president of lifestyle and entertainment for Reebok. "That's the one. No one had ever made Jordan look like that on a single move. He made Jordan look human."

Or maybe it was the day of the draft in 1996?

"I knew from that day," said Sonny Hill, a senior adviser to the Sixers, the founder of the Charles Baker League for pros in the summer and various youth leagues, and an acknowledged historian of the game. "I said, 'This is electricity, that there would be electricity in the building.' I said he would be something special, not just as a player but as a connection to the city, that he had an aura about him. If you want to say the defining moment beyond that was the crossover on Michael, OK. To me, that was more like reaching a crescendo."

How about before all of that? Bill Walton, a Hall of Fame player and now a TV analyst, recalled meeting Iverson for the first time at the John Wooden Award presentation in Los Angeles.

"This was after, I think, his second year at Georgetown," Walton says. "I had seen him play a little, but had never talked with him. This was the beginning of my media career, and I was blown away by his stage presence, his command of the moment."

Walton was aware that Iverson had had a difficult upbringing, that he had spent four-and-a-half months on a prison farm after an incident in a bowling alley as a high school student.

"He has been able to overcome so much," Walton says. "Not that this is the same thing, but it's like my stuttering problem; it's something you have to deal with every day."

Go ahead, look back at Iverson's two seasons at Georgetown.

"I remember him flying around the court," says Sixers coach Maurice Cheeks, an assistant to Johnny Davis when Iverson was a rookie. "But I didn't know then that he was a superstar. When he first came in to the NBA, he was pretty good, but my definition of a superstar is someone who does it year after year after year. I think maybe he was at that level by his fourth year, as he kept getting better, getting more productive. There have been guys who have won awards early in their careers and haven't turned out; he just continued up the ladder."

Stay, for a moment, back at Georgetown, then ruled by coach John Thompson.

"He got John to change his style of play, and that was something that opened everyone's eyes," says John Nash, the Portland Trail Blazers general manager. "John went from ball control to pushing it, and that was an awakening."

Keep flipping back the pages of time, keep searching for clues, and you find . . .

"You might have to go back to high school, when he was in trouble," says Pat Williams, the Orlando Magic's senior vice president. "That's my first memory of him. It was so traumatic, but he was an incredible athlete and people went to bat for him. Eventually, John Thompson took his life over, became a mentor, a leader, a most impactful force. Here was this young kid with superstar ability from a difficult background, and the world was rooting for him. If he hadn't been helped then, he never would have emerged; he would have been just one of millions."

Gary Moore, Iverson's personal manager, insists he knew Iverson was a superstar at two distinctly different stages of his development.

"I knew first probably when Allen was 11," says Moore, then directing a youth football program in the Tidewater area of Virginia. "He was eight and a half, maybe nine when he came into our program in Hampton. At nine, he was playing at a level reserved for the kids who were 12 and 13.

By 15, he was leading his AAU basketball team to a national championship. What I saw, even then, was that the tougher the competition, the better he played. At Bethel High, he led a mediocre team to a state championship."

The second time Moore knew was the day of the NBA draft in '96, the day the Sixers made Allen Iverson the No. 1 overall pick.

"The obstacles he overcame, he really shouldn't be in the NBA," Moore says. "Others who would have had to face the situations he faced would probably have succumbed to the pressures. Because of his athletic prowess, Allen was accused, tried, convicted and sentenced for a crime he never committed. Most young black kids would not have survived that, or may have allowed that to destroy any opportunities at a fair share in life. I've never seen any bitterness in him about that."

This is who Allen Iverson is. He hasn't won a championship with the Sixers, he draws controversy to him as if he were a human lightning rod. He stoically insists there are a million people out there who love him and a million who hate him, but no one has ever been able to log an actual count. He wears his mantle as if it were a huge chip on his shoulder, daring anyone to try to knock it off.

He has the necessary unique skill set: physical talent, magnetic personality, fan appeal and marketing appeal that help create superstardom. He hasn't won nearly enough, and you can point to many reasons why, including, but not limited to, a lack of talent around him, a lack of a firm hand from coaches and management, or an unwillingness to alter his style.

But he has broken records and broken barriers. Philadelphia has seen this before, just never in a 6-foot, 160-pound package.

MJ ON MJ

Philadelphia Daily News
April 17, 1998

AS WILT CHAMBERLAIN, Shaquille O'Neal and Karl Malone have defined sheer physical strength in basketball over the years, as Allen Iverson eventually might define the blinding brilliance of speed, Elgin Baylor and Julius Erving once defined grace, style, flair and dynamics in space.

Until Michael Jordan.

Jordan has, as his predecessors once did, left everyone gasping for more, trying to fight the reality that, no matter when he leaves, it will be too soon.

Is Jordan's leaving imminent? Is he about to walk away? Could the show finally be over? Or will it linger at least another season, in part easing the transition for the league's sometimes funky Generation Next?

Jordan diplomatically says that "under certain circumstances" he will play on. But those circumstances seemingly include Phil Jackson being retained as the Bulls' coach and Scottie Pippen returning with a fresh, rich contract that, at least to some degree, makes up for his having been underpaid all these years. Whether management will allow all of those elements to remain in place remains, at best, unlikely.

One more time for Jordan? He says, "If people think I can still play the game, that's a great time to leave." But he will not say whether he is leaving, couching his thinking with, "It's still pretty much up in the air."

In sessions after practices, shootarounds and games in Washington, D.C., Orlando and Atlanta, he addressed questions about himself, about his career, about his profession. In some cases, Jordan was direct, offering glimpses of himself. In others, he fenced, parried, yielding as many questions as answers.

Question: Do you agree with the premise that you have come to define space on the court?

Answer: In retrospect, to some degree, yeah. But there were guys before me who did basically the same thing—Doctor J, some of the other guys who played off the floor with their styles. I may have innovated it to some degree.

Q: Could Allen Iverson, as he continues in his career, eventually define speed?

A: He could, but he had guys before him, [such as] Calvin Murphy. He takes it another step with his athletic [ability] and the way that he plays. What you see within us is always an extension of the older players.

Q: Do you have a relationship with Iverson?

A: We've talked a couple times; we have the same agent [David Falk]. I have a lot of respect (for him). He's going to learn. He's got the game. He is getting better. You can see it. He's poised on the court, he's becoming more of a true point guard, [yet] he's still being himself. It's just a part of growing up. He's gone through a lot. He's made it thus far and he will continue to get better. That's the good thing about Allen. He's willing to learn, and he's willing to make certain changes, to adapt.

Q: Is he someone you would sit down with, or does he have to initiate that?

A: I would rather he come to me. He has his own support group. He has his own trust factors, so sometimes you don't want to intervene with those people because those are the guys that have stood for him for a long time. If he wants to step outside that arena in some respect and get some advice, sure, I'll be there to help.

Q: As you come into each arena, what do you say to people who want to know whether it's for the last time?

A: It could be. Then again, it could not. Either way, the respect they pay me is greatly appreciated. It motivates me to go out and do my job.

Q: Has that made this an even more challenging season?

A: It's been different, but we're still in a position to do what we have to do. I'm very happy with what we've accomplished with all of this.

Q: What's your take on the owners reopening the collective bargaining agreement?

A: It's all positioning and leveraging at this point—who can leverage to get the other side to give and take on certain issues, issues that probably need to be dealt with. I'm pretty sure management thinks salaries should be dealt with, as well as the players saying licensing money should be talked about. You have to be very cautious in terms of how greedy you become. You have to be able to compromise within reason where the league and the credibility of the game is not at stake.

Q: Is it accurate that you want to have a role in negotiations?

A: I said I would consult. I'm a player. I will contribute my focus to that. That's my prerogative. Hopefully, it can be a peaceful negotiation to where it does not end up in a worst-case scenario, which is a lockout.

Q: What about problems in the league with bad behavior?

A: It's definitely a concern. The precedent [Latrell] Sprewell set is, you have a clause in your contract, a morality clause. What defines that? That's the biggest thing that comes out of that. It was a gray area to this point. Now it hasn't really been defined, even with this action.

Q: What did you give up by being Michael Jordan?

A: I don't know. I can't say, "What if? What if I wasn't Michael Jordan?" What things would have been different? Sure, maybe I would have been able to move around in public a lot easier and sometimes I wish. But there are a lot of other things that came along with being Michael Jordan—the respect, the admiration, certainly the business outside has been great—but to say, "What if?" My wife asked me, "What if you could change anything right now?" You know what? I wouldn't, because I know what I'm dealing with. When I go back and change, some other things might come into play that I never really thought about.

Q: So it's a fair trade-off?

A: I think it is, because I'm comfortable with where my life is right now.

Q: Would you like to be able to go to a mall? To a movie?

A: I go to the movies. I just don't go as often as you or some other people may. We went [in March], saw "Zero Effect." I went at 9:45, last movie [of the night]. Everybody's gone. Mondays and Tuesdays are good days.

Q: Do you still enjoy all this?

A: Yeah, I do. It's fun. I've learned how to curtail some of the media exposure. I may not talk to the media as much as I used to. I don't think I have to, because I think people know me, know my opinions on different things.

Q: What's the worst part of all of this?

A: That one day it has to end.

Q: And yet it's your decision?

A: Always. And I like it that way.

Q: How do you feel about fans coming out now not just to see you play, but to show some appreciation?

A: It's great appreciation. I take it as that. I've always been dedicated to going out and doing my job for the fans to enjoy the game—and try and beat their team. But they've always showed true respect for me. I guess going out and playing hard is my way of paying them back.

Q: Does being in a place for what might be the last time carry any added weight?

A: Every time I play somewhere it may be the last time. I try to play hard. I'm not going to change that whole approach. I've been successful with the same approach, and I will know—I will feel—it may be the last one, but it shouldn't alter my game.

Q: How about the people who want you to stay?

A: I know, it's great. I appreciate that. It's always great to be wanted. But I don't think it's in my best interests to walk out when I can't play at the same level that people are expecting to see. I think they expect me to play until they start to see parts of my game start to break down. I don't want to leave the game that way.

Q: Yet you understand their feelings?

A: It's understandable. Everything is up in the air. No one knows. Why not just live for the present? That's the way I've taken it.

Q: Is there one thing left that you want to do that you haven't?

A: I can't say, other than winning. To me, winning meant a lot. It meant a lot of hard work, pleasing a lot of the fans. I just want to make sure that when I walk away, I've done everything I can to entertain the people that are watching. Individual accolades, I've had my share, [and] I'm very happy for that. That doesn't drive me as much. I want to maintain my consistency and play, because I think that's what people judge me on. But in terms of team success, I just want to finish on a good note.

Q: Do you ever just sit back in amazement and reflect on what you've created?

A: I never take the credit. I always feel I contributed. I think that's a great feeling, that you've been able to expand on the opportunity that other former players have given to you, to the point where you get [57,000 people attending a game in Atlanta] that's not a playoff game.

Q: Why do you think you have been so successful in marketing?

A: I think my personality is well-liked and respected by a lot of people. I just try to be myself in that respect. It's surprising it's lasted this long. I'm just trying to do my job.

Q: Is burnout at all a factor?

A: No. My love for the game was resurged when I came back [from baseball], when I took the two years away and I came back.

How preciously I treasured that. And I treasure the game, and I will always because I have a better understanding about what it meant to me. So even if I'm not playing next year, I'm still going to have the same love for the game.

Q: You came back from baseball only to lose a playoff series to Orlando, which has been what could be looked at as your only failure since your return. How do you look back at that?

A: It was an eye-opening situation. I was naive about what I could do coming back from baseball, and the situation [with Orlando] forced me physically to focus a little more on some of the things it took to play the game of basketball. I came back from baseball, thought I could just turn it on. The failure I had [against the Magic] woke me up to say, "Hey, you have to put forth the effort, you have to put forth the work and results will come back." In a way, I'm glad that happened, because I would have taken a whole different perspective getting myself mentally and physically prepared.

Q: How much of your decision to return or walk away will depend on the status of Phil Jackson or your relationship with [owner] Jerry Reinsdorf and [operations chief] Jerry Krause?

A: It's going to be my decision, and no matter what happens, no matter what decision management makes and Phil makes, it's going to be my decision.

Q: What has been the effect of Pippen returning from an early season injury?

A: His leadership is so welcome at this time of the season. You don't have to beat someone's head to think about focusing on our jobs.

Q: Kids want to know, when they grow up, what's the key to beating you on the practice floor?

A: [Laughing.] Don't play me.

Q: Are you still honored by opponents double-teaming, and sometimes triple-teaming, you?

A: Oh, yeah. If I'm not getting double- and triple-teamed, I need to get out of the league. That means my game is starting to diminish.

Q: So you will stick around?

A: [Laughs.]

Q: How much of a factor is conditioning?

A: When you think about my age [35], I missed my second year [with an injury] and two more years when I was out of the game, so actually I'm playing at the age of 32 in terms of actual playing time. That makes a big difference.

Q: Do you sense that people coming to the games now seem to feel a mixture of pleasure and sadness watching you play?

A: Someday you knew it would have to come to an end. I know I can still play, but they'd rather see me walk out, limp out, and I'd rather see myself run out.

Q: You didn't want a retirement tour, did you?

A: No. I think it's very distracting from my objectives, which are to continue to win and be successful. I just want to quietly walk away.

Q: Did you understand the Jason Caffey trade? [At the Feb. 19 trade deadline, the Bulls sent Caffey, a forward who frequently filled in for Dennis Rodman, to Golden State for unproven—and since-waived—David Vaughn.]

A: No. Do you? That's two of us. The family was connected. We didn't see where a trade would benefit us. David [would have had] to learn our system—that's a three-year process. It's really hard to do that. You look at trends this year—if you don't think you can sign [a player who can become] a free agent, you get something for him. That was management's choice.

Q: You work with management, don't you?

A: No, I don't. I work with 12, 15 other guys. Management doesn't come down and put on a uniform. They do what they do in the off-season. Different decisions have to be made, [but] in the course of the season there's nothing I have to confer with them about.

Q: Would you entertain becoming a player-coach?

A: No.

Q: There was a rumor that you're buying your own island in the Bahamas.

A: What does that have to do with you? Tell them I said no comment.

Q: If you're facing your last appearance at any arena, would you prefer a knock-'em-dead performance?

A: You always want to play your best. You also understand every night's not going to be like that. I'm not too good to realize that I'm going to have a bad night. If you win the game, that's the overall I'm happy.

Q: When you do leave, would you still go the gym, to the playground, still play?

A: I probably will. I'll get conversations from local guys, from some of my buddies, to see if I still can play the game. That's still fun to me. I still get that from my teammates, in camps all fun games.

Q: Is there a feeling of closure as the season goes on?

A: [Nods affirmatively.] Things have been so great. I want to finish it the right way. This has been a great run. The best way to do that is to win a championship.

Q: You have fans all over the world. What do you say to them?

A: Hello. [Laughs.] I appreciate the support.

TO SIR, WITH LOVE

Philadelphia Daily News
March 30, 2001

CHARLES BARKLEY HEARS young players in the NBA talk about "keepin' it real," and wonders about their definition of real.

Barkley remembers trying to talk to Allen Iverson, then a 76ers rookie, during All-Star Weekend in 1997, and wonders if Iverson remembers what Barkley remembers.

"All I wanted was for Allen to grow up and understand his responsibilities," Barkley, 38, was saying, reconstructing snippets of his 16-season career that began in Philadelphia in 1984.

"You know what real is? It's that he's one of the best players in the world, making more than $10 million a year. That's real. It doesn't matter where he comes from, or any of that other stuff. Just accept the responsibility. That's the only thing that's real.

"Being from a poor neighborhood, from a single-parent home, things like that, that's somewhat real, but where do you think I'm from in Alabama? I grew up in Leeds, in a single-parent home, a welfare baby. It took me a while to grow up and mature. That's all I ever wanted for Allen."

Time and experience, Barkley learned, can be magnificent teachers.

Barkley will be at center court at halftime of the 76ers' game against Golden State tonight, seeing his jersey retired. Iverson, his painful left hip permitting, will be the Sixers' leader in the game, in the homestretch of his finest season, in part the result of his willingness to finally buy into coach Larry Brown's program.

"He's a marquee player, really talented, really good," Barkley said.

Barkley, who enjoys the swirl of attention as people try to figure out whether he will attempt a comeback, is equally happy with what he has seen from Brown, building the Sixers into one of the league's best teams.

"He's somebody I respect and admire," Barkley said. "I'm glad he hung in with Allen, trying to make him do things the right way. What's happening in the league is, a lot of coaches are cowards, afraid to challenge guys.

"Pat Riley [the Miami Heat coach] sent [Anthony Mason and Duane Causwell] home because they were late for a meeting; I loved it. I see what goes on with [the Los Angeles Lakers' Kobe Bryant and Shaquille O'Neal]; they can have their cake and eat it, too, and they're bitching about it. That's so disappointing and frustrating for me.

"I wasn't easy, but Billy Cunningham [his first coach with the Sixers] made me do things the right way. Matty Guokas and Jimmy Lynam came after him, and they didn't let me get away with things.

"But some of the stuff that goes on in the league today . . . I mean, Rasheed Wallace in Portland; all they do is defend him, say the referees are picking on him when he gets technicals. That's bull.

"In the old days, we disciplined each other. Me, Mike Gminski, Rick Mahorn, we kept each other in line, on the court, in the locker room. Rasheed won't talk to the press. Talking to the press, that goes with it. When I messed up, I was always a man about it. I would have killed to play with a team as talented as the Blazers. Karl Malone would have. Patrick Ewing would have."

Barkley had his share of controversial moments. He was stopped by the New Jersey State Police on the Atlantic City Expressway and cited for having a gun in the car in 1988. He punched out a guy in Milwaukee. He tossed a guy through a window in Orlando, spit at a fan in New Jersey and inadvertently hit a little girl. But he also became the shortest (6-4 7/8) player in the modern history to lead the league in rebounding, went to the NBA Finals with Phoenix, was a Most Valuable Player, was named to 11 All-Star teams, earned two gold medals in the Olympics.

When—not if—he enters the Naismith Memorial Basketball Hall of Fame, he will do it as a Sixer, even though he went on to play for the Suns and the Houston Rockets. He still wants to be the governor of Alabama, but not until he's 45, because he wants some "quiet time" first. He is carving out a career as a Turner Broadcasting analyst, just being Charles, saying exactly what he thinks and making you laugh as he says it.

He credits Jack McMahon, the late, great coach and scout, Moses Malone and Michael Jordan for helping mold his career. He wishes the atmosphere had been different when he played in Philadelphia, wishes the rules makers would leave his beloved game alone, wishes Bryant and O'Neal would find a way to coexist.

You name the subject, he has an opinion and doesn't hesitate to offer it. He loves a debate, enjoys the sharing of ideas. Regrets? Maybe a few.

"My only regret about my time in Philly is, I didn't get the credit I deserved," he said. "I was obviously at my best there as a player, but I went to Phoenix [in 1992] and all of a sudden, I was this great player. The one year we had me, Derek Smith, Gminski and Mahorn in Philly, we won the division, had a really good team, but most of the time I got handicapped by the players I played with there, by some of the trades the Sixers made. It was a mixed bag of tricks.

"People ask me about the Hall of Fame, and I say you go into the Hall for being a great player, and in Philly is when I was at my best. One year ['86–87], I averaged 23 points and 14 rebounds, led the league in rebounding, the best I ever played. But whether I belong in the Hall, that's for others to judge. I'm happy with my career. It's not for me to tell people how good I was. What I did speaks for itself."

Basically, Barkley did everything but win a championship.

"That's something I couldn't control," he said. "Like Malone and John Stockton in Utah; they haven't won one, either. But as a player, you have no control over draft picks, trades, who your teammates are. I wish I could have had Brad Daugherty as a teammate. I wish I had had Moses longer, that we had kept Gminski. I wish I could have had more say-so when we made trades. But that never happened. You kind of played at the discretion of the general manager and the owner."

The fascinating story lines intersect everywhere. The Sixers traded the chance to draft Daugherty to Cleveland in 1986 for Roy Hinson and $800,000, a deal that worked beautifully for the Cavaliers. The same day, the Sixers traded Malone, Terry Catledge and two first-round draft choices to Washington for Jeff Ruland and Cliff Robinson. It is a day that is recalled as the darkest in Philadelphia pro basketball history.

But if people see Iverson as rebellious with today's Sixers, that's the way the early Barkley was, too. He recalls Malone, the workhorse rebounder, as "the most influential person in my career, who taught me to work hard, who taught me the ropes." He recalls McMahon as "the only person who really believed in me from the start, who told me nobody could guard me, who told me I could average 10 rebounds, who told me that from Day 1."

"It sounds like a cliché, but Michael Jordan has been there for me the entire time," Barkley said. "The Bulls would beat us in the playoffs, he'd call, tell me to keep my spirits up. He'd tell me, 'You don't have any players around you.' The success I had in Phoenix, I wish I could have had that in Philly."

On the controversies:

He knows people ultimately will ask about the controversial incidents, and why he couldn't avoid them.

"I felt the media in Philly was really unfair," he said. "If three guys jump me in an alley, what am I supposed to do? I've carried a gun in my car every day for 16 years; you only heard about it one time. The [state trooper] tore my car to shreds looking for drugs. [The charge of illegal possession of a handgun was dismissed when the search was ruled unconstitutional.]

"I'm sitting at a table with a group of friends in Orlando and a complete stranger throws a drink on me; I don't regret any of those incidents. The spitting incident was something I learned from; it was a blessing for me.

"In Milwaukee, I hit the first guy, the other two ran. I went back to my room that night and went to bed. Later, the police came and said I jumped on the guy because I wouldn't sign an autograph for him. Obviously, I won that one in court. But I thought a lot of the media characterizations were a little far-fetched and overblown."

He became a lightning rod for controversy, sharing the distinction locally with Eagles quarterback Randall Cunningham.

"I didn't know what they wanted from me," Barkley said. "I remember the Dave Hoppen situation, when we had to cut two players and a guy asked who I thought we'd keep. I said I didn't know, but that some people might be offended by an all-black team. Next thing I knew, all hell broke. I really like Dave Hoppen [who is white]. I don't think Dave had a problem with me.

"What did people want me to say? Did they want me to fabricate an answer? Or not say something? I wasn't really sure how to answer questions, so I made up my mind to answer and whatever happens, happens. And I'll defend it when it needs to be defended."

He defends the game itself, wishes the players had come out better in the most recent collective bargaining agreement, wonders why owners complain about their financial situation.

"The game is fine," Barkley said. "We've got to do something about the young kids coming in, because they're not ready for the NBA. We have a lot of guys 19 and 20 who aren't ready for the media scrutiny, and you've got to admit that the media is a totally different animal nowadays. Put together those two things, and you're going to have problems.

"The media is more negative now. The money involved has added a certain amount of jealousy, created some serious attitude problems among the players, the public and the media. I think there's some resentment from the media; I know there's resentment from the fans. People don't even talk about players anymore; they talk about the money the players make.

"The owners beat us down with the collective bargaining agreement. Now, they control the salaries, but they haven't lowered ticket prices enough. I think the prices in the whole upper bowl of the arenas should be lowered. It's not a good seat, and you've got to get the regular people back to the games.

"The owners know exactly how much everybody is going to make, except themselves. They have creative control, but they haven't given anything back to the fans. Obviously, the luxury suites and the lower-bowl seats are going to go to the corporate people, and rightfully so. But the owners are making money; they're not selling their teams, so they must be making money.

"The biggest crock I've heard the entire time I've been in the league is that the players are overpaid. Well, the owners are billionaires. For some reason, they don't sell their teams. The franchises appreciate in value by ridiculous amounts. These guys are too smart to make bad business decisions. When was the last time an NBA team—any pro team—sold for nothing?"

Jerry Colangelo, the president of the Suns, is leading a select committee charged with making recommendations on rules changes. Do they need to adjust illegal defenses, the three-point line, the shot clock? Do they need to allow zones?

"The NBA has done everyone a disservice because they keep changing rules to make it easier to play," Barkley said. "You can't touch guys, can't push. Why don't they lower the rim if everybody can't dunk?

"They've changed rules and scores still haven't gone up. That wasn't the problem. The problem is, guys don't know how to play. My saying is, 'They run like deer, jump like deer, unfortunately they think like deer.' I'm embarrassed to a certain degree. Trying to find a good game to watch is like trying to find Einstein's theory of relativity. There are a lot of good players, but good teams? You have to go through brain surgery to find a good game. When I'm working for Turner, we'll have 10 games on in the studio, three will be worth watching.

"They've got to come up with a minimum age, because kids get better in college than they realize. You have kids with a year or two of experience, they're very talented, but that's it. Then the coach gets fired, the next coach brings in his system and the process starts over again."

On today's stars

He loves watching San Antonio's Tim Duncan, Minnesota's Kevin Garnett, Shaq.

"I like watching Iverson—my daughter, who's 11, loves him," Barkley said, laughing. "He's terrific. But I've been on him all season, because he's not going to hold up physically. That's another reason I don't like the Sixers to go all the way. He's got to get on an aggressive weightlifting program, or by the time he's 30 he's going to be in really bad shape.

"His body isn't big and strong, and the league is too physically grueling for a 150-, 160-pound guy to last 82 games and then all those playoff series. It gets more grueling as you get older.

"I wish I could hook him up with Tim Grover, Jordan's trainer. I did Tim's program the last two or three years I played and I felt better than I had in years. People don't know that Michael lifted weights every day, even game days."

Encore?

So, are the rumors true? Is Barkley, bad knee and all, coming back? Is Jordan?

"Michael spent some time with me in Phoenix," Barkley said. "We scrimmaged a few days, trying to get in shape. I was 337 pounds, just too much. He had gained 25 pounds himself, felt he needed to get rid of it. Now, everybody's kind of running with it.

"Would I come back? Right now, I'm content to be retired, but . . ."

Always a but. That's pure Barkley. Entertain you, inform you, leave you hanging, eager for more.

INDEX

Andy Jasner is a freelance sportswriter whose work has appeared in the Associated Press, the *New York Times*, the *Boston Globe,* and *Hoop* magazine, among others. The son of Phil Jasner, he is also the author of the book, *Baltimore Ravens.*